TIBET, TIBET

TIBET, TIBET

A PERSONAL HISTORY
OF A LOST LAND

Patrick French

HarperCollins*Publishers*

HarperCollins*Publishers*
77–85 Fulham Palace Road,
Hammersmith, London w6 8jb

www.fireandwater.com

Published by HarperCollins*Publishers* 2003

1 3 5 7 9 8 6 4 2

The author asserts the moral right to
be identified as the author of this work

A catalogue record for this book is
available from the British Library

HB ISBN 0 00 257109 9
TPB ISBN 0 00 716678 8

Maps by MAPgrafix

Set in PostScript Monotype Apollo by
Rowland Phototypesetting Ltd, Bury St Edmunds, Suffolk

Printed and bound in Great Britain by
Clays Ltd, St Ives plc

To Ab

CONTENTS

MAPS

My brother said to me . . . 'If you shut your eyes to a frightening sight, you end up being frightened. If you look at everything straight on, there is nothing to be afraid of.'

AKIRA KUROSAWA, *Something Like an Autobiography*

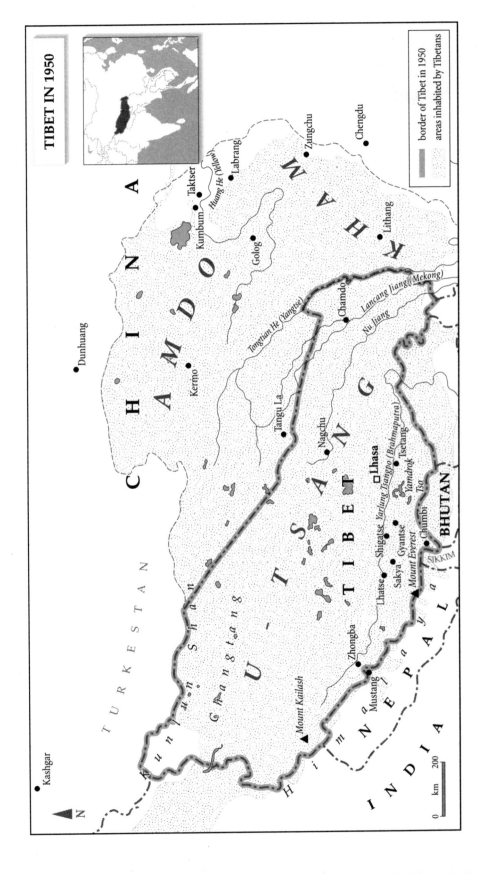

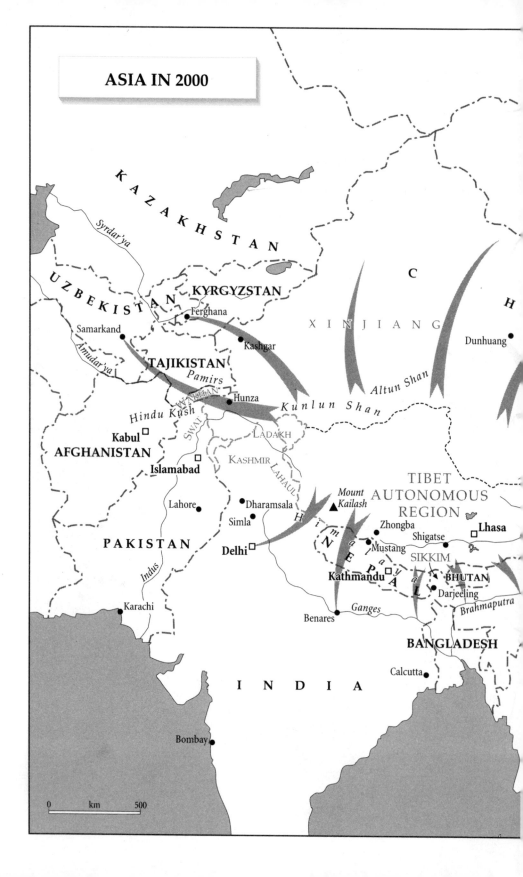

ASIA IN 2000

KAZAKHSTAN

Syrdar'ya

UZBEKISTAN

KYRGYZSTAN

Ferghana

Samarkand

XINJIANG

Kashgar

Dunhuang

Amudar'ya

TAJIKISTAN

Pamirs

Altun Shan

Hindu Kush

WAKHAN

Hunza

Kunlun Shan

Kabul

SWAT

LADAKH

AFGHANISTAN

KASHMIR

Islamabad

LAHAUL

TIBET
AUTONOMOUS
REGION

Mount
Kailash

Lahore

Dharamsala

Zhongba

Lhasa

Simla

Shigatse

H

Delhi

N

Mustang

SIKKIM

PAKISTAN

i
m
a

E
P
A

BHUTAN

Kathmandu

L

Darjeeling

Indus

a
y
a

Karachi

Ganges

Brahmaputra

Benares

BANGLADESH

Calcutta

I N D I A

Bombay

0   km   500

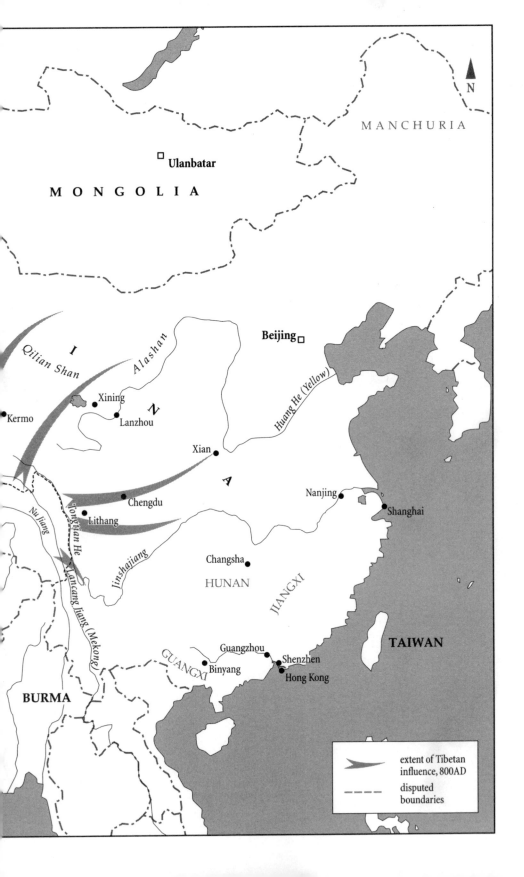

N

MANCHURIA

□ Ulanbatar

MONGOLIA

Qilian Shan

I

Alashan

Beijing □

Kermo

Xining

Lanzhou

N

Huang He (Yellow)

Xian

A

Nu Jiang

Tongtian He

Chengdu

Nanjing

Lithang

Jinshajiang

Shanghai

Lancang Jiang (Mekong)

Changsha

HUNAN

JIANGXI

TAIWAN

BURMA

GUANGXI

Guangzhou

Binyang

Shenzhen

Hong Kong

extent of Tibetan
influence, 800AD

disputed
boundaries

TIBET IN 2000

N

X I N J I A N G

C
H

K u n l u n Altun Shan

S h a n

C h a n g t a n g

T I B E T

▲ *Mount Kailash*

A U T O N O M O U S

H
*i
m
a
l
a
y
a*

N
E
P
A
L

Zhongba

Saga

Mustang

Lhatse

Sakya

Shigatse

Gyantse

Lhasa □

Yarlung Tsangpo (Brahmaputra)

Tsetang □

*Yamdrok
Tso*

□ **Kathmandu**

▲ *Mount Everest*

Chumbi ●

□ **Thimbu**

SIKKIM

B H U T A N

| 0 | km | 200 |

I N D I

BANGLADESH

Zungchu	Tibetan name
(Songpan)	Chinese name
– – –	disputed boundaries
	land over 3 000 metres

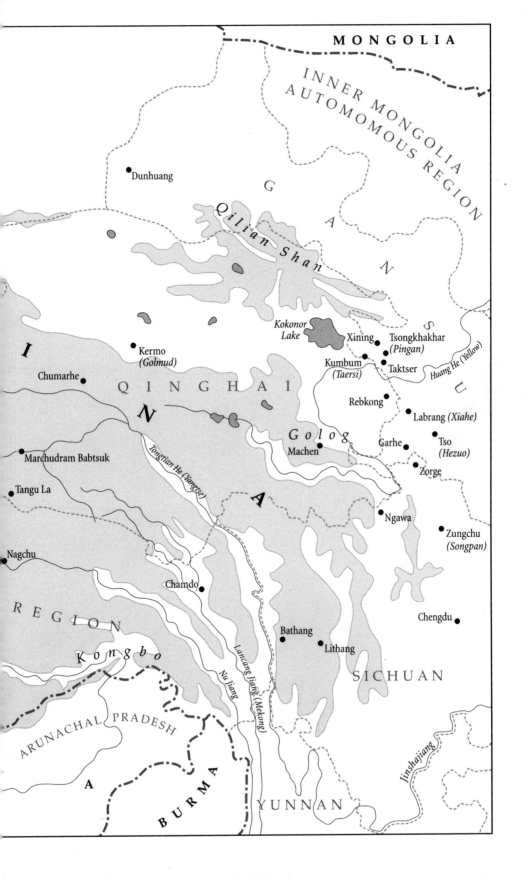

I

ONE

I was living in a room at Tsechokling monastery, below the Himalayan village of McLeod Ganj, the centre of exiled Tibetan life. It was 1987, and demonstrations were breaking out in Tibet for the first time in decades. At the end of the summer I had to return to Europe, but for the moment I was just where I wanted to be. It was simple. Each morning I would wake early, wash in cold water and walk down through the forest to the library above Dharamsala. The place was poor and insanitary at that time, with hunched old women clutching rosaries, and second-generation hustlers parading in slogan T-shirts and shades. There were a few post-hippie travellers, some Hindu pilgrims who came to visit the shrine at Bhagsunath, and students of Tibetan culture from places like Israel and Japan.

There was one man at Tsechokling who was attached to the monastery, but was not a monk. He lived alone in a hut he had built on the hillside, and could be seen herding cows, collecting firewood and occasionally helping out in the smoke-filled monastery kitchen. His name was Thubten Ngodup. He was quiet and shy, with a worn face that was marked with experience: he had escaped from Tibet after the Chinese Communist invasion of 1950, and worked in pitiful conditions on a road gang before joining the Tibetan section of the Indian army.

Ngodup had learned to cook when he was a soldier, and one of the monks suggested he might make a living by providing food for the occupants of the few monastery guest rooms. I was asked to help him set up the operation. We communicated in fits and starts, using fragments of shared language; looking back, I think that he felt awkward dealing with a foreigner during our fleeting, symbiotic friendship. A feasible menu was agreed (tea, soup, omelette, momo, shabalay, thukpa) which I copied out in English and distributed to likely customers. The arrangement worked well. Ngodup became dedicated to the purchase and preparation of food, anxious, maybe too anxious, in an ex-military sort of way, to provide perfect service. He had a role, and it made life easier for him.

You can see Ngodup at Tsechokling as the sun comes up over the wooden houses high on the ridge, carrying a bashed aluminium tray, on it china cups and saucers, a bowl of sugar and a beaker of hot milk, a cracked pot of tea and a plate of cooling buttered toast. He stands, leaning over the table, half-smiling and half-embarrassed, placing the breakfast things before us, bowing slightly, instinctively, in the Tibetan way. When he has finished, he picks up the tray and, holding it flat against his side, goes down the stone steps of the guest house, back towards the monastery kitchen, hitching up the patched brown trousers that hang loosely from his hips as he walks. He is forty-nine years old.

Eleven years later, during a demonstration in New Delhi, Ngodup made his choice. By his own free will, he ran to a hut where the cleaning fluids for the banners were kept, and poured gasoline across his body, drenching his clothes, his head, his hair, his face, the smell of the clouding vapour enough to make you reel. With a spark and a roar, he burst from the hut and ran into the square, blazing.

The date was 27 April 1998, just as the sun came up. Six Tibetan refugees were holding a hunger-strike at Jantar Mantar, encouraged by hundreds of supporters and frequent visits from the world's press. The target of their protest was the poor, useless United Nations. There were several demands: a plebiscite over Tibet's future, a rapporteur to investigate human rights abuses, and a debate on long-forgotten UN resolutions.

The hunger-strike had been going on for forty-nine days, and several people were close to death. Ngodup was in the next batch of protesters, lined up ready to replace those who died. There was a hitch: a Chinese visitor was expected. The chief of the General Staff of the People's Liberation Army, Fu Quanyou, was arriving in India on an official visit, and the authorities did not want his stay to be marred by dying Tibetans. Indian police were told to clear the site. As day broke, the police crashed in, wielding boots and lathis, dragging hunger-strikers into ambulances and beating back protesters. Choyang Tharchin, an official from the exiled Tibetan government in Dharamsala, picked up a video camera and began to film the scuffles.

I watched the footage over and over, and each time it seemed more shocking.

Indian police are bustling about. There are Tibetans in traditional dress, more traditional than anything you would find in Tibet, and the police are shoving them, grabbing their arms, poking them with lathis. In the corner of the frame, you can just catch sight of Thubten Ngodup, pushing the wrong way through the crowd, red-faced and desperate, like a runner ending a race. He disappears from view. A minute or so later the camera moves away jerkily from the barging police and protesters, and focuses on an orange light surrounded by a white light. As the picture becomes clearer, you can make out a figure at the heart of the light, a Giacometti, moving, jumping, skipping. As the shape comes nearer, you see that this is a man, burning to death, holding his palms together in the Indian *namaste* greeting, moving his arms rhythmically up and down as he runs, imploring. You can see his face and just hear him shout in a reedy, high-pitched voice, above the noise of the screaming crowd, '*Po Gyalo! Po Rangzen!*' He turns away from the camera and moves towards the crowd of Tibetans, still framed by the orange light. Ngodup is stumbling now, dancing and stumbling, but he still holds up his joined hands towards the crowd, as if he is praying, or pleading for his life. He falters; someone acts, a policeman maybe, and pushes him to the ground. Ngodup is whacked with blankets and sacks as he cowers on the ground, shielding his head. The orange light fades, the film runs on, fixed now on the prone figure and the people running in confusion. Above the scene, you notice a hand-painted banner.

UNO

WE WANT JUSTICE

TIBETAN WOMENS WELFARE GROUP

The film flickers, and stops.

In the hospital, his nerve endings still functional, Ngodup was visited by the Dalai Lama, who told him that he should harbour no feelings of hatred towards the Chinese. Ngodup tried and failed to sit up, signalling that he had understood, and seemed happy, and died just after midnight.

Ngodup's death shook me. There was something about its directness and logic that was hard to put from my mind. It was a very Buddhist death, a suicide bomber who turned his violence inwards, killing only himself, protecting others. Ngodup had no way to make himself heard. He was a powerless, ageing refugee in a country with enough problems of its own, so he burned himself to death, as a protest. For the Tibetan exiles and their supporters, he became a martyr, a symbol. A picture of him wreathed in flames was syndicated across the world, returning Tibet to the front pages, displacing Lewinsky and the Nasdaq, briefly.

Writing about Ngodup's life and death, the essayist Jamyang Norbu offered an explanation for his actions.

> In his last photograph taken before the hunger-strikers' tent in Delhi, Thubten Ngodup is smiling . . . There is no hint of anger or fanaticism (or alcoholic depression) in that smile. He was a simple man (he only read Tibetan haltingly) but when I look at his photograph I feel I am seeing the calm happy face of someone who has discovered a simple truth about life; something that has always eluded our leadership, but which traditionally Tibetans have regarded as basic to any major undertaking, especially the effective practice of the Dharma — *thak choego ray*, you have to make a decision, and act on it.

There were things that kept him on my mind.

That he had shouted, '*Po Gyalo!* Victory for Tibet! *Po Rangzen!* Free Tibet!' even as he was being killed by flames.

That people in the crowd had said they heard popping noises as his body began to burn.

That he knew what he was doing, and why he was doing it, even as the flames consumed him.

Ngodup had always seemed such a shy, quiet man when he brought me tea and toast at Tsechokling. I had not thought of him for years until I saw his picture in the paper.

TWO

Some nations have access to their history; some never had their history recorded, except in conversation; others had records once, and knowledge, but the coherence was destroyed by outsiders. Writing this from a place of security, a rented office in southern England, connected by fibre-optics to precise information about all sorts of irrelevant contemporary subjects, I can see from the window a stream and a hillside, with cows grazing on the fattening grass. I can find out, with no trouble at all, a depth of detail about what went on here in the past. I can learn that more than a thousand years ago, this hillside was owned by Christian nuns, who were granted the land by Edwy, the first Saxon king of England. I can read the names of the nuns' tenants, who farmed the hides of land that ran down from the hillside, using – it is recorded – four plough teams to prepare the ground for planting corn. I know that six centuries on, the village clergyman was entitled to graze seventy sheep and five 'beasts' on this land, and that his curate, though known to be a drunk, was kept in post because his church services remained orderly. I can learn that a piece of hunting ground on the far side of the hill was sold by one land-owning family to another, and know that now, four centuries later, the same name owns it still.

The land here has not been invaded. The people have not been driven out. There is an at times oppressive weight of continuity, a continuity that you only notice clearly when you have been to other places where the past has been torn up and the history of the land and the people who came from that land has become a story of loss and longing, of partial and absent memory, of lasting exile and the destruction of collective identity. As the song of the Sixth Dalai Lama says,

> White crane!
> Lend me your wings,
> I will not go far . . .

From verifiable sources, you can learn much about the Tibetan empire of the seventh and eighth centuries, or the history of particular monasteries, rulers or Buddhist lineages. What has disappeared for those inside Tibet is the link between the past and the present. This link has been broken systematically by the imposition of an alien political ideology, exported from industrial Europe, and the physical destruction of texts and objects. The effect of the period of mental cleansing – which was at its most intrusive in the 1950s and sixties – has been to kill the processes of thought and memory that define a society, and enable the people within it to communicate and interact. This rupture has left those in Tibet, both Tibetans and Chinese, in a state of something like atrophy. As Nadezhda Mandelstam wrote in *Hope Against Hope*, her memoir of Stalin's terror, 'An existence like this leaves its mark. We all became slightly unbalanced mentally – not exactly ill, but not normal either: suspicious, mendacious, confused and inhibited.'

It was only towards the end of my time in Tibet in the fall of 1999 that I came to understand the extent of the abnormality. The Lhasa hotel I was staying in, the Raidi, was under surveillance. There was nothing peculiar about that. I had been in the Tibet Autonomous Region for too long, and try as I might, the places I went to and the people I met prevented me from seeming the tourist I claimed to be. So there were men, Chinese men in double-breasted suits, who came to the hotel each day and asked questions and examined my room when I was not there. A man with a wide-brimmed hat sat in the window of the shop opposite, watching people going in and out of the hotel.

All this I could accept, although it made me sick with tension. What shocked me was the discovery, a little later, that the smiling, joking Tibetan receptionist, barely out of her teens, with whom I chatted casually most days, was working for the PSB, the Public Security Bureau. I was told that she was required to report foreign tourists who behaved suspiciously: if they met the wrong sort of people, if they spoke Tibetan, if they had professional-standard film cameras, if they knew too much. She did not want the job. Her father had been compromised by the PSB over a minor irregularity; she had no choice but to do it.

To Tibetans in Lhasa, none of this seemed strange. It was how things worked. Anyone, even a member of your family, might be betraying you. Most of the betrayers betrayed not for political or financial gain, but because they felt they had no alternative.

Around this time, I was talking to a very old Tibetan man, a doctor, at his house by the Barkhor. He said in passing that he felt like screwing up his new Conduct Agreement and trampling it beneath his feet. I asked him what a Conduct Agreement was, and he produced it, a document that every resident of his part of Lhasa had been made to sign.

It was titled *Responsibilities of the People*, and there were headings such as 'Defending the Security and Stability of Society' and 'Education in Political Ideology'. The tone was threatening, with talk of fines, neighbourhood committees, model compounds and model families, like China in the days before Deng.

> The people must love their motherland, oppose splittists and defend the unity of the motherland and the friendship and solidarity of the nationalities. The townsfolk must show their respect for Party policies by refraining from engaging in activities that are detrimental to the image and interests of the Party and the government. They must display their political loyalty clearly by opposing the splittists resolutely, not participating in political disturbances, refrain from watching such political disturbances, show no mercy to the splittists and avoid spreading rumours ... Upon becoming aware of or coming into contact with a suspicious-looking person, they must immediately report the person to the authorities instead of hiding them.

The redundant political jargon was as bad as the content: the people, the Party, the motherland, the elusive solidarity of the nationalities and the danger of those who thought their own thoughts about how Tibet should be run; the splittists. It went on. There were rules on gatekeepers, rules on how to report your neighbour, rules on how much you should be earning, rules on contraception, rules on hygiene and rules on who could visit you and when.

Moments like this – the discovery of the existence of Conduct Agreements, or the plight of the chirpy young PSB agent – made me feel that I had fallen through a trapdoor to another level of comprehension. The place was ruled not by terror, as it had been once, but by constant mental supervision; the absence of freedom.

The people of each nation are formed in part by their physical geography: the level of the Netherlands, the ice of the Arctic, the islands of Greece, the jungles of West Papua, the climate of England, they all create a culture, a way of seeing and doing. Tibet has always been varied and diverse, a nation of interactors and travellers, rather than the hermetic, forbidden land of European repute. A geographical treatise written by a Tibetan monk in around 1820 contains references to Louisiana, Rio de Janeiro, the department system in France and the imprisonment of a Corsican general named 'Na-pa-li' on charges of conquering most of Europe.

Tibet's inaccessibility has long driven its people to roam, whether to spread religion, to trade or to fight. Thousands of years ago, its cultural borrowings extended to distant lands. Important roots of the Tibetan language can be found in the West, rather than in a Chinese or Sino-Tibetan proto-language. Some of the oldest words in Tibetan have Indo-European origins, including such linguistic staples as cow, wheat, pig, wheel, dog, rice, birth, star, kin and government. The linguist Christopher Beckwith has observed that 'The famous Indo-European root that gives words for "king", "royal", "right", "rights", "reckoning", and so forth, namely *reg*, "to touch" . . . is represented very richly in Old Tibetan.' There are 'remarkably good correspondences between Old Tibetan and Proto-Indo-European'.

As far back as 715, Arab soldiers joined forces with Tibetan imperial troops in a gruesome battle in Ferghana, a Central Asian outpost closer to Constantinople than it was to Changan (or Xian), the Tang dynasty capital of China. A case has even been made for the conceivable influence of the First Book of Kings on an eighth-century Tibetan historical narrative, *The Testament of Ba*, perhaps via 'Nestorian Christians, Manichaeans, and Jewish merchants operating along the Silk Road'.

Today, ethnic Tibetans stretch from northern Amdo to the Kunlun Shan, across the Changtang to the Himalayas and over to Sikkim, back through the high deserts and snow mountains to Lhasa, up to Chamdo, on to Lithang and down to the hot forests on the border of Burma. The common bond is indefinable. Religion, language, jokes, appearance, dress and social convention all go some way towards explaining it. The historian Tsering Shakya delved into tradition and came up with the eating of *tsampa*, roasted barley flour, as the defining mark. 'During the height of Tibetan resistance to Chinese rule in 1959,' he observed, 'a letter appeared in the only Tibetan newspaper, *The Mirror*. It was symbolically addressed to "All *Tsampa* Eaters". Here the writer has gone back to the most basic element which united people . . . *tsampa* is the sub-particle of Tibetanness. It transcends dialects, sects, gender and regionalism.'

Tsampa-eaters have never had the security that comes from a soft, pliant landscape and fixed national boundaries. Survival depends on constant self-reliance. If you walk too far east from London, or too far west from Tokyo, you will fall into the sea; but on the vast, sprawling continent of Asia, borders are uncertain. Where does Tibet begin and China end? Where does India end and China begin? The Chinese government lays claim to much of the Indian state of Arunachal Pradesh. India lays claim to territory inside the Tibet Autonomous Region. The exiled Tibetans lay claim to parts of Sichuan.

In the days of empire, Tibetan power stretched as far north as Turkestan, as far east as Changan, as far south as the banks of the Ganges and as far west as Afghanistan. It was a massive, fluctuating sphere of influence, pulsating out from central Tibet, sustained by frequent battles and a network of shifting alliances.

A millennium later, ethnic Tibet and political Tibet had become disjointed. Tibetans were spread across the Himalayas and up into China, but although their ultimate spiritual loyalty may usually have lain in Lhasa, political allegiance varied. The source of authority in different parts of the giant, impervious Tibetan plateau ranged from the Lhasa government, to the Chinese emperor, to a temporarily dominant warlord, to a large local monastery.

During Tibet's brief period of *de facto* independence between the First World War and 1950, the Tibetan government controlled territory roughly corresponding to the borders of today's Tibet Autonomous Region. Like the Balkans, Tibet's fringes have long been inhabited by a patchwork of different ethnic groups: a Han Chinese village, a Hui Muslim village, a Qiang village and a Tibetan village may sit side by side. In the Chinese provinces of Qinghai, Gansu, Sichuan and Yunnan — which border Tibet — there has for many years been a substantial ethnic Tibetan population, living on untamed land that was often under no clear external control. In modern times, Beijing's response to this diversity has been to carve out nominally autonomous Tibetan counties and prefectures within the four border provinces. More Tibetans now live there than in the Tibet Autonomous Region itself.

According to official Chinese census statistics (which are regarded by demographers as wanting but usable) there are 2.5 million Tibetans in the Tibet Autonomous Region and 2.9 million in Qinghai, Gansu, Sichuan and Yunnan. But if you take the province of Qinghai, for instance, which has almost all of its land under 'autonomous prefecture' designations, you find there are eight hundred thousand Tibetans and six hundred thousand Chinese living in Tibetan prefectures, and another 1.3 million Tibetans and seven hundred thousand Chinese living in a Mongolian prefecture. In Sichuan, a large province of eighty-five million people, there are 1.1 million Tibetans living in Tibetan prefectures, but the same areas also contain seven hundred thousand non-Tibetans. So although the autonomy of these prefectures and counties is largely fictional and their boundaries are often inept, it is apparent that the different ethnic groups within them could never be easily disentangled.

The exiled Tibetan government in Dharamsala ('by far the most serious' government-in-exile in the world, according to the *Economist* magazine) has responded to this complex, historic demographic problem in a dramatic way. To keep things simple, it lays claim to all land inhabited by Tibetans, covering a total of 2.5 million square kilometres, more than twice the area of the Tibet Autonomous Region. Astonishingly, this territorial sleight has been swallowed and endorsed by most foreign supporters of the Tibetan cause, despite much of the land, especially in the north and east, never having been administered from Lhasa.

I had tried asking the Dalai Lama's foreign minister, T.C. Tethong, why the exiled government maintained a claim over territory that it did not control before 1950. Surely this position weakened its chances of ever reaching an accommodation with the Chinese government? His response was loose: they were 'still looking into it'. The border was based on 'ancient claims', as well as on oral history and the demands of different Tibetan exile groups. 'We made our map so as not to leave out any Tibetans,' he said, 'so that they didn't feel isolated. We are going for the whole of Tibet. But I accept there will have to be give and take. His Holiness the Dalai Lama wants a fair compromise.'

The demand for a greater Tibet is rooted in the politics of displacement. In order to maintain the unity of the émigré community after the Dalai Lama's flight across the Himalayas in 1959, his exiled administration developed the idea of a giant, theoretical Tibet. In the early 1960s, with the arrival in India, Nepal and Bhutan of large numbers of Tibetan refugees (many of them from the border areas close to China, who had endured the worst of the reforms and suppression), it became necessary to develop a pan-Tibetan identity. Its focus was the idea of '*Po Cholkha Sum*', the unity of the three historic regions of ethnic Tibet: Amdo, Kham and U-Tsang. People who had previously identified themselves with a particular region now became consciously Tibetan.

A sense of Tibetan nationhood was created deliberately, in exile. The Lhasa dialect served as the basis of a shared refugee language; a regimental banner devised in the 1920s by a wandering Japanese man (which had been displayed at the Asian Relations Conference in India in 1947), featuring red and blue stripes and a pair of snow lions, became the Tibetan national flag; a song written by the Dalai Lama's tutor Trijang Rinpoche (himself a reincarnation of the Buddha's chariot-driver) was adopted as Tibet's national anthem; the Dalai Lama's birthday became a day of popular celebration; and an invocation used at the new year festival of *Losar*, '*tashi delek*' or 'good luck', was promoted as a versatile greeting, which could be picked up easily by foreign helpers.

THREE

My mental involvement with Tibet had started in the early 1980s, when I was about sixteen, provoked by an encounter with the Dalai Lama, whose style and exoticism caught my eye. I was being educated in vice and morality at a school for boys in northern England, physically and culturally isolated from the rest of the world, run by Roman Catholic monks. The Dalai Lama had expressed a wish to see a Christian monastery in operation, and we were the chosen venue. There was great anticipation. We were instructed to wear suits, since he was, after a fashion, a head of state. There were security preparations involving dogs and detectives. A documentary film was shown about the history of Tibet, which I remember in detail: the landscape shots, a caravan of horses and yaks making its way jerkily through a mountain pass, tall yellow hats, images of a religious ceremony, which I think must have been archive footage of the Dalai Lama's own enthronement. I can even remember the angle at which I was watching the screen, from the back, on the left, in a wooden-panelled common room.

Some of the monks, our teachers, communicated the view that the visit was a great, historic honour. Others spoke in sardonic tones, debating the ethics of allowing a prominent denier of Christ into the hallowed sanctuary of the abbey, the monastery and the school. There was one old monk who spread a story which I think he must have gained from one of the fantastical travel books of the early twentieth century, or conceivably from Voltaire's *Dictionnaire Philosophique*. He said that anywhere a Dalai Lama defecated at once became a Buddhist shrine, so foreigners of various kinds would now be bound to treat the place as a site of lasting pilgrimage. There would be no way of keeping them out, the Orientals, who would certainly come in numbers to revere the sacred excrement. The more simple-minded schoolboys appreciated this line, discussing the mechanics of the worship.

The Holder of the White Lotus arrived in rain with police cars and an entourage of Tibetan monks and Indian security men, some displaying automatic weapons. We stood in a rough line, waiting. He was in his forties, so young and uncelebrated, I realise now, looking back and seeing him against the backdrop of the heavy stone buildings, the distant sports fields, the old-style police cars, the drizzle, the memory of the England of my childhood, far from Tibet. He wore platform flip-flops and a maroon robe, vivid against the sombre black habits of the receiving monks. Joy poured from him; there was no trace of piety, the great Christian virtue. I remember having an urge to be noticed by him, to be picked out. He smiled and laughed and leaned forward, gripping each person's hand in turn.

A little later, as he came out of the school theatre, he was intercepted by a long-haired American woman, fresh from Chicago. She was howling. In our isolation, far from women and far from America, such a sight was hardly imaginable. I got as close to the action as I could. She looked a little like Joni Mitchell. The gist of her message, communicated in noisy sobs, kneeling, hugging the Dalai Lama's knees while damp security men darted about, was that the world needed him. She had been told in a dream to go to him, wherever he was, and help humanity in whatever way he thought best. I was struck by the seriousness with which he dealt with her, listening carefully to each word, unconcerned by the gawping schoolboys and his embarrassed hosts.

That was the beginning of my obsession with Tibet – or from this distance what looks like a beginning, although it did not feel like one at the time. I read a leaflet, issued by the Dalai Lama's office, which explained the principles of reincarnation, and how he was chosen as the reborn version of his predecessor.

In 1935 the Regent of Tibet went to the sacred lake of Lhamo Latso, and had a vision of a monastery with roofs of jade green and gold, and a house with turquoise tiles. In 1937 high lamas and dignitaries carrying the secrets of the vision were sent to all parts of Tibet in search of the place that the Regent had seen in the waters. The search party that headed east was under the leadership of Lama Kewtsang Rinpoche of Sera Monastery. When they arrived in Amdo, they found a place matching the description of the secret vision. The party went to the house with Kewtsang Rinpoche disguised as the servant, and a junior official disguised as the leader. The Rinpoche was wearing a rosary that had belonged to the Thirteenth Dalai Lama, and the little boy of the house recognised it and demanded that it be given to him. Kewtsang Rinpoche promised to give it to him if he could guess who he was, and the boy replied that he was 'Sera aga', which means in the local dialect 'a lama of Sera'. Then the Rinpoche asked who the leader was and the boy gave his name correctly; he also knew the name of the real servant. This was followed by a series of tests that included the choosing of correct articles that had belonged to the Thirteenth Dalai Lama, including a walking stick and drum. In 1940 the Fourteenth Dalai Lama was enthroned.

I was captivated by the romance of this scene: the search party setting off, finding the house with the turquoise tiles, disguising the lama as a servant and identifying the chosen child, who could recognise a walking stick and a drum. It was only some years later, when I read the memoirs of a member of the Dalai Lama's family, that I saw the background was more complex. The Dalai Lama's great-uncle and elder brother were important reincarnate lamas in Amdo, his uncle was financial controller of nearby Kumbum monastery, and the region's notoriously brutal Muslim warlord, Ma Bufang – who was personally instrumental in choosing the Dalai Lama – turned out to be a friend of his mother's family.

I began to read about Tibet, its life, religion and traditions, its rulers and ruled. Looking back through sheared, overlapping memories, trying to get a glimpse of the past, it is hard to be sure what made me feel such instinctive devotion to Tibet. I can see another version of myself responding, with similar instincts but different knowledge.

In essence, there were two things that drew me: the place and the spirit.

Tibet was as far as you could go. It was a harsh, remote, untouched land, outside time and geography, where ideas could be projected and dreams could be lived, a high plateau the size of western Europe, the most mountainous country on earth and nearly the most sparsely populated, a place of physical angularity and limitless expansion where perceptions of space and distance altered, a land of blue sheep, blood pheasants and barking deer, ringed by snow peaks and impassable high-altitude deserts, dropping to fields of jasmine, sky-blue poppies, apricot orchards, incandescent turquoise lakes and hillsides of juniper; a place of serenity, where the enlightened chose to return after death and reincarnate themselves in human form for the good of all sentient beings; of names that rolled from your mouth: Pandatsang, Chomolungma, Dekyilingka, Dorje; of ancient monasteries with smoking butter lamps, wrathful deities, prostrating nuns, flailing oracles, revelatory trances and shaven-headed incarnations in maroon robes, cloistered in meditation, the low cry of human thigh-bone trumpets and the rhythm of soft, guttural chanting flowing down the valleys with the snow-melt; nomads and herders, amulets close to the skin, children wrapped in sheepskins, pushing flocks of yak and dzo, the yak–cow crossbreed, through the mountain passes, heading for the fragrant grasslands as their ancestors had always done. This was Tibet, before I went there: a place of dreams, a place to feel at home.

I was not the first to fall for such an idea of this remote land. Later, I came to know that it had been coveted in this way for centuries, and that my fellow travellers included Tintin, Franklin Roosevelt, Heinrich Harrer, Madame Blavatsky, Sherlock Holmes and Lara Croft. Sometimes I felt that most of the Western world saw Tibet as a place of distant realisation. 'Do you know what the Lama says?' asks Bill Murray's character in the cult comic movie *Caddyshack*. 'He says, "Oh, ah, there won't be any money, but when you die, on your deathbed, you will receive total consciousness.'' So I got that goin' for me, which is nice.' The computer game heroine Lara Croft, with her erupting breasts and 9mm Uzis, sees Tibet as a place of initiation into heroism. She throws off her aristocratic past and begins a career as an adventurer when her plane crash-lands in the Himalayas, returning to Tibet on a mission in *Tomb Raider II*. In John Updike's *Rabbit at Rest*, failing, dying Harry Angstrom tells his lover Thelma, 'The only country over there I've ever wanted to go to is Tibet. I can't believe I won't make it. Or never be a test pilot, like I wanted to be when I was ten.' Angstrom has 'always been curious about what it would feel like to *be* the Dalai Lama. A ball at the top of its arc, a leaf on the skin of a pond.' A decade on, at the end of the millennium, his grandson Roy returns to the theme in *Rabbit Remembered*, e-mailing his grandmother: 'What really took my interest in the news is this Tibetan boy just my age who was the second most important lama in the world and escaped by walking several days through a blizzard in the Himmeleyas, hes called the KARMAPA. On the same website I read where the Dolly Lama (the most important lama) said of YK2 ''Millennium? The sun and the moon are the same to me.'' '

Tibetans themselves believe they come from somewhere special. Implicit in Tibetan Buddhist teaching is the idea of Tibet as a sacred land. The prophecy of Shambhala, found in the scriptures of the Kalachakra initiation, projects a huge, mythical kingdom ruled by a congenial monarch, shaped like a lotus and encircled by a range of snow peaks. The kingdom may be in the mind; or it may be real. The nineteenth-century Hungarian scholar Csoma de Körös suggested with admirable precision that Shambhala was to be found 'between 45° and 50° north latitude . . . where the increase of the days from the vernal equinox till the summer solstice amounted to twelve Indian hours, or four hours, forty-eight minutes, European reckoning'. It was an idea taken up by James Hilton, the author of the mawkish *Goodbye, Mr Chips*, in his 1933 novel *Lost Horizon*, when he coined the now universal term 'Shangri-La', to mean an imaginary secret paradise. Hilton's Shangri-La was a place where wisdom and knowledge were preserved from the ravages of the madding world by an elite gang of old men, led by a Capuchin monk named Father Perrault, in the Valley of the Blue Moon, somewhere inside Tibet. A mountainous region on the Yunnan–Sichuan border now markets itself to tourists as the 'real' Shangri-La.

Hugh Richardson, Britain's last representative in Lhasa, who in 1943 signed the treaty which gave up British extra-territorial rights in China, once mentioned to me in a letter 'a quotation from Newbolt which I can't find, "The mind's Tibet where none has gone before".' I liked this phrase. Everyone has a Tibet of the mind, a notion of a pure, distant land, a place of personal escape, the heart of lightness. For some, it may be glimpsed through music, or fasting, or drugs, or prayer, or excessive exercise, or perfect love. It is the imaginary paradise, the cool correlative of the desert island with palms, coconuts and Gauguin's women. I searched for the phrase 'the mind's Tibet' in the writings of the patriotic British poet Henry Newbolt, zipping through lines on a database, but without success. I decided to ask Hugh Richardson if he could remember where the phrase came from, but before I could, he died, at the age of ninety-four, while Al Gore and George W. Bush squabbled over chads, and the last link in a shared history was broken, leaving 'the mind's Tibet' elusive and unlocated.

In 1986 I travelled through the Tibetan borderlands as a tourist, spending time in Kumbum and other parts of Amdo, as well as in Chinese cities such as Xian and Beijing. I realise now that I saw and comprehended little of substance. I was looking for the wrong things, concentrating on the experiences of travel and the reactions of the foreign tourists around me, rather than on the place itself. Aspects of Tibetan and Chinese conduct that I took to indicate ignorance, hostility or insipidity I see now to have been no more than automatic, conditioned fear, the responses of a society emerging from trauma, of people who have passed through terror and know that nothing will be gained from frankness, certainly when dealing with something as unstable as an outsider.

I felt I was perceiving things more clearly when I spent the next summer living in the monastery at Tsechokling, near the headquarters of the Dalai Lama's exiled government. I learned the exiles' view of their native land, seeing this as necessarily more authentic and truthful than the controlled version I had seen the year before. The scale of Tibet's dislocation seemed to become clear then, viewed from a distance in the relatively free society of India (politically chaotic, but unconstrained), so that the suffering and victimhood of the entire Tibetan people in the years following 1950 replaced my own memories of the place I had seen. Tibet became for me, at that time, a land of certainties: an independent country had been invaded by Chinese Communists, who destroyed six thousand monasteries and killed 1.2 million people, an exact figure, one-fifth of the population.

Tibet became the cause to which I attached myself, writing leaflets, making speeches, going on demonstrations. Much of this attachment was a reaction to my own world, a case of what George Orwell called 'transferred nationalism'. A movement that has since been termed post-Seattle politics was beginning. Ideologies were viewed as weights from the past, discredited by the ways they could be seen to have failed. Party politics were being replaced by particular causes and concerns. The Tibetan cause became a central part of my life, and many friendships and relationships developed from it. When I was leaving university, determined above all to live on my wits and not be an employee, the chronicling of Britain's 1904 invasion of Tibet and its leader Francis Younghusband became an obvious route out.

Spending time over the years with Tibetan exiles, but not returning to Tibet itself, my image of a promised, damaged land grew. Coming from a materially rich but spiritually confused world, I could not help but be drawn by the character, feeling and serenity of many of the Tibetans I met, by their capacity for dealing equably with whatever life threw at them. Many had passed through intense personal suffering, but seemed to have found a way, through their religious or cultural beliefs, of coping with it. Sometimes, their pain was internalised and liable to emerge in another form, but often it seemed to have been faced, and dissolved.

Poverty can kill you, but widespread affluence does not bring happiness. It is one of the gravest problems of overdeveloped societies. Depression, stress, weight fixation and loose rage flourish in rich countries; in poor countries, people have other things to worry about.

I remember a moment in a pristine shopping centre in southern England. There were clean metal elevators, themed shops, designed spaces, corporate brands and coffee bars. As I rose sleekly from one floor to another, looking down through the glass and light, I felt that few people in this shoppers' paradise seemed content. There was an air of anxiety, as if time was running out for all of them. It brought me back to a moment in Tibet, to a memory of a group of men and women sitting, laughing, on the edge of a field of barley after a morning's harvest, wearing wide-brimmed hats to keep off the strong sun, each one spinning wool on a spindle, or carving a wooden peg, telling a joke, passing the day. In the free world, the invented world, there is little time for being. Each step is managed, and you have to work ever harder to get the money to buy the things that will keep you from falling out of the system. The people in the shopping centre had everything, but all they wanted was more, because having everything did not make life easier for them; they had to run just to stand still.

For Tibetans, the idea of self-loathing or of loneliness in a crowd is hard to comprehend; there is no way to translate, for instance, the concept of low self-esteem into Tibetan. You are what you are. Mental disturbance or illness is understood, but formless anguish is not. This is something that the Dalai Lama has noticed and tried to respond to, and is one of the reasons for his global allure – the hope that he might provide some answers.

In his book *Freedom in Exile*, he wrote:

> There are a lot of people in the West who live very comfort-
> ably in large cities, but virtually isolated from the broad
> mass of humanity. I find this very strange – that under the
> circumstance of such material well-being and with thou-
> sands of brothers and sisters for neighbours, so many
> people appear able to show their true feelings only to their
> cats and dogs. This indicates a lack of spiritual values, I

feel. Part of the problem here is perhaps the intense com-
petitiveness of life in these countries, which seems to breed
fear and a deep sense of insecurity.

An old Tibetan refugee who lived in India once told me about
a trip he had made to see his daughter, in Zurich. It was a baffling
experience. They went to visit friends, but everyone was too
busy to stop and talk. Sometimes, you would go to someone's
house and they would not even invite you in to sit down, or offer
you anything to eat. Children would spend their time addressing
computer games rather than talking. If you went to a party, you
would be expected to arrive and leave at a certain time, and to
bring a bottle of alcohol with you. Machines, rather than humans,
were used to mend the roads, but unemployed people were
funded generously by the state. Oddest of all, he said, in a land
where people always seemed too busy to stop and chat, was their
behaviour when they had a chance to relax. On hot days, the
residents of the city would go to a park filled with people, but
once there they would try to avoid contact or conversation, and
pretend they were alone. Although he had been intrigued by his
time in Zurich, the common social behaviour there was outside
his comprehension.

In the wealthy world, the pervasive sense of lack drives people
to worship at the oddest shrines, and to seek a solution to their
formless malaise in bogus shamanism, crystal therapy, hands-free
massage, rebirthing, sun salutations, flotation and pesticide-free
food. Some people abandon the search for a transcendent explanation quickly, settling on materialism as an alternative, while
others continue it for a lifetime. The process of being born and
raised within the rituals of an established religion, which has
been automatic for most people through the whole of human
history, becomes rarer with each year that passes. For many
people in rich countries, the certainties of earlier generations now
seem implausible, especially the theories and dogmas of revealed
religions.

For me, Tibetan Buddhism was a workable approach. Leaving
the Roman Catholic faith of my childhood was not hard. It had
long seemed less than credible, although its rituals could be

reassuring and I liked the emphasis on moral inquiry. But the creator god, the conjuring of bread and wine into flesh and blood, the ban on contraception, the promotion of Christ's sexless mother as an example to women, the harassment of dissident clergy, the thought that *ex-cathedra* pronouncements by the Pope should be taken seriously — all of these things had pushed me away from my inherited faith.

Buddhism appeared to create contentment among its followers, and reincarnation seemed a fair explanation of what happened to the spirit after death. So my admiration was partially utilitarian: it felt good to be around Tibetans, and if their religion brought good to them, it was worth pursuing. The outward aspects of Tibetan Buddhism, and the celibate male hierarchy running the show, were what I found least appealing, although I still respected the Dalai Lama. It was the Buddhist explanation of life, the universe and everything that drew me, rather than the ritual or the theology.

I was also drawn by the central principle that suffering is universal and pleasure is transient. In secular Western thought, an expectation of permanent satisfaction has become deeply ingrained, and is an important cause of the prevailing discontent. People believe that they can expect fair treatment from life. The idea that loss, death and suffering are to be expected has become obsolete, and a relatively minor trauma can provoke great emotional upset. The Buddha taught in the First of the Four Noble Truths that 'discontentment, unhappiness and disappointment are universal . . . all the things we desire and cherish, not least our own lives, must eventually come to an end'. The Second Noble Truth states that suffering is caused by desire, and that the immediate satisfaction of desire brings only illusory, passing pleasure. By surrendering the self and attempting to break down the delusions of desire, ignorance and hatred, it is possible to find freedom from suffering, and to attain a state of liberation. This free state of mind should be our aspiration. The Dalai Lama has gone as far as to say that 'the very purpose of our life is happiness'.

Buddhists use the Sanskrit term *samsara* to mean the cycle of existence, the way we live, the endless round of birth, death and rebirth, where the imprints of the actions of earlier lives and delusions return to mark the present. Our state of existence is characterised by the forces of *karma*, the law of cause and effect, the idea that everything that you do, will, in time, rebound upon you. The only way I could make sense of random suffering (a child mutilated in war, the numerous victims of famine, a loving parent dead in a pointless accident) was by believing that it was linked to earlier actions which had, in some way, returned. This is a deeply unfashionable belief, which offends the sensibilities of both Christians and secularists. When the England football manager Glenn Hoddle suggested that disabilities might be caused by misdeeds in earlier lives he was obliged to resign, with Britain's prime minister, Tony Blair, leading the chorus of derision against him. In fact, Hoddle was merely expressing, in a slightly muddled way, a principle that is followed by around a quarter of the world's population, Hindus and Buddhists, who believe that every action has an eventual reaction.

At its worst, a belief in *karma* – what Tibetans call '*las*' – can lead to fatalism of a stultifying kind, where a person's distressed condition is blamed on actions committed many lifetimes before. In orthodox Hindu society I had seen this attitude taken to an extreme, with individual poverty and suffering treated with ritual indifference and blamed on an immutable law of nature that had led people to low birth. I did not perceive cause and effect in this way, but more as a recognition that negative actions can rebound in unexpected ways. People who are violent may be drawn to conflict and end up suffering a violent death; those who are bewitched by money may be consumed by fear and worry about maintaining their wealth, and destroy any pleasure they had hoped to obtain from it; those who are cruel to animals are more likely to be attacked by them; the angry and frustrated can become imprisoned within their own frustration.

The other principle that attracted me to Tibetan Buddhism was its stress on empathy and compassion, for all living beings. This was something which seemed to work in practice, as well as in theory, and to give a richness and constancy to Tibetan lives. The Dalai Lama has pointed out that it is a doctrine with wide implications, and that 'whilst generally translated simply as compassion, the term *nying-je* has a wealth of meaning that is difficult to convey succinctly ... It connotes love, affection, kindness, gentleness, generosity of spirit and warm-heartedness. It is also used as a term of both sympathy and endearment.' For a Tibetan, it is a principle that has to be adhered to even at times of hardship and provocation, as an expression of shared suffering. Although I had met Tibetans who were untrustworthy and aggressive, there did seem to be a shared, culturally embedded sense of *nying-je*.

As I studied Buddhism more closely, some of the failings began to show, and I noticed the schisms, bigots, frauds, hypocrites and predators that you would find in any ecclesiastical system. I was put off too by the tone of many of the foreign converts, who thought they could strip the tradition of its tough ethical underpinnings. They were implausible, with their showy accoutrements of conversion, their beads and bracelets, their devotion to instant spiritual empowerment, their reliance on airport-hopping teachers who were not always taken seriously by Tibetans. Then there were the prominent blunders: the teacher and promoter Sogyal Rinpoche, served with a lawsuit for seducing a student; and the Nyingmapa monk Penor Rinpoche who, in the most dubious circumstances, identified the high-kicking Hollywood action hero Steven Seagal (*Marked for Death, Hard to Kill*) as a reincarnation of the seventeenth-century master Chungdrag Dorje.

I was also cautioned by the Dalai Lama's own refusal to proselytise. After long observation, he had decided that conversion usually led to confusion, and that without the support of the prevailing culture, it was hard to maintain your spiritual practice: 'In the West, I do not think it advisable to follow Buddhism. Changing religions is not like changing professions. Excitement lessens over the years, and soon you are not excited, and then where are you? Homeless inside yourself.' Sitting cross-legged in a Buddhist temple in the Himalayas or listening to silence in a Renaissance church in Florence, it is not hard to feel a sense of the spiritual. The difficulty comes at times of everyday frustration, like when your car breaks down in traffic, or you find yourself shopping against the clock in a packed supermarket. In these situations, the cerebral and the sublime disappear and the transcendent becomes irrelevant.

As time passed, some aspects of Tibetan Buddhist teaching

remained with me, becoming part of my life, while others faded. I did not anticipate liberation from the cycle of existence, or an end to the experience of desire, however illusory I might know its satisfactions to be. When I had passed through the various stages of learning, inquiry and rejection, I was left with techniques of meditation and the philosophy of Buddhism; a way of looking. I felt no need to go through a process of declarative conversion, as you would when joining a revealed religion like Islam or Christianity. Instead I slipped into something near it, avoiding classification, borrowing and incorporating bits of another culture to make my own life easier.

Between 1987 and 1989, repeated protests and riots broke out in Lhasa. Disparate events began to lock together. Tibet Support Groups formed in the world's wealthier countries, composed largely of people who had been moved by an encounter with Tibet or expatriate Tibetans. We gathered for the first time in 1990 in Dharamsala, listening to former prisoners' testimonies and talking urgently of the need for networking and international coordination. There may even have been mention of e-mails and the internet, an invention that was over the next decade to transform the speed, extent and nature of our campaigning. Being around people with the same obsession, the same determination, was stimulating. We sat in the tea shops of McLeod Ganj, deliberating. Everyone tried hard to treat Richard Gere as if he were just another regular activist. There was a sense of momentum, that we were on the cusp of change. The approach might best be summed up in the mawkish words of Melissa Mathison Ford, screenwriter of both *Kundun* and *E.T.*: 'I believe the Dalai Lama will return to Tibet, having saved His country, having completed the task set before Him in childhood. If He does not, we will all share in the blame. But if He does, we all share in the glory.'

Television documentaries and properly researched press coverage on Tibet's plight started to appear. The Dalai Lama travelled more widely, without the restrictions of the past, being received by presidents and prime ministers. (His first visit to the USA had only been permitted in 1979.) He became an instantly recognisable global figure, with a moral weight behind him. Tibet stopped being obscure, a change that has its marking-point – the sort of arbitrary marking-point that writers of history enjoy – in a 1988 edition of the literary magazine *Granta*, when the writer Amitav Ghosh published a short piece titled 'Tibetan Dinner'. The article described a fund-raising event in New York, staffed by fashionable people eating salmon and asparagus momos, with a displaced Tibetan monk sitting at the end of the table. Ghosh thought the man looked 'a little guilty . . . Or perhaps he was merely bewildered.'

> It cannot be easy to celebrate the commodification of one's own suffering. But I couldn't help feeling that if the lama, like the actor [Gere, again], really wanted to make Tibet a household word in the western world, he wasn't setting about it in the right way. He'd probably have done better if he'd turned it into an acronym . . . And sold the rights to it to a line of detergents or even perhaps a breakfast cereal.

This is, in a roundabout way, what happened. Tibet – the export version, the mind's Tibet – went from being obscure to cult-fashionable to mainstream in a decade.

The tone of the support altered. I remember a meeting in the late 1980s of the world's oldest Tibetophile organisation, the Tibet Society of the UK, in a draughty hall near Trafalgar Square. I was sitting near the front in unkempt trousers with sparse rows of retired colonial servants lined up behind me. There was a long debate about a letter that the organisers – the Council, I think they called themselves – were sending to *The Times*. Their last letter had not been published, and there was discussion about the possible reasons for this, and the appropriate form of the next letter. Later in the proceedings, a woman stood up and offered fraternal greetings to the Tibet Society from the newly formed Tibet Support Group.

I decided to join the Tibet Support Group. We got an office the size of a cupboard, and an Apple Mac LC. More members appeared. Media coverage grew. Someone held a party to raise money for a fax machine. Events and stunts unfolded. I joined the executive and edited the magazine. We moved to a bigger office, and the membership grew into thousands. There were long and frequent meetings to discuss strategy. We took on more paid staff, held exhibitions and marches, boycotted exploiting companies and changed our name to Free Tibet Campaign. Celebrities (some serious, some frivolous) attached themselves to the cause. The movement grew rapidly across Europe and North America. Students for a Free Tibet swept through the campuses of the United States, expanding to hundreds of chapters worldwide. The Washington-based International Campaign for Tibet gained a formidable public profile, bringing Hollywood on board.

Tibetan imagery started to appear in the press, as well as in transitory media such as fashion catalogues, advertisements, flyers, artworks and magazine covers, carrying a weight of meaning that would have been impossible in the past. Across the rich world, every shop window seemed to carry a poster promoting the Dalai Lama. Musicians incorporated Tibetan Buddhist notions into their lyrics. There was a group called Nirvana and a song called Shambhala. The magazine *Vanity Fair* had the sentence 'A Lhasa-ing we will go . . . Diki Tsering, revered as "Grandmother of Tibet", offers tales from the bearskin rug in her autobiography, *Dalai Lama, My Son.*' Such lines made me recall the days when you had to say, 'Lhasa, the capital of Tibet,' in the way you might say 'Ouagadougou, the capital of Burkina Faso.' Young British Tibetans become models and designers, appearing in *i-D* magazine dressed in Duffer of St George and Paul Smith, spurning the immigrants' jobs and immigrants' clothes of their parents.

Everything seemed to be going well. Free Tibet Campaign was thriving. The plight of Tibet was becoming mainstream. Governments hardened their line and lobbied China over Tibetan political prisoners. Bill Clinton promoted the need for dialogue with the Dalai Lama at a historic joint press conference held with Jiang Zemin in Beijing in 1998, and broadcast live across the People's Republic of China. 'I have spent time with the Dalai Lama,' he declared. 'I believe him to be an honest man, and I believe that if he had a conversation with President Jiang, they would like each other very much.'

I took some time to realise that none of this seemed to have had the slightest effect on the Chinese government.

It was a wish to get back to Tibet, to see it unmediated by the versions or hopes of others, that set me on the road to Lhasa in the summer of 1999. More than a decade had passed since I had been there, and I was drawn back by a sense that the practicalities of daily life were being drowned out both by Communist restriction and the white noise of foreign sympathy. I wanted to move forward from the image I had created for myself during the years among exiles and campaigners.

There were many obstacles. I did not want to leave those I loved, my wife and my children in particular, with the practical and emotional problems that months of absence would bring for them, and for me. Beijing's political control was so tight that anyone I came into contact with might be compromised; I was a known activist, tainted. By meeting someone, or doing an interview, I would be attracting neighbourhood snoopers, or at worst the PSB and their gruesome cousins the SSB, the State Security Bureau. I would have to disguise names and locations when writing about the trip. I rejected the idea of travelling above board as a journalist, since it would involve a brief Potemkin tour in the charge of Communist officials, during which I would see nothing. There were linguistic problems. To speak with people in the provinces of ethnic Tibet (Kham, Amdo, Tö and U-Tsang) I would need several dialects of Tibetan, and at least two dialects of Chinese. I spoke none of these languages properly, and would have to find interpreters who could be relied on both professionally and politically.

The trip took much preparation. I avoided the network of contacts used by foreign journalists and campaigners, in particular the helpers linked to the Dalai Lama's exiled government, who had in the past been compromised. Instead, I followed the advice of people I trusted, and decided to move as informally as possible, looking like a tourist, starting in the border regions of Sichuan, where political control was comparatively lax. From there, I would make a gradual, fluid journey of around 2500 miles across mountains, plains and grassland, travelling mainly by local bus and truck, through the border province of Gansu to Xining, visiting the Dalai Lama's home village of Taktser, before threading down to the Tibet Autonomous Region, along the old trade route to the capital, Lhasa, on past the crab-claw turquoise lake the Yamdrok Tso to the Panchen Rinpoche's historic seat at Shigatse, and out towards the sacred snow peak, Mount Kailash, trying to link the Tibet of the mind to a modern, physical reality.

FOUR

In the early eighteenth century, a Dalai Lama grew his hair, practised archery and wrote erotic verse. I enjoyed the paradox of this epitome of celibacy and asceticism trying to live like an ordinary man. The Sixth Dalai Lama, the 'ocean of pure melody' Tsangyang Gyatso, is still loved by Tibetans for his transgression, and for his songs. He would descend from his high white palace, the Potala, and pass the evenings singing and wooing lovers in the drinking dens of the village of Shol. He was tall and sensual, a dancer and a drinker, an aesthete dressed in blue silk with rings on his fingers and braids in his hair. In the words of a street song of the time,

> In the Potala, he is Tsangyang Gyatso.
> In Shol, he is the licentious Dangzang Wangpo.

It was an idea of protest, the king coming down from his palace to be among the people. To Tibetans, he set a kind of example, yet his life was to come to a pitiful end as a pawn in a power struggle between Tibetan Buddhists, the Chinese state and intemperate, roaming Mongol tribes. In 1706, the year in which the Société Royale des Sciences de Montpellier was founded, the Sixth Dalai Lama was murdered in secret by Mongol soldiers near Kokonor Lake.

Before his death, he had prophesied his own rebirth in a famous song that is always associated with him, the beautiful, haunting, mournful lines,

---

Chade trung trung karpo,
Nga la shok tsel yar da,
Tak ring gyang la mi dro,
Litang kor ne leb yong.
(White crane!
Lend me your wings,
I will not go far, only to Lithang,
And then I shall return.)

The Sixth Dalai Lama's reincarnation was discovered, fittingly, in Lithang, but with Tibet facing incursions and internal turmoil, the future of this new child Dalai Lama was uncertain. The boy was taken west and installed in the Potala, but his return came at a terrible cost, since his guarantor was none other than China's ruler, the Kangxi emperor, whose troops had carried him to Lhasa. As disruption and civil war rumbled on in Tibet, the Chinese emperor sent a garrison of two thousand soldiers to oversee the Lhasa administration, and the new Dalai Lama was only able to function at the discretion of his overlord.

So in 1720, more than two centuries before the arrival of Chairman Mao's People's Liberation Army, Tibet's time as a free land came to an end.

When I thought of Lithang, it was of what one traveller called the 'barbaric grandeur' of the place: the rasping air, the rugged mountains, the blood feuds between the clans and the brutality of the suppression of the 1950s. I could picture tough Khampas in fur-lined *chubas* (the long, wraparound Tibetan robes), and the Sixth Dalai Lama singing his mournful song, and the little boy, the reincarnation, being taken away to the fastness of the Potala under the guard of Qing soldiers.

There was the symmetry of the liberated saint, Tsangyang Gyatso, Dangzang Wangpo, choosing to be reborn in a new body at Lithang, where his white crane had flown before returning. So it was a disappointment when I read a footnote in a book by the scholar Michael Aris stating that the Sixth Dalai Lama was unlikely to have been the author of 'White Crane'. It was not included in his body of work in the eighteenth or nineteenth century, and appeared under his name only in the twentieth.

Since then he has slipped into being the author. It sounds like the Sixth Dalai Lama's poetry, it has the right tone, so the attribution gets repeated. This made me wonder whether, like so much of Tibet's history, it may have been no more than a version, a version that was hard to dislodge.

Despite these doubts, I went on connecting the Sixth Dalai Lama with Lithang as I descended the azure mountains of Kham towards the fertile plains of Sichuan. He was universal, outside time, the maverick holy man, the poet.

> If I could meditate upon the Dharma,
> As intensely as I muse on my beloved,
> I would certainly attain enlightenment,
> In this one lifetime,

he wrote, a plea evoking sympathy and recognition.

> Peacocks from eastern India,
> Parrots from the depths of Kongbo,
> Though born in different countries,
> Come together at last in the holy city of Lhasa,

ran another song; but it was on the road from Lithang that my own journey, for all practical purposes, began.

On a hot summer's day, I met up with Wangdu. This was his first trip home since his escape, held tight at the front of his grandfather's saddle as they galloped away through fields of broad beans and barley on a moonless night to the village with the stone bridge. For forty-two years he had been in exile: in India, in Europe, in the USA; as a sweater salesman, a teacher, a bank clerk.

Wangdu and I were on a bus, descending from Lithang to a place where the air was thick and misty, the earth a deep rich red and the rivers a rushing ochre. Peanut- and orange-sellers squatted by the roadside under low, dripping ferns, and Chinese women marched steadily, carrying pails on the ends of bamboo poles, as their ancestors have done for centuries. The miles went by, the road widened and traffic and billboards appeared, and before long we were in Chengdu, the great city that has become, together with Chongqing, the arbiter of south-western China.

Walking in the evening rush hour, the crush was unmediated, people pressing in close, on bicycles, on the street, in shops and restaurants. Roads and buildings were being built and dismantled, pipes and cables had been pushed through surfaces, scaffolding was being erected. The old houses, with a brick base and wooden cladding rising to tiered, tiled roofs, like the ones Marco Polo saw when he came to Chengdu in the thirteenth century and compared the city to Paris, were being razed. A metallic smog lay across the stagnant river. On the main square, behind a large grey statue of Chairman Mao, his arm outstretched in greeting, rose a giant picture of a suave European man smoking a cigarette. Outside a video arcade, a tall chair was occupied by a twitching salesman, yabbering away into a microphone like a rapper. A willowy figure with hooded eyes stood by a department store with a bulky plastic barrel on his back and a nozzle in his hand. You purchased a cup; he filled it with Future Cola.

Chengdu was rich, compared to Lithang and the Tibetan borderlands, with glittering shop-fronts and long hotels draped with gaudy tentacles of light. Office workers clipped down the arcades in sharp suits and short skirts, mobile phones clasped to the side of the head. The city felt relaxed, like much of urban China, with no obvious sense of being supervised or coerced, except by market forces. This was a capitalist metropolis, on the Asian model, with barefoot bicycle-rickshaw drivers straining alongside family cars and delivery trucks. The only people who seemed different – separate – were the Communist Party officials I saw, once or twice, speeding through traffic in long, dark limousines, windows tinted to keep out the gaze of the masses.

Chen Kuiyuan, ruler of the Tibet Autonomous Region, lived here in Chengdu, and only flew the two hours to Lhasa when his presence was required. His predecessor as Party Secretary, Hu Jintao (who was now heir apparent to Jiang Zemin), had even lived in Beijing for the last two years of his tenure. The official explanation for this was that both men suffered from respiratory problems at high altitude. Another reason, which I learned some weeks later, was that Chen was so despised by Tibetans, including those who worked within the Party bureaucracy, for the severity of the crackdown when he arrived in Lhasa in 1992, that he tried to avoid going to Tibet at all. The wandering British mathematician Thomas Manning had noticed a similar problem in 1811, writing: 'The Chinese lord it here like the English in India . . . it is very bad policy thus perpetually to send men of bad character to govern Tibet. It no doubt displeases the Grand Lama and Tibetans in general, and tends to prevent their affections from settling in favour of the Chinese government.'

Party Secretary Chen was an old-style ideologue, resolutely against the political flexibility encouraged by elements within the Party leadership in Tibet. He often lashed out at the Dalai Lama and Buddhism, which he called a 'foreign' religion. His speeches did not inspire confidence that he had anything to offer his fiefdom but further repression. In a radio broadcast in 1994, he had said:

> As long as Party organisations around Tibet remain pure, strong and capable of fighting, the disturbance caused by the splittist forces is nothing to us . . . We should never give up our education and guidance to the people and should not allow a *laissez-faire* attitude towards religions under the pretext that people are free to profess a religion. Communists are not allowed to have any religious belief, much less participation in religious activities.

So Tibet was run from Chengdu, by remote control, in the colonial way. The rulers of empires are rarely interested in those they rule; they administer and deal with them, trying to project a sense of permanence, but find their subjects frustrating and ungrateful. The colonised reciprocate with resentful over-interest, looking to conspiracy to explain their plight, thinking their rulers must have some overarching idea or policy towards them, when really they are doing no more than muddling through, defending their position, trying not to lose control. No Chinese paramount leader – not the emperors of old, not Mao Zedong, not Deng Xiaoping – has been to Tibet, although the Tibetan plateau makes up almost a quarter of China's land mass. Jiang Zemin visited

Lhasa in 1990 before he became president, but has not been back since.

Wangdu, nearing fifty, had last seen his sister Pasang when he was five years old. She was a peasant now, with many children and gold-capped teeth, living in a house with doors of unseasoned wood, strips of raw pork fat hanging from the kitchen rafters and *thangkas* (Buddhist paintings, protected by silk curtains) hanging from the walls. Wangdu came from a world of subways, chinos and schedules. Such dislocation was expected here, for Tibetans.

He took me to a family lunch in a small village two days' journey north of Chengdu. I must make his story anonymous, he explained, to protect his relatives.

The house stood alone, with a fence and a spiked metal gate. Wangdu, myself, his wife and daughter, his old father and sister Pasang, secure in her *chuba* and *pangden* (the Tibetan apron striped like a coloured barcode), had been ushered in with great ceremony past beehives and a potato patch. Outside was a river, lush with mountain water, with barley growing on both banks. Local workers were quarrying sand from the riverbed, standing in the icy running water, shovelling it into a trailer while a miniature tractor shot black smoke into the cold air. This was a coveted job; sand and gravel extraction permits were coveted and costly to obtain.

The house was spacious, with four rooms. It belonged to Wangdu's cousin Zhaxi and her husband, a Chinese farmer and veterinarian who was spending the morning making bricks at a neighbour's farm. When her mother died, during the bad times, while her father was in prison, Zhaxi had been taken in by a Chinese family. Now she spoke the local Chinese dialect, and could remember no Tibetan.

The receiving room had damp, discoloured walls, concrete blocks licked with limewash. There was a couch, some chairs, a low table, a plastic tree and an unplumbed top-loading washing machine. A shabby poster of a Chinese pop star in a shirt and tie, bright-eyed with bouffant hair, was stuck to the wall. Zhaxi, excited and anxious at having to entertain us, was small and broad, with chunky round shoulders and red cheeks, wearing tailored trousers and a slippery blue shirt with an embroidered collar. She bustled about, looking at us shyly, making little clucking exclamations of surprise. Clearly this was a new experience, her first encounter with guests from abroad, and her aim was to fête and receive us, rather than to have a conversation.

A television was carried in. There was a performance with the aerial, stretching it round the back of the chairs, moving the table, moving the television, moving us, until everything was settled, precariously. She brought a tray of plums and some boiled broad beans, and we watched folk-dancing for several hours, drinking black tea and syrupy barley spirit while the meal was prepared.

When I returned from a visit to the toilet, a shallow hole in the ground with a rough plywood seat, guarded by a pair of enormous, snorting pigs, Pasang was telling a story about the illness of her youngest son. Soon after he was born, the boy developed a distended stomach. Conventional and herbal remedies were tried, but he remained weak. On a summer's day, they were having a picnic by a lake when a Chinese couple came past. They started talking and the woman cuddled the boy, whose stomach was very painful that day. He stopped crying at once. Realising that this was a good omen, Pasang suggested that the Chinese couple take him as their own child, nominally, so as to deceive the spirit that was making him ill. They agreed. Offerings were made and the boy was given the name of one of Pasang's deceased nephews, whose soul was known to live peacefully at the base of a particular tree in the valley. This change of name was a variation on the traditional Tibetan system of not naming a child until it was six years old, or giving it a 'bad' name such as 'Dog' or 'Blacksmith', in order to preserve its life from evil spirits, as the spirits would have no name by which to call it. A month later, the boy was able to come home, although some of his clothes and possessions had to be left with the Chinese couple in order to deceive the bad spirit. To be safe, they changed his name a second time, on the advice of a lama, and paid for prayers to be recited. Now he was five years old and in good health.

Pasang told us this in a detailed, matter-of-fact way, in the Amdo dialect of Tibetan, as if it was an ordinary, unquestioned part of daily life that a dead boy's soul should reside under a tree, and an evil spirit would be deluded by a change of name. We were in a different world, far from the streets of Chengdu. Her interest was less in the philosophical systems of Tibetan Buddhism than in folk superstition, ritual and blind veneration. I saw clearly for the first time that spiritual devotion still lay at the core of the identity of most rural Tibetans.

The television was removed. We sat around the table, which had been covered now with a thin sheet of plastic. There were about a dozen of us: some cousins, neighbours and a pair of semi-adopted children.

A Chinese cadre, Mr Li, arrived late, although he lived only next door. There was a flurry as everyone shifted and shook his hand. He was a short man with a green jacket buttoned over a weighty belly, smiling and magnanimous. It turned out that he was a retired mid-level official from the forestry department in the local town, and a Party member. After a while I realised, from his manner and his lateness, that Mr Li had been invited to the lunch to confer status.

'*Ji tui shi xiang!*' he barked. 'The chicken's foot is a delicacy!' He waved a chicken's foot.

The cadre loved his food. Most of all he loved the yellow chickens' feet that Zhaxi brought in on a large plate. He would bite off a toe, masticate noisily, eject a small piece of bone, then bite the next toe until he had the pad all to himself. Then he would start on a new foot. He puffed on a cigarette throughout the meal, offering grunts of appreciation.

Plates came: cold cucumber swimming in soy and chilli, cured duck eggs which gave off a strong smell of fish, chopped tomatoes with sugar, pickled white radish, wind-dried mutton with sesame seeds, cubes of cold pork fat, oily spiced celery, and finally a big tub of clear soup. The green, pungent duck eggs were coveted. When Wangdu's teenage daughter Sonam refused even a mouthful of them, everyone laughed and the plate was pushed towards her again and again. Back in America she was a fashion model, hoping to move from New Faces to the Main Board, more at home in New York or Paris than here in Amdo, and she was not to be persuaded to eat cured duck eggs.

Zhaxi's husband opened a bottle of strong fruit spirit. The cadre became expansive, praising the scenery and the tourist spots of Sichuan province.

'A toast to Jiuzhaigou National Park!' he said, raising his shot glass and exposing snaggled teeth, the colour of the chickens' feet. He plucked a piece of toilet paper from a roll in the middle of the table and rubbed it across his lips.

Everyone drank.

The cadre had come across foreigners before, he told me, when he entertained members of a German tourism delegation. Life in Ngawa prefecture was good these days. The minority nationalities lived in harmony with the Han. They were like brothers. He was happy to share a meal with a Tibetan family. Wangdu should leave America and come home. There would be plenty of opportunities for him here.

'A toast to the beauty of the Sichuan mountain waterfalls!'

Everyone drank.

The next day, I went with Wangdu and his father to visit the local town. Rain streaked down in sheets, melting the red earth. The People's Armed Police jogged down the street, in formation, past old wooden buildings. A pair of Tibetan women, with lumpy red coral jewellery, scarlet head-scarves and dark braiding and coins attached to their aprons, made way for them. Lungs and tripe were draped over a length of wire at the meat stall, where a glass cabinet displayed yak hooves, tongues and hairy fetlocks. Another stall had fox pelts, their furriness illuminated by a dim lightbulb dangling from the end of a stick, like bait from a fishing-rod. A porter pushed past us, stooped under the weight of a huge, bloody yak skeleton.

The communities were physically distinct in this border town: Chinese, Tibetans, Qiang and Hui all huddling in separate groups in shop-fronts and restaurants. They traded, but marriages, like that between Zhaxi and the veterinarian, were still rare. There was a mosque used by the Hui, two Chinese temples, one of which looked as if it had recently been built, and several Tibetan Buddhist temples. Some of the more picturesque buildings were administered by the state as tourist sites, for despite its profession of atheism, the Party has no qualms about making money from religion. It was this desire for revenue, in part, that lay behind the cadre's toasts and conversation. There had been a subtext to the encounter at the family lunch, which only became apparent when Wangdu went with his father to pay a courtesy call on two local officials, one Chinese, one Tibetan.

Later, Wangdu told me what had happened.

The officials had a proposition, communicated gradually over several cups of tea in a squat government block off the muddy main street. Wangdu would be given a senior position in the tourism department if he returned from exile. There were great new opportunities coming up. Tourism was booming, with the forests and lakes of northern Sichuan already attracting the adventurous new rich from cities like Chengdu. The trouble was that local people lacked knowledge of the outside world. Wangdu was an educated man. He spoke English. He knew what tourists would enjoy, and would be able to improve the town's commercial prospects. He should return to the place of his birth, where he would be honoured as a favoured son.

Wangdu was dismayed by what he heard. He had a good clerical post in a bank in Seattle. The idea that he might abandon the life he had worked so long and hard to create in order to live in such a backwater was inconceivable. Returnees were known dismissively by the exiles as 'gyal tshong pa', or 'country-sellers'. His wife Pema, also a Tibetan although from another part of Tibet, had a job selling white goods in a department store in the suburb of Maple Leaf. Their children, one still in college, the other two just starting out on their careers, would laugh at the idea of migrating to Communist China. They knew the plight of their homeland; even the official statistics looked bad. According to a recent report from CPIRC, China's state body on population, 60 per cent of people in the Tibet Autonomous Region were illiterate, against a national average of 16 per cent. It had the lowest rural per capita income of any province, and was the only one where life expectancy dropped below sixty years of age, against a national average of sixty-nine. Infant mortality towered at ninety-six per thousand, eleven times the rate in Beijing. Here in the ethnically mixed borderlands the situation was a little better, but the underlying privation was the same.

Wangdu tried to explain all this to the officials as politely as he could. They were not convinced. Naturally, he should bring his wife and children with him; the paperwork would be arranged. The town needed people like him. The pitch continued, and it became apparent that Wangdu's father, a strong and resolute old man, conscious of the respect that was being shown to his son, was in favour of the plan. He told Wangdu that he should take up the post, but not join the Party. There were several young Tibetans in influential positions in the town who would look out for him; the days had long gone when Tibetan officials were mere stooges, with Chinese 'secretaries' controlling their every move.

Repeating a refusal became embarrassing, so Wangdu left the meeting, saying he would think it over. He let the matter drift for a few days, hoping it would go away, despite frequent remarks from his father. He had his return air ticket. His daughter Sonam was keen to get home. I knew that he found it awkward and painful to be put under pressure in this way, and that he would never be persuaded. He was displaced, an exile; it would not be possible for him to feel a true sense of belonging in his ancestral land – or not until Tibet was free.

Wangdu's dilemma struck me. A Tibetan was being sought for a prominent post in a Chinese province. According to the material put out by Western pro-Tibet groups, much of which I had read and some of which I had written, the authorities discriminated systematically against Tibetans. Words like apartheid, racism and genocide cropped up. Yet from what I had seen so far, the regime was far from homogeneous. Most officials in China seemed to be unsophisticated, poorly educated and badly paid, and envious of those who had made lives abroad. Local people paid fortunes to criminal gangs to smuggle them to Australia, Europe and North America. Although the top Party jobs were occupied by Han Chinese, who make up more than 90 per cent of China's population, the middle and lower ranks of the bureaucracy in these border regions included many Tibetans, Hui and other minorities. The official newspaper the *People's Daily* said that nearly three-quarters of the officials in the Tibet Autonomous Region were ethnically Tibetan.

I asked Wangdu why his father was so keen for him to move back to Amdo. Surely he understood that his future lay in America?

'I guess he doesn't see it like that. He was in prison for eighteen years,' said Wangdu, in an offhand way, 'and he wants the family to be reunited before he passes away.'

Eighteen years. A friend of mine who spent three years in prison in Britain had found the squalor and tedium extreme. How could Wangdu's father have spent eighteen years in prison here? What were his crimes? During the long lunch at Zhaxi's house, he had sat with his hat pulled well down over his brow, a quiet, taciturn, stoical old man. What lay behind the hard set of his jaw, the deep creases on his brown face, the silence in his eyes?

Wangdu's father, Dawa Tsering, told me some of his story, reluctantly, a bit at a time, making light of his own misery and tribulation, and emphasising the suffering of others, in the Tibetan way.

When the Reds first came to Dawa Tsering's village in the early 1950s, they reformed the trading of crops and the registration of land. The villagers were nervous, but the changes made no immediate difference to their lives. They knew about the Communists from the days of the Long March, back in the 1930s, when fighters had passed through their district while retreating from the Guomindang, the Nationalist Party. Many of the Communist soldiers had starved at that time, eating grass and leaves, and some had stooped to eating their fallen comrades. These men had fought a big battle to the east of Dawa Tsering's village, and some years later his cousin found a pair of high-powered binoculars on the battlefield, which he sold to a local Chinese trader, and got himself started in business.

In 1958, during the period of *Minzhu Gaige*, or Democratic Reforms, life changed. There were a few Tibetan members of the Communist Party, but nearly all the new ideologues were Chinese, from outside the region. They were not like the Chinese that Dawa Tsering knew in neighbouring villages. His family were classified as rich peasants, the same background as Mao himself, and were forced to move out of their house. Soon afterwards, while the Communists were holding a public struggle session there, an associate of Dawa Tsering burst in and stabbed the leader of the Party work group and his bodyguard. The stabber escaped, but after that, life in the village became very dangerous.

The Communists confiscated the wealth of the Buddhist monasteries of Sichuan. They took money, gold, carvings and grain reserves. Many people had brought their most treasured possessions to the monasteries, thinking they would be safe there. One Tibetan monk, Kesang Chompel, had joined the Reds, and after his monastery had been looted, he returned on horseback in a raiding party and smashed the monastery's protector deity in front of people from nearby villages, who had been made to come and watch. He challenged the deity to strike him down, saying that he was not afraid and that he condemned religious superstition. Kesang Chompel smashed open the big statue and removed a sacred relic, the skull of a famous monk, a great spiritual practitioner, with the Tibetan letter 'ah' inscribed naturally upon it (the letter had been there from birth). The raiders took the skull and threw it away, telling the villagers that religion was poison and monks were parasites. Leaving, they managed to cross the river safely, except for Kesang Chompel, whose horse stumbled and threw him. He drowned in the river. His death reinforced local faith in the protector deity, despite the terrible things that had happened to their monastery.

The ordinary monks were disrobed and sent back to their villages. They were forced to marry. Some took their lives rather than break their religious vows. The senior monks and reincarnate lamas remained, under the supervision of Party officials, but were not allowed to go into their own rooms. Signs were put on the doors saying 'Confiscated Property, Do Not Enter'. Farmers from another region were brought in to live in the monastery. Not until 1982, after liberalisation in China, were the local people allowed to rebuild the monastery. Funds were raised from local Tibetans and money was given by the government. A local woman had a dream that the monk's sacred skull was near a certain rock in the mountains. It was found there, and has now been installed again inside the statue of the protector deity.

In 1958, believing that everything he knew and valued was being destroyed, Dawa Tsering decided to join the Amdo men who were fighting the Communists. He sent his daughter Pasang to live with her aunt, and told his wife to take Wangdu to Lhasa to be close to Gyalwa Rinpoche, His Holiness the Dalai Lama, their guardian.

Dawa Tsering arrived in Lhasa just before the uprising of 1959. The city was full of people from Amdo and Kham. It was the first time he had been there. The resistance fighters had few weapons. One night, when he was a little drunk, he and three others broke into a Chinese military base. They knew that it contained an arms depot, and thought they might be able to get away with rifles or even machine guns.

Inevitably, they were caught, and he was sent to a prison in Bathang, then transferred east to a labour camp. His strongest feeling was one of sheer loss, that the Chinese had control over Tibet and the Dalai Lama had become a refugee.

China was now in the grip of the Great Leap Forward famine. The hunger was constant. Dawa Tsering had a cup of porridge made of barley or maize flour twice a day, and sometimes a piece of turnip. Many people were starving. They thought about food all the time, about how they might be able to get something to eat, even if it was only a cabbage leaf or a plant or something small. They were so weak they just wanted to lie still. But you had to work. If you were digging in the earth and came across an earthworm or a caterpillar, others would try to grab it. If you got a worm, you would usually save it until the evening, then boil and eat it. Planting willow trees near the prison fence, they found the skeletons of prisoners who had died of starvation and been buried by the guards. Prisoners started to eat the leather from their own boots. They would cut a small piece from the top and chew it through the day to try and get some sustenance.

Each day, a little less of the boot would remain, until their feet were bare.

As the famine got worse, the guards allowed files of cadaverous prisoners out into the grassy valley around the camp and let them hunt for insects, worms and berries. Many of the older and weaker prisoners never returned. The guards did not search for them. Years later, nomads reported finding human skeletons in the upper reaches of the valley, some resting against a boulder, some lying beneath a tree or by a riverbank. Many of the skeletons were reported to be huddled together in an embrace of death, for comfort maybe, hoping or praying for a better rebirth in the next life.

In the early years, the prisoners were chained and shackled, and there was constant hunger; there was nothing else to think about but the hunger. The sanitation was disgusting, just a pot in the middle of the large cell, emptied once a day, and a constant smell of excrement and filth. There were bugs and lice all over their bodies, and they had no way of getting rid of them. Their clothes were rags. They did whatever the guards told them. 'If a small boy is told that the west is the east,' Dawa Tsering said, 'he will have no choice but to agree. That is what it was like for us in the camp.'

After about twelve years, at the beginning of the 1970s, the prison camp became less strict. It began to feel normal to live in that way. They still had to do hard physical work – chopping down trees, making tiles, moving stones. These conditions continued until the political situation in China improved with the death of Mao Zedong in 1976, when a few people were released from the camp, or transferred to different prisons. In 1979, Dawa Tsering was released. When he returned to his home village, the place was so different it was hard to recognise the houses and the fields. He felt that he was in another world. Many people had died during the terrible famine of the early 1960s, victims of Chairman Mao's Great Leap Forward. Dawa Tsering was able to find his daughter Pasang and other members of his family, the ones who had survived. He felt as if he had been in prison for his whole life.

For two years, he saved money. He knew by then that his wife and his son Wangdu had escaped into exile in India after the 1959 uprising. He crossed the border into Nepal, where an unbribed local guide gave him away. The police caught him, but he was released and finally reached Siliguri in India, where he boarded a train to Calcutta; his first time on a train. He got to Howrah station and stood there waving his arms, trying to get the Indians to understand him. He found it incredibly noisy. There were huge crowds of people, more people than he had ever seen. Someone found a Tibetan monk at the railway station, who came and spoke to Dawa Tsering in the Lhasa dialect. The monk helped him to meet other Tibetan exiles in India, and finally, after several months, to locate his wife.

She was married to another man.

Not knowing whether he was dead or alive all those years, she had found a new husband. Dawa Tsering tried to persuade her to come back with him to Amdo. She refused. He returned alone. The Chinese police caught him, and gave him another year in prison for crossing the border illegally. Then he came back to his home village and started up in business, trading this and that. He was not doing too badly, he told me, but he was getting old; his main wish was to reunite his family.

Dawa Tsering did not wish to talk about the loss of his wife or the injustice of his imprisonment. His emotions had been cauterised, in order to survive. His final remark to me, looking straight ahead, hat pulled down low over his brow, was, 'I had a certain destiny. My children have a different destiny. *Da de min rey ci shad ji.* That's all there is to say.'

Wangdu flew back to America with his family. His father seemed to be reconciled. He still had Pasang. Dawa Tsering was not a broken man, for all that he had been through.

FIVE

There was a bus heading for northern Amdo, deeper into ethnic Tibet, towards the limitless grassland. I took it; I could return to Chengdu and city life later.

The strangest thing about my time with Wangdu and his family, looking back, as we drove through the lush fields of Sichuan, was the normality, the way they spoke so calmly of persecution and starvation. Tibetan families in the borderlands expected that people would have died, gone missing, become refugees. The theft of Dawa Tsering's adult life was not unusual. It was part of the local past, the wrenching of brothers from sisters, husbands from wives, parents from children. The younger generation had found ways to deal with what had happened, and to survive in the present. Zhaxi and Wangdu were escapees (Zhaxi to China, Wangdu to America), but many participated in the political system, taking salaried jobs in the bureaucracy where they could, quietly, help other rising Tibetans. Some went back to traditional pursuits like farming and herding. Others broke away.

I had met Pemba, a friend of a friend, in Chengdu, and been amazed by her open political disaffection. She was a squat, canny, flat-faced woman, heavily pregnant, from Rebkong, a Tibetan town in northern Amdo known for turning out writers and free-thinkers, most famously the mercurial, opium-smoking monk Gedun Chompel, who was known to have debated publicly with eight different people at the same time, like a grand master playing simultaneous chess. (On being arrested in Lhasa in 1947 he was found to be in possession of a subversive history of Tibet, revolutionary pamphlets and a rubber woman.) Pemba had spent a year studying in India, illegally, and I felt that this period of freedom lay behind her irreverent view of Chinese politics. She said the quality of education in the Tibet Autonomous Region was so bad that serious students either went to secondary schools and universities in China, or escaped over the border to India to be schooled with the exiles.

Pemba spoke of those who governed the country in the name of the proletariat as if they were parasites propping up a failed system. Communism had been abandoned by the Chinese Communist Party in favour of a market economy, but the Party still ruled. Corruption had become systemic within Chinese politics, to the point that distinguished senior officials were being targeted through the courts in an attempt to bring it under control. A provincial deputy governor, a vice-mayor and a city police chief were shortly to be executed for taking bribes, while the wife of a senior Party boss was being investigated over a multi-million-dollar smuggling scandal. Pemba regarded high-level arrests of this kind as being little more than a symptom of the power struggle within the leadership. Chengdu was the collecting point for officials from across Sichuan, Tibet and Yunnan who were in search of relaxation and business opportunities. Many were involved in construction and tourism projects, winning contracts which generated money for those in positions of greater power.

A graduate of Sichuan University in Chengdu, Pemba had to conduct her life on several different levels. The city's Tibetan residential quarter was targeted as a centre of likely subversion. There were frequent visits from the police, checking papers, and from the PSB, taking in known suspects for interrogation. There were Tibetan informants, which reduced the sense of trust within the community. Still, the subversion continued. Pemba's friend Lobsang distributed pirated DVDs of the banned Hollywood movies *Kundun* and *Seven Years in Tibet*, and had not, so far, been caught.

The last time I had been in China, in the mid-1980s, there had been a respectful fear of the country's leaders. Having spent time in Eastern Europe, this was a surprise to me; I had imagined all totalitarian regimes to be plagued by dissent. Soviet satellites such as Poland and Czechoslovakia were full of people whispering jokes about their rulers.

'How many leaders rule Russia?'

'One and a half, because Chernenko is half dead and Lenin is still alive.'

'Can Canada become Communist?'

'No, because it would have nowhere to import grain from.'

There was none of this open impiety in China at that time – or none that could safely be shared with a visiting foreigner. The years of Maoist rule had inculcated a seemingly genuine respect for the Party leadership and the functioning of the system. Dissent was not encouraged; Mao's one-time anointed successor, the paranoid former soldier Lin Biao, said he had prospered by following these personal mottoes:

DO NOT BE CRITICAL

DO NOT REPORT BAD NEWS

DO NOT MAKE CONSTRUCTIVE PROPOSALS

Pemba spoke good English and fluent Chinese. She still used Tibetan at home, but saw Chinese, pragmatically, as the language of progress and communication. Even when speaking in Tibetan, she would break into Chinese to transmit a piece of data, such as a telephone number. Like the younger generation of Tibetan fiction writers, she felt that the Chinese language offered a way to reach out and speak to a larger audience. Pemba had no view on this; unless you used the tongue of the dominant power, you would go nowhere. Many of her friends were Chinese. She avoided discussing Tibet's political status with them, but otherwise they had similar views on the need for change in China, and matching scorn for the corruption within the Communist hierarchy. 'It's not the Chinese that are the problem,' Pemba had said, 'it's the Communists.'

The bus skirted a wide valley, passing fields of maize, cabbages and onions, and spacious wooden houses with rooftop satellite dishes. It seemed incredible that such fertile land had ever known starvation. Yet every family in Sichuan – Tibetans and Chinese, revolutionaries and reactionaries – had been damaged by the famine of 1958–1962, caused by Mao's catastrophic Great Leap Forward. The death rate for the province in 1959 was forty-seven people per thousand, more than three times the national average. The days of the great hunger were a memory now, of gnawing pain, lethargy and swollen bellies, of having to eat boiled grass, roots and tree bark, of parents lying down by the roadside to rest and never getting up again. The Communist Party still claimed it was a mistake caused not by human agency, but by such matters as bad weather and international debt – what might be called Acts of God. Younger people knew little of it; even those who spoke of the wrongs of the Cultural Revolution had only the haziest idea of the famine.

I felt, travelling north, steeped in paper knowledge of the past while observing the present, that history had gone into remission, to be walked over for as long as it would stay down. Everything had to be tempered; so much could not be mentioned, for fear of the consequences.

We drove through Zungchu, a town the Chinese call Songpan, an ancient frontier post, a place of trade and ethnic overlap, stemming from a collision in the seventh century between its Chinese commander and a Tibetan imperial army which laid siege to the town and demanded that the emperor of China send a bride to marry King Songtsen Gampo of Tibet. Now the communities lived side by side. For the surrounding nomads, Zungchu was the metropolis, a place of things where they could buy provisions and manufactured goods. Urban Tibetans with knowledge of the wider world intersected with their own wild past, the world of yaks and horses, swords and skirmishes.

'*Cho ngotsa mepe dundro! Cho talokpa, tso zong dashar!* You shameless little animal! How dare you do that, you insolent heathen? You're going to get it!'

The voice was loud and piercing, beside my ear. I had fallen asleep as the sun came up, and woke to find an old man climbing on top of me, trying to stab a young nomad with a dagger as the bus lurched into potholes. The old man lunged forward and managed to jump from my lap onto a sack of grain that was wedged in the aisle, lashing out at the nomad and ripping a gash in the front of his sheepskin *chuba*. Everyone on the bus was shouting now, taking sides. Outside it was pouring with rain, soaking the fields as we drove between them. The young nomad, using his bare right arm, his fighting arm, pulled a short sword from his belt to retaliate, but someone grabbed the old man from behind to keep them apart.

For a few moments, everything was calm.

'How dare you behave like that, bringing shame on your community? Do you call yourself a nomad? Where is your respect? You little bug, how dare you do a thing like that, behaving like a foreigner? That's what you're doing. Look at you, you're behaving like a foreigner.'

The old man, his face dark and lined, went on with the tirade, gesticulating. The nomad, handsome, perhaps twenty, with nearly Mongolian features, matted long black hair and sharp cheekbones, his *chuba* bound at the waist with a band of scarlet cloth, looked frightened. His friend, of a similar age, held up his hands and stroked the air, indicating apology and contrition.

The elderly attacker was wearing a khaki reefer jacket, which he took off now, still muttering with anger, tying the sleeves around his waist tightly and deliberately, smoothing down the sides over his legs, until he was wearing the jacket like a *chuba*. I realised now that he too was a Tibetan nomad, and that this was a preparation for more fighting. The dagger blinked, and he was onto the younger man, pushing him back into a seat, trying to find elbow room to strike a decent blow. They wrestled, wedged in by the crush of passengers, puffing and cursing until they were pulled apart. The younger man was pushed roughly to the front of the bus, his head cuffed by other passengers as he went. The driver stopped, the door opened, and he was left on the roadside in the rain.

The bus had left Wangdu's village before dawn, packed with farmers, nomads, traders and sacks of *tsampa*. There were two young Chinese women on board, wearing sexy silk shirts and knee-length skirts, with clips in their hair, going on holiday. In Chengdu, their clothes would have been unremarkable, but in the countryside they looked defiantly urban and racy. The young nomads had made the most of the opportunity, joking with them in broken Chinese, singing romantic songs about mountains and eagles. The Chinese women enjoyed the game, flirting back, a little nervous of the roughness and crudity of their suitors, but clearly excited and amused.

This had continued for several hours. I fell asleep, wedged in beside the old man in the reefer jacket, unaware that the display represented a major breach of protocol. The mistake came, I learned later, when one of the nomads took the hand of one of the Chinese women, with her consent, and began to stroke it. For my old neighbour, this was an unacceptable way to behave. It broke the social conventions; a member of his own extended community was behaving 'like a foreigner'. He drew his dagger, clambered on top of me, and lunged at the manifestation of modern manners.

Things returned to normal quickly. The bus had to cope with the overlap of modernity and tradition, the gulf between the placid Tibetan farmers of Zungchu, the nomads and the wide-eyed Chinese visitors. In the old days, Tibetan farmers and nomads had little interaction, except for meeting at certain times of year to trade and barter, but since the disruption of the 1960s, both groups had fractured. The radiance of the landscape caused further complications, attracting urban Chinese tourists who had no point of reference with either community. Casual fights, the sudden flash of a dagger and immediate physical action to resolve a problem were part of nomad culture. There was none of the lenient, cuddly pacifism that foreigners might expect from Tibetans.

By midday, we had risen out of the farming land of Sichuan and into the true grassland, covered in little yellow flowers and aromatic herbs. The altitude was too high for crops to grow, and every few miles you would see clusters of tents and small herds of yak and dzo grazing in the distance. Our progress was slow. There was no proper road, just a snaking, muddy indentation running alongside the river.

We stopped. A dozen trucks and a handful of buses were backed up in front of a crater, where torrents of rain had dissolved the track.

A gang of nomad men, who looked as if they had appeared magically out of the landscape, but had in fact only discovered a foolproof way to make money, were collecting rocks and stones from the riverbank to throw into the crater. The repairs were done with swaggering theatricality to entertain the onlookers, in particular the Chinese tourists who stared with faces of horror and fascination from behind the windows of a minibus. A middle-aged Chinese man, dressed in white pumps, white trousers and a cream zip-up jacket with a kangaroo embroidered on the collar, stepped down daintily from his bus to inspect the crater. He had the air of a tour leader. As he leaned over, a wide wave of cold, muddy water came shooting up onto the shoes, the trousers and the zip-up jacket, dispatched by a nomad's careful lob of a large rock. He retreated to the minibus soaked, filthy and irate, while the thrower made comical expressions of surprise, as if the drenching had been an unhappy accident. A pair of nomad women standing on the track laughed infectiously, showing their gold teeth.

The urban Chinese tourists viewed the nomads as savages. Their attitude reminded me of the line taken by the chronicler Athanasius Kircher, who in 1667 wrote of the Tibetans in *China Illustrata*: 'Since, in religion, they never wash themselves with water, but with a certain oil, which is so putrid that they exhale an intolerable stench, they are so stained by the aforementioned oil, that you would say they were not humans, but witches.' The nomads played up to the role, knowing they had an audience. The Tibetan farmers, whose bus I was on, mixed disapproval of the nomads' behaviour with amusement at their panache.

The lead truck inched forward. Soon, many engines were revving. The nomads, some of them on horseback now, levied an impromptu toll, demanding to be paid for their work on the road. The drivers were compliant, and any who had doubts were soon persuaded by the arrival in their cab of a couple of uninhibited types, smelling of dung smoke and livestock, fingering the daggers at their belts. As we drove away through exhaust fumes and muddy water, I could see whooping nomads galloping across the grassland, stuffing banknotes down the front of their *chubas*.

There were two small landslides during the journey, but as the day began to fade we reached Zorge, a town stuck out on its own in the middle of the grassland. It had taken us eleven hours to cover about a hundred miles.

Zorge was not what I had expected. There were two long, dusty streets, municipal and Party offices, a court and a jailhouse. That was it, apart from the ceaseless dust. Nothing happened in Zorge. The stores sold basic goods: enamel bowls, synthetic fabric and thermoses. The eating places, run by Chinese or Hui Muslims, offered only yak meat, noodles and boiled bones. Visiting nomad men played snooker on pitted open-air snooker tables. Two monks from Tagtsa monastery rode into town on horseback, followed by a boy in dark glasses astride a backfiring motorbike. Muslim women in full black veils walked along in pairs, knitting as they went. A Chinese policeman wobbled by on a bicycle. Sometimes a truck would appear, which got the place going.

On the map, Zorge had looked like a remote outpost of the mind's Tibet – a town, a place, an event – but it turned out to be no more than a dirty, temporary, run-down creation, with no organic life of its own. A friend in India who came from Zorge, a Tibetan exile who now worked in New Delhi, had described it to me as a place of adventure, romance, monasteries, nomads and galloping horses. I realised that this must have been an imagined memory, to give some shape to the family and places he had left behind; or perhaps he had just told me what I wanted to hear. Many of the remoter Tibetan towns and settlements were, like Zorge, no more than places of colonial administration, the fallout of the policies of central government, hardship postings for police and officials. Such towns had no purpose but the impossible one of trying to administer landscape. The real Tibetan world continued out in the grassland with the nomads, their tents, their yaks and their faith.

Later, I spoke to an old nomad man, and asked him what or where he had regarded as the ultimate source of political authority before 1950. He thought for a while and answered Labrang, meaning Amdo's big monastery, south of Xining. When pressed, he mentioned Lhasa, but said that Lhasa was a source of spiritual rather than political authority. The further our discussion went, the more I realised that my question was meaningless. There had been his tribe of nomads, and the other tribes it ran up against, and then there had been Labrang, where boys would be sent to become monks and crucial religious ceremonies would be conducted. Beyond that, there was nothing. Political influence could not be exerted on nomads in empty grassland.

I decided to visit Labrang; it would only be a small detour on the way to Xining. A bus set off from Zorge before the sun rose, pushing a convoy of canvas barrel trucks up through the rising green hills, the drivers surly and still drunk from the night before. The escarpment broke sharply into roll after roll of shining hillside and an intense, expanding landscape. We stopped at a police checkpoint on the boundary between Sichuan and Gansu. Hefty Chinese men in dark glasses sprawled beside their four-wheel drives eating a picnic while their juniors inspected papers. The others on the packed, pungent bus were Tibetan, mainly nomads, but since I was on an 'open' tourist route I had no difficulties, only stares.

I got down before Garhe, at a windblown crossroads. There were two people on the roadside, a man and a woman, their *chubas* bulging with possessions, heading home from a pilgrimage to Labrang. The man was carrying a set of scriptures wrapped in cloth. I could feel the emptiness of the land, the sweep of the stretching sky, our smallness. A golden eagle circled above the crossroads, watching.

After waiting for several hours in the piercing sunlight, I caught a lift on a little tractor-trailer going down the dusty road to the south. I rode on the back, bumping, until we reached a wooden bridge, and then walked along the river to some rickety buildings. There I found a bus for Tso, the prefectural capital which the Chinese call Hezuo. It was going nowhere. A very dark, toothless man prodded the engine interminably with a metal spike, and then set to work on it with a spanner. There was a lot of conversation about the engine. The sky was growing heavy. I drank green tea and ate *thukpa* and *tingmo*, the little steamed dough buns. After exchanging parts with another bus, and borrowing a fan-belt from a tractor driver, we set off into the dusk, the low sun casting long shadows across the land. Two days later we were in Labrang.

Rising from the banks of the Sangchu river, framed by bare

hills, the great three-hundred-year-old monastery of Labrang Tashikyil had been restored since the damage of the Cultural Revolution. In those days it had housed four thousand monks; there were a few hundred now. The town of Labrang (which the Chinese call Xiahe) buzzed with raw energy. Tourists from Lanzhou, the capital of Gansu province, drove Nissan four-wheel drives and VW Santanas up the long, dusty main street, speeding past cycle-rickshaws and motorised carts. Tibetan and Mongolian monks in maroon robes crowded into cafés to watch martial arts videos. The guest houses had running water and the shops had signs, some of which had been machine-translated into English.

ALL KINDS OF VASES RACIAL CAPS OLD BOWLS AND
    NEW ROTA
THE CENTRY OF DAINTY SNACKS
THE NATIONAL ARTIC HAS LONG HISTORY OF LA-
    BU-LENG (OLD AND FAMOUS)
MAKE A SEEING TEST AND MIX GLASSES

At the end of the street, overlooking everything, was the great monastery and its temples.

I met Alang, not quite by chance, in a restaurant. He was approaching old age, a thickset man with rosaries wrapped round his wrists and a smooth, oval face. His voice was thin. He had begun again, coming back to the place of his childhood, having fled to Lhasa in the mid-1950s. In exile he had done well, working in Nepal during the bad times, trading in carpets and jewellery, in particular the amber, turquoise and orange coral that the nomads love. The coral was imported from Japan and Italy, the amber from Lithuania and the turquoise from Arizona; he had a low opinion of the quality of local stones.

Alang was distantly related to Tibet's second spiritual leader, the Panchen Rinpoche. After Mao's death, he had helped him set up a branch of the Ganggyen Corporation, the trading company which the Panchen used to fund the restoration of monasteries and temples. Alang was instinctively apolitical. His aim was to separate religion and politics, and to devote himself to his faith, in its purest form. Religion was his means of survival in the Communist system.

When he first returned to Labrang in 1982, the buildings were in ruins and basic goods were unavailable. He and several others had extracted government grants and private donations for rebuilding, and had watched the place grow into what it was now: a functioning religious centre under close external control. For him, the political restrictions and the police informants inside the monastery were a fact of life that had to be tolerated. Labrang was a place of religion, not a place of politics. Alang's main concern was to be home, and not a refugee.

'It is too dangerous to think about politics here,' he said. 'We are serving the Dharma. We have no freedom; that will come after my lifetime.'

Underlying his words was the current political tension. The government had a lama problem.

Alang discussed this with me in more detail the next day, in a large chapel by the monastery. He positioned himself near the entrance, so that he could see who was coming in and out.

The old Panchen Rinpoche had died in 1989, he said, amid unproven rumours that he had been poisoned by Chinese security officers. Traditionally, the child chosen as his reincarnation would be authenticated by the Dalai Lama, because of the close spiritual relationship between them, the two senior figures in Tibetan Buddhism's predominant Gelug sect – Nyingma, Sakya and Kagyu being the other sects, with their own devotional, philosophical and sartorial traditions.

Despite its atheism, the Chinese Communist Party considers itself the guardian of the transmigration of Buddhist souls, and has taken control of the identification of reincarnate lamas. Briefly, it looked as if a compromise candidate might be found, but owing to intransigence from Beijing and tactical misjudgement by the Dalai Lama, two rival claimants were declared. The 'real' Panchen was promptly locked up by the Chinese authorities in 1995, while they tried to generate popular support for their own boy. To do this, they put intense pressure on four eminent monks with links to the old Panchen Rinpoche, encouraging them to participate in the selection process and endorse the pretender.

Alang explained to me what had happened.

The four senior monks were unwilling to support the impostor, who was, inevitably, the son of two ardent Party officials. Agya Rinpoche, head of Kumbum monastery, where the old Panchen had spent much of his childhood, fled into exile in the USA, after refusing to denounce the Dalai Lama or to promote the synthetic Panchen. Chadrel Rinpoche, the influential head of the Panchen's own monastery, Tashilhunpo, was publicly condemned as an enemy of the motherland for having secret contact with the Dalai Lama, and was now in an isolation unit in a Sichuan prison. Gungthang Rinpoche, a respected religious scholar from Labrang, was seriously ill. I had been told his illness was political (a means of avoiding publicly supporting the pretender), but Alang said it was genuine. Only Jamyang Shepa, or Laughing Jamyang, the reincarnate head of Labrang, whose predecessor had initiated the Panchen Rinpoche as a monk and been his spiritual guide, had acquiesced. He had agreed, unwillingly, to act as tutor to the Beijing candidate.

Alang did not condemn Jamyang Shepa for what he had done. He said that for the last two decades he had walked an impossible tightrope, trying to plead the Tibetan cause from inside the system without compromising his integrity. The only alternative was flight, but as Alang said, once all the high lamas had fled, who would be left inside China to speak for the Tibetan people and their religion?

In the meantime, the lack of popular support among Tibetans for the imposed Panchen Rinpoche had led the authorities to promote the young Karmapa, the head of the Karma Kagyu sect, as the patriotic lama of the moment. It was whispered among Tibetans, however, that the teenage Karmapa Rinpoche had refused to recognise the bogus Panchen. Still, the Karmapa was produced on state television, performing ceremonies and apparently backing Communist rule. Jiang Zemin had said optimistically that he hoped the Karmapa would be 'a patriotic Living Buddha' and 'contribute to the economic and social development of Tibet'.

Alang said it was too dangerous to go on talking any longer. He gave me a small plastic image of Je Tsongkhapa, the charismatic fourteenth-century teacher whose disciples founded the Gelug order, and slipped out into a courtyard. I never saw him again.

Walking back towards the main street, I stopped at a temple. There was a shrine featuring a picture of the Dalai Lama (a display which would be illegal inside the Tibet Autonomous Region) and photographs of both Jamyang Shepa and the old Panchen Rinpoche. The new Panchen, in either of his boyish incarnations, was nowhere to be seen.

SIX

I have three photographs of the old Panchen Rinpoche.

In the first, he is young, not much more than a teenager, standing with the Dalai Lama in Beijing, holding a bouquet of flowers. They are on a state visit to the capital. It is the time of the early reforms, when both men were optimistic about the changes that Communism might bring to Tibet. He is wearing an ornamental hat and elaborate silk and brocade travelling robes, of the kind that high lamas once wore when going on important journeys. He looks amused, confident, slightly arrogant, with the air of authority that is expected from an influential *tulku* or reincarnation.

In the second picture, taken a decade later in Lhasa, the Panchen stands on a podium behind several large, old-fashioned microphones, with a sad, wounded look on his face. He is unshaven. Surrounding him is a crowd of people, from the winning side, wearing the drab uniform of the time, pointing accusatory index fingers in his face. This picture shows a public 'struggle' session, or *thamzing*, a form of persecution used widely during the Cultural Revolution. This session lasted, day in, day out, for seven weeks. Years later, only days before his death, the Panchen said in a speech, 'I was criticised, struggled and educated. I was confined in darkness. This is my personal story. Other spiritual figures suffered the same fate or even worse. My big name ensured me a slightly better treatment.' His eyes are closed, his head framed by a halo of stars from the Chinese national flag, and behind him hangs the long forehead of Mao Zedong, the instigator, watching the scene from a photograph. The Panchen is about to be given the 'hats', or labels, of 'anti-people', 'anti-socialist' and 'anti-Party', and to be taken away for another twelve years of imprisonment and harassment.

In the last photograph, another two decades have passed. The Panchen, out of prison, is standing at the top of a set of metal steps, looking down at the camera, magnanimous. He is waiting to descend from an aeroplane which has brought him back to Tibet, where the streets are lined with people holding *katags*, the diaphanous white scarves of religious greeting and respect. The expression on his face is astute and authoritative: nothing that happens now can break me, it says, for I have been through persecution and emerged. He is beyond fear.

The Panchen Rinpoche was no plaster saint. He was a passionate, short-tempered and notoriously frank man, and by the end of his life he had grown extremely fat. He loved music, mutton, horses, fine restaurants and aviation – had his destiny not been decided at birth, he said, he would have been an airline pilot. In his later years he abandoned monastic celibacy, marrying a Chinese woman and having a child with her. Despite this, he remained a hero for many Tibetans, who would secretly exchange cassettes of his outspoken speeches.

The Panchen Rinpoche was only twenty-four years old when he dared to challenge the Communist Party over what it had done to Tibet. Like many eminent figures in the pre-Communist regime, he had been co-opted and given a sinecure, in his case as acting chairman of Uyon Lhenkhang, or PCART (the Preparatory Committee for the establishment of the Tibet Autonomous Region), following the flight of the Dalai Lama into exile in 1959.

After touring the Tibetan border areas in 1962, he prepared a detailed report, in the form of a petition to China's prime minister, Zhou Enlai. It was written on specially imported Indian paper, and translated into Chinese by a trusted team. There were desperate scenes among his entourage as they tried to persuade him to tone down the petition, but the Panchen was resolute. He said that he was speaking on behalf of the Tibetan people, and that there was no reason why their rulers should not receive honest criticism. In the preface to the English translation (the full text of the petition emerged only in 1996), the writer Robert Barnett states that there is no other known document 'in which a senior official attacks so explicitly and in such detail the policies and practices of Chairman Mao'.

The petition uses the formulaic, overblown Marxist language of the period, larding 'our great, correct and wise leader, Chairman Mao Zedong' with praise, and condemning 'exploiting elements' such as 'the Tibetan upper strata' and 'the imperialist powers and their running dogs'. At first this tone jars, confounding your expectations, but as the petition continues, the Panchen's carefully worded criticisms emerge, and the formality and restraint of his literary style redouble its effect. The reader senses the climate of dread in which he was working, knowing that he was putting himself at intense personal risk, but conscious that his grievances had no chance of being heard unless they appeared in the jargon of the prevailing ideology. The Panchen made skilful use of Mao's own slogans, claiming for instance that the report was merely 'seeking truth from facts'.

Although the petition, which was later labelled 'The Seventy-Thousand-Character Document of Reactionaries', ranged over many subjects, three principal themes emerged: religion, cruelty and starvation.

The Panchen's case was strengthened by the genuine support he had previously shown for reforms to Tibetan society, such as reducing the political and economic power of the large monasteries. He thought the Party was right to 'thoroughly eliminate all feudal privileges and the systems of oppression and exploitation which are inconsistent with the profound doctrines of Buddhism'. But, he added, the way in which the reforms were taking place was wrong.

Anyone who displayed religious faith in Tibet, the Panchen explained, was persecuted as superstitious, and Communist work teams in monasteries and nunneries went as far as 'lining up monks on one side, and lining up nuns and secular women on the other side, and forcing them to select someone from the other side'. Monasteries were left in charge of people who had 'illicit relations, went with prostitutes, drank excessively and took other such unscrupulous actions; they regarded ignoring their vows as nothing, and publicly and unscrupulously engaged in liaisons with women within the monasteries . . . Consequently, these days, when the conduct of monks is raised, people shake their heads and feel sick.'

Much of the persecution of monks was carried out by local Tibetans, at the instigation of Chinese officials. Paper scriptures were used as fertiliser, and prayer books were made into shoes. Statues of the Buddha were looted. 'They recklessly carried out wild and hasty destruction of monasteries, Buddhist halls, mani walls and stupas, and stole many ornaments,' the Panchen wrote. Places 'looked as if they had been accidentally destroyed by bombardment and a war had just ended'. The effect was to drive almost all of Tibet's nuns and monks from religious life, forcing them to abandon the homes they had lived in since childhood. 'Before democratic reform, there were more than 2500 large, medium and small monasteries in Tibet. After democratic reform, only seventy or so monasteries were kept in existence by the government.'

The phrase 'democratic reform' occurs frequently in the petition, referring to a process which started in China in the mid-1950s, when 'mutual aid' groups were set up, land was redistributed and existing social patterns were disrupted. It is a shock to realise that this period stands at the heart of the Panchen Rinpoche's complaint. The destruction of much of Tibet's physical heritage was complete before the Cultural Revolution.

The Panchen believed the intellectual core of Tibetan Buddhism was being destroyed: debates, philosophical discussions, prayer ceremonies and the oral transmission of learning could no longer take place. 'Due to this, the sweet dew for "teaching, debating and writing" and "listening, thinking and contemplating" has dried up . . . and so we see the elimination of Buddhism, which was flourishing in Tibet and which transmitted teachings and enlightenment. This is something which I and more than 90 per cent of Tibetans cannot endure.'

Next, the Panchen dealt with the Tibetan rebellion of 1959. He denounced it as 'counter-revolutionary in nature', but pointed out that in the aftermath, countless innocent people were labelled as criminals and put in prison, where they were treated with great cruelty, deprived of proper clothing and accommodation, and denied food and medical attention.

> Old prisoners in their fifties and sixties, who were physically weak and already close to death, were also forced to carry out heavy and difficult physical labour. When I went back and forth on my travels and saw such scenes of suffering, I could not stop myself from feeling grief and thinking with a compassionate heart 'Why can't things be different?', but there was nothing I could do.

During struggle sessions, minor officials of the old regime were categorised as agents of feudalism. Their property was confiscated and they were subjected to 'vicious beatings'. Even those who admitted to past errors, such as the Panchen's own father, had to undergo 'public confrontation and fierce beating'. Their hair was pulled, and they were punched, kicked and clubbed.

> This resulted in bleeding from the seven apertures in the heads of those who were being beaten and in their falling down unconscious and in their limbs being broken; they were seriously injured and there were even some who lost their lives during the struggle.

The Panchen then explained how Tibetans were humiliated by visiting Chinese work teams. Anything specifically Tibetan – flagpoles, the whitewashing of outer walls, *chubas*, hairstyles, headdresses, festivals and traditional sports – was depicted as 'backward, filthy and useless'. There were hardly any interpreters, so people rarely understood what was happening. Remarkably, even PCART documents were issued only in Chinese, so the Tibetan members of the committee were unable to read them. Tibetans who gave their support to the new regime were required to wear Chinese clothes; if they failed to do so, they were 'scarcely treated as human'. As a result of this, he wrote with painful understatement, most Tibetans had only 'a weak perception of the motherland'.

Finally, the Panchen tackled the famine in remarkably out-spoken terms, slicing into Mao's pet project. 'Although there was a Great Leap Forward on paper and in speech, it is not certain whether there was one in reality.' A 'fierce wind of ignorant commands' from Party officials had led to chronic food shortages. During 1959 and 1960, traditional Tibetan practices of barter were outlawed, and there was no exchange of grain and meat between peasants and herders. 'In some places, many people directly starved to death because the food ran out; therefore, in some places, there was a phenomenon of whole families dying out.'

This problem was worst, wrote the Panchen, in the Tibetan parts of Qinghai and Gansu provinces, where large communes were established at breakneck speed and private ownership was abolished. The public canteens had failed to supply adequate food.

> Because the amount of grain was not enough to feed even those with the lowest requirements, the fire and bitterness of hunger was ignited, and so dregs of fat, grain husks and so on which formerly in Tibet were fodder for horses and donkeys, bulls and oxen, became hard to get and were considered nourishing and fragrant foods. Also, in order to make the [amount of] food appear more and to dispel one day's hunger and bitterness, the responsible people in the canteens, apart from gathering together a lot of grass, which was more or less edible, even gathered tree bark, leaves, grass roots and grass seeds, which really were not edible . . . They made it into a thin gruel like pig food and gave it to people to eat.

'In the past,' wrote the Panchen Rinpoche, 'although Tibet was a society ruled by dark and savage feudalism, there had never been such a shortage of grain.'

Mao Zedong was a utopian, and it irritated him that people were so human, with their traditions, their individuality, their habits and their limitations. Within a few years of seizing power in 1949, he was frustrated by China's lack of progress towards a pure Communist society. Agriculture had been collectivised, but output remained static. The takeover of private businesses had failed to generate a boom. Mao wanted a fresh start. He decided that the Chinese people would all link hands in a great leap, a Great Leap Forward.

At the heart of his programme lay the communes, where households would come together for joint labour, eating and political meetings. In the summer of 1958, the senior leaders of the Communist Party visited the seaside resort of Beidaihe, where they ate good food and enjoyed the cool breeze blowing from the Gulf of Chihli. They passed a resolution stating that the commune system was increasing crop yields 'by about 100 per cent, by several 100 per cent ... In this way the ideological liberation of the people is further promoted.' The claim was manifest nonsense, but by now, nearly a decade into the Communist revolution, with much of eastern Tibet in open mutiny, truth was less important than adherence to the line emanating from the Chairman.

By the end of 1958, nearly all rural Chinese families had been herded into communes. Yields would be made to rise by whatever means necessary. Regions which planted one crop of rice a year would start to plant two; Tibetans, who grew barley because of the high altitude, would grow wheat; farmers would plant five times as many seedlings per acre as before. Sparrows, rats, flies and mosquitoes would be eliminated under the 'Four Pests' campaign, with armies of schoolchildren with drums chasing birds until they died from exhaustion. China would overtake Britain's steel production within seven years. Soon Mao was claiming that China would surpass Britain by 1959, and the USA by 1962. Do-it-yourself steel and iron furnaces in every commune would enable them to meet their targets; China's sheer weight of population would ensure success.

These ambitions were preposterous, but because the state statistical system was being closed down and false data were now bandied about with ease, they went unchallenged. Agricultural production fell, but the mock statistics cascaded upwards. Everyone wanted to promote and share in the enthusiasm of the Great Leap; no one wished to spoil the excitement by exposing the truth. Buoyed by the claims of pseudo-science, people reported cabbages weighing a quarter of a ton, and fields yielding fifty-three thousand pounds of grain per *mu* (a sixth of an acre) when once they had produced 330 pounds per *mu*. Han Suyin wrote in her ludicrous prophetic tract *China in the Year 2001* that after the Great Leap, China had 'a pool of six million peasant-scientists who not only knew about soil and seed improvement but could carry out experiments, hold conferences, and pass on their knowledge at scientific meetings'.

Mao went on tours of rural China in his private train. The night sky was lit up by the red glow of the backyard steel furnaces, where woks, knives, railings and shovels were being melted down to make useless lumps of scrap metal. When the Chairman inspected a furnace, samples of genuine steel would be brought from a factory. In Hubei province, the party secretary arranged for rice plants to be transported to the fields along Mao's route. They were planted so close together that electric fans had to be set up to circulate air to prevent the plants from rotting.

Intoxicated by the exuberance of their own statistics, Party leaders plied the communal canteens with food, using up the nation's reserves. Food was left to rot; food was not grown; grain was exported abroad; crops died from the exigencies of bogus agriculture. Famine loomed. There was an escalation of expenditure and a curtailment of income: in 1959, there was a 14 per cent deficit between government revenue and expenditure. Some regional Party figures began to express their fears, but there was great nervousness about passing on complaints to Beijing.

One senior leader challenged the consensus of lies: Peng Dehuai, a blunt, stocky soldier with a shaved head and a face like a bulldog. He was China's defence minister, a senior civil war veteran and one of the few Party leaders to come from a genuinely poor peasant background. Taking time off from commanding the brutal military operation to suppress the Tibetan revolt, he wrote a careful, deliberate letter to Mao, stating that although the Great Leap had achieved great things, mistakes were being made and production figures were being inflated. Characteristically, Mao distributed the letter to the Politburo and asked for a reaction. Most members were guarded, but a few spoke out in support of Peng. Mao paused, then pounced. The defence minister was a 'bourgeois democrat' who wanted to 'usurp the proletarian banner'. 'You are devious,' Mao told Peng in front of his colleagues. 'I tell you, you've fucked enough.'

Peng Dehuai and his supporters were purged, the Great Leap Forward continued and a new period of 'class struggle' began. The People's Republic of China starved. In 1960 the famine was exacerbated by typhoons and a drought which hit all parts of the country except Tibet and Xinjiang. Returning to his home village in Hunan some years later, Peng said to local officials, 'Ai! I was afraid of hunger in the old society, and so I joined the revolution. I never thought that twelve years after the victory of the revolution our people would still not be able to fill their stomachs. What a profound lesson!' He thought backyard steel furnaces were about as much use as 'beating a gong with a cucumber'. Peng's rehabilitation was considered in 1962, but according to his wife, Pu Anxiu, 'he didn't want to accept the appointment, he only thought of going back to his village to cultivate his vegetable garden'. During the Cultural Revolution he was put in prison, where he died after years of humiliation and medical neglect, a simple, direct old man who had done no more than tell the emperor he was wearing no clothes.

For many years the scale of the suffering in China and Tibet during the famine remained concealed. Writing in 1976, the commentator C.P. FitzGerald suggested that although there may have been passing food shortages, they were soon solved by the commune system. He wrote breezily, 'In 1960–62, not even the most virulent critics of Mao Tse-tung's China claimed mass deaths by starvation, or mass migrations. There was certainly no political disorder.'

Although some scholars and researchers have made estimates of as many as forty or fifty million deaths during the Great Leap famine, most academic studies now put the figure at around thirty million. A computer reconstruction of population trends by the demographer Judith Banister produced 'an estimated thirty million excess deaths during 1958–61', although she warned that 'official figures may actually underestimate China's mortality during the crisis years . . . Deaths among a destitute population engaged in a fight for survival are not likely to be properly registered.' The political scientist Dali Yang has described it as 'the worst famine in human history'.

Starvation in China reached its peak in 1960. Three of the five provinces where mortality rates were highest that year (Gansu, Sichuan and Qinghai) bordered Tibet. Their average death rate was a massive 45.3 per thousand, approaching double the national average of 25.4 per thousand. China's overall mortality rate grew by 115 per cent during the period 1959–62 (against a base of 1956–58), but for these three partially Tibetan provinces it grew by a mean average of 233 per cent. If the increase in the death rate for Gansu, Sichuan and Qinghai had applied across the whole of China during the years of famine, it would have pushed up the estimated total number of excess deaths during the Great Leap Forward from thirty million to a horrifying sixty-one million.

Credible population data for central Tibet does not exist for this period, making it impossible to be sure how many people died there. The savagery with which the revolt against Chinese rule was suppressed masks whether deaths were caused by hunger, rather than by disease, warfare or persecution. It would be tempting, but probably inaccurate, to assume in the absence of clear information that central and western Tibet suffered as badly during the famine as the eastern and northern borderlands. Anecdotal evidence suggests that starvation was in fact less widespread in central Tibet, because the harsh, diffuse nature of the rural economy meant there was less reliance on grain than in places such as Gansu and Sichuan.

Reading the charts, looking at the numbers and trying to quantify death from data, I felt that the clearest picture of what happened to Tibetans at this time came not from statistics, but from the Panchen Rinpoche's report.

When he first submitted his petition, in an act of bravery which surpasses that of Peng Dehuai (an ambiguous hero, especially for Tibetans), Zhou Enlai commended it and summoned Tibet's top leaders to Beijing. Then Mao, relaxing at Beidaihe in the summer of 1962, spoke. He said that class struggle should return to the heart of the Party's agenda, and that the Panchen's petition was a 'a poisoned arrow' fired at the Party by a 'reactionary feudal overlord'. Zhou, who in the words of the historian Roderick MacFarquhar 'seems always to have taken the line of least resistance, bending with whatever Maoist wind was blowing, be it leftist gale or rightist zephyr', smartly abandoned the Tibetan leader.

The Panchen was taken for struggle sessions.

He was put under house arrest in Beijing.

He was beaten in front of huge rallies of Red Guards.

Fifteen years later, following the death of Mao, the Panchen was released from detention. Needing the support of a credible Tibetan leader during the period of liberalisation, the Chinese government returned him to an official position.

The Panchen Rinpoche did not stay silent. He announced that he hoped the Dalai Lama would soon be able to return to Tibet, and, famously, that since 1950 'there has certainly been development, but the price paid for this development has been greater than the gains'. He said that his petition had understated the extent of Tibet's calamity. In it, he had written that 5 per cent of the population of Qinghai were in prison, but 'according to my information at that time, it was between 10 and 15 per cent. But I did not have the courage to state such a high figure. I would have died under *thamzing* if I had stated the real figure. These are serious matters as far as Tibet is concerned. If we pay only lip service to these kind of mistakes and do nothing to redress them there will be equally serious consequences.'

That was in 1987. Since then, the Chinese government has stopped paying lip service to the 'mistakes' and done little to redress them, beyond occasionally repeating, when pressed, the mantra that the Cultural Revolution was '70 per cent good' and '30 per cent bad'.

At night, huddled in my Labrang hotel room under cold cotton quilts, I would watch China Central Television: advertisements for unfeasible medical products, ten minutes of Jiang Zemin clapping himself as he toured a factory, a protracted mini-series about Mao Zedong's life in advance of the looming fiftieth anniversary of the Communist seizure of power. There was no suggestion there that the Great Helmsman had made mistakes. One day I read in a newspaper that China's state propaganda chief, Ding Guangen, was complaining about media stories which 'purposefully ignored the first thirty years of development of the People's Republic'. Newspaper editors were instructed to mention China's 'vigorous

development in the 1960s, with special emphasis on its development of the atomic bomb, which it exploded successfully in 1964,
and the launch of its first carrier rockets, to balance coverage'.
No reference was made to the thirty million people who were
killed by ideology in the 1950s and sixties.

SEVEN

When I went to China in the mid-1980s, it was hard to buy a railway ticket. I would go to the booking office and stand in line, and when I reached the little booth the clerk would stare through me and address the next customer. Or she would laugh in an apprehensive way and cover her face with her hands. Or she would slam down the hatch. Often, the only way to get a ticket was to ask a sympathetic local to buy one for you. Foreigners were strange and unmanageable, and nobody wanted to take responsibility for dealing with us.

Of all the cities I visited at that time, Xining, the capital of Qinghai province, was the one most firmly stuck in the isolationist past. Walking down a street, I would be followed by dozens of people, marvelling at the freak in their midst, an experience that was more wearing than frightening. Across China, clothes were dowdy and monochrome, but in Xining, men and women still wore Mao suits and caps. The billboards advertised nothing but industrial machinery. There were plenty of bicycles on the roads, but no motor vehicles except buses, trucks and tractors. Getting a meal was almost impossible. Dining halls would turn me away. Most difficult of all was winning a bed at the city's sole 'open' hotel. Arriving at reception, I was told that although there were plenty of empty rooms and I was theoretically allowed to stay there, the correct paperwork for the registration of foreigners did not exist. I was therefore unable to check in. The receptionist explained this impassively. I found myself an empty room, and stayed in it for several days, without registering. Everyone looked through me. Nobody lost face.

Going back to Xining a decade and a half later, the shape of the city was hardly recognisable. I had crossed the tall, stark ochre mountains from Labrang by truck, and was now intending to head for the Tibetan heartland, down to Kermo and on to Lhasa. New factories sent out thick smoke, covering the place in a film of grey dust. Tower blocks and lines of buildings had been thrown up. Houses had grown by several storeys. Foreigners were no longer a spectacle. There was a sense of opportunity, as there had been in Chengdu, but in Xining this energy was tempered by shoddiness and squalor. The blocks of new housing were cumbersome and badly built, the roads marred by craters and jammed with traffic, the big hotels filled with smacked-out prostitutes and hard-faced men muttering into mobile phones, dressed like gangsters. Everything was growing, and nothing had been thought through.

The city had once, a millennium ago, been a centre of Tibetan culture, but was now inescapably Chinese. Even in the 1940s, Hisao Kimura, a Japanese spy who was travelling under the name Dawa Sangpo, noted: 'There were comparatively few Chinese and most of the inhabitants were Muslims, who appeared distinctly Turkish with their hooked noses and reddish-brown beards. Amdo Tanguts, the Tibetan tribesmen of Kansu and Xinghai, swaggered along the streets with one shoulder bare and a long sword thrust into their waistband.' Now, small huddles of Tibetans and Salar sat outside on the street by the main bus station, but were peripheral and unprotected. They belonged in the countryside, like the forced labour camps that litter the desolation of Qinghai.

The powerless can still dream. In 640, a Tibetan envoy named Gar travelled to the Tang court to win a royal bride for his king, Songtsen Gampo. He was instructed to compete for the hand of the emperor's daughter in contests against other aspiring suitors. One hundred mares and one hundred colts had to be matched up. Gar corralled the colts and gave them plenty of grass, but no water. 'The following day the thirsty colts were turned loose among the mares, and each colt by nature sought out the whereabouts of its own mother-mare for milk.' Next, each suitor was given a hundred lengths of pine, and ordered to work out which ends came from the top of the tree. While the other men pondered and floundered, Gar threw the wood in a stream, knowing that the root end would be heavier, and sink a little in water. After further contests, in which he was again victorious, he won the hand of Princess Wencheng.

The Chinese, however, kept Gar as a hostage to ensure her proper treatment when she went to live among the barbarians. Ingenious as ever, Gar put some rotting animal hide beneath his bed, which gave the impression that his body was corrupting. He smeared vermilion on his cheek and rubbed phlegm and blood on his body, 'then fastened a string to the horizontal beam on the roof over the couch and connected the string to his genitals and when he placed his head to the ground, it made all the blood in his veins boil from pain'. The worried emperor sent an expert physician, who diagnosed 'a consumptional disease'. Gar suggested that the sight of mountains would soon cure his illness, and was sent off in the care of four trusted athletes. He gave them dried meat to provoke a thirst, followed by plenty of beer. Having lamed their horses for good measure, Gar galloped to Tibet. Back home, he said, 'Generally, we have been treated contemptuously by the entire Chinese population. Aside from one Chinese hostess, not one single sympathetic Chinese was found.'

The current Chinese view of Princess Wencheng is that she brought civilisation to the Tibetans, together with maize, potatoes, horses, donkeys, camels, medical treatises and industrial techniques. She stopped them from painting their faces red and taught them how to grow crops, grind wheat and make wine. Tibetan accounts tend to stress the prestige and power of the Tibetan empire at this time, and the ingenuity of Gar in winning Princess Wencheng's hand for King Songtsen Gampo. Like the epic tales of the great King Gesar, this story still has strong resonance for Tibetans today, as they dream of outwitting the ruling power.

When I had found myself a hotel room in modern Xining, I set about meeting Nyima. She was a young Tibetan nun from Lhasa, on a visit to the city to prepare manuscripts for a cultural publishing project. I had made a vague arrangement to see her, but knew this would only be possible if we could find a setting where she would be completely safe, and able to speak freely. An intermediary told me that I was to meet Nyima at her aunt's apartment, off Wusi Lu.

The streets down by the river were bustling. A Muslim man wearing a big turban, like a bird's nest, was packing chillies into bamboo boxes. At the rendezvous point, a shop which sold large, gaudy photographs of landscapes, there was a difficulty. Nyima's aunt had gone to hospital with a sore leg. I was told to come back the next day.

When I returned to the shop the following day, I was guided to the apartment. It was reached through a courtyard, and the courtyard had a guardian, whose job it was to report comings and goings. I would have to wait until he went for his midday meal. He left, finally, and I walked through the entrance gate, my heart thumping, head down, listening to the sound of a barking dog, trying not to move too fast. Strings of washing dangled from metal balconies. The place smelt of drains and vegetation. There was a musty narrow passage, then a steep staircase which led to the apartment. It was cramped and dirty in there, with pots and pans, clothes and religious books all stacked together, too many people living in too small a space. I was shown to a bench covered by a strip of carpet. A child with iodine-stained scabs on her arms, a cousin, stared wide-eyed at me before falling asleep in a huddle under the bench.

Nyima, extremely beautiful, with almond eyes, the highest cheekbones and cropped hair, was twenty-five, although she looked ten years younger. Watching her, I could not help thinking of Gedun Chompel's lines:

> The beggar pretends to frown on others' gold,
> The hungry guest pretends to spit on food,
> Everyone pretends to dislike sex,
> But in the mind sex is the only thing
>   everyone likes.

When Nyima started to speak, her inner resolution and maturity showed through, and I saw the strength behind her chaste vocation. She had made choices early in her life which had fixed its course, and they gave a weight to her words. At the age of seventeen, she had decided to become a nun in a rebuilt nunnery to the east of the old city of Lhasa, and had resolved to oppose the government. These choices had lethal implications. Nuns and monks had been at the vanguard of public protests in Tibet in the late 1980s, and there were many documented cases of their being molested, tortured and killed, or driven to suicide while in prison. Nyima was aware of this when she joined the nunnery. Several of her friends had been carted off to Gutsa detention centre, and one had died from renal failure after a severe beating.

The fiercest and bravest advocates of Tibetan nationalism and religious freedom were often extraordinarily young – in their twenties, or younger. They had not lived through the horrors of the Great Leap or the Cultural Revolution, and had grown up at a time of relative political laxity, when many of the trappings of 'old' Tibet had been physically erased. In theory, they might have been expected to accept the prevailing order. Yet their devotion to Buddhism, the Dalai Lama and the idea of Tibetan nationhood was clear, absolute and impassioned. It was this devotion that made me want to meet Nyima, and to hear the story of a new generation.

She answered my questions in a thoughtful, deliberate way, speaking in a quiet, rhythmic voice.

'I get up each day at around six o'clock, do the cleaning, put out the water offerings on the altars, check the butter lamps and prepare breakfast. In the afternoons I say prayers, study or do jobs around the nunnery. We are part of a community, looking out for each other.

'We do all sorts of different rituals in the nunnery. Every lunar month we do seven religious ceremonies for the deities, organised by a senior nun, the Lobpon. People come to us if they want prayers said for a member of their family who is sick, or if someone has died. That's one of the ways we get funds. There are all sorts of rituals we perform. For example, on the eighth day of each lunar month, we chant prayers for the Medicine Buddha. One of the most important prayers is for the longevity of Gyalwa Rinpoche, His Holiness the Dalai Lama. The problem is that the Committee – the Democratic Management Committee – have forbidden us to recite it. So we have to do it in secret, or silently, alone.

'We know that His Holiness has said that we shouldn't put ourselves at risk in Tibet by saying prayers for his long life, but we all want to. It's part of our religion.'

I asked Nyima about her family background.

'They are nomads, over by Nagchu. We were brought up to practise our religion and to respect all living beings. My parents did not want me to become a nun. They wanted me to get married, like my elder sister. It took me three years to persuade them to let me become a nun. I always felt very spiritual, in a private way, when I was a child, although I didn't know all that much about the teachings of Lord Buddha. Then a great wandering lama came to Nagchu and we travelled to the big monastery to receive his blessing. My auntie went with me. She had been a nun when she was young, but during the black times she was expelled from her nunnery. She lives as part of our extended family. She is still a spiritual practitioner, although no longer as part of a nunnery.

'We went to the wandering lama and told him of my vocation. I took my vow in front of him, there and then. It gave me a special feeling inside. I told my parents, and they accepted what I had done. I shaved my head and started to dress like a nun, in the plainest clothes. My family made me a special *chuba*. I acted like a nun. I felt that the ways of the world were an illusion, and happiness lay in religion.'

I wondered how other people in her community had responded to this decision.

'They respected it. I still spent time with the other girls of my age, looking after the livestock, going into town or whatever. When men were around they would be respectful towards me. They would make jokes about sex or marriage, but that's just how people are. They took my vow seriously, just as they would with any other religious person. To be honest with you, there were times when I wondered if I should have got married and stayed in Nagchu. But once I joined the nunnery, I knew I'd made the right choice. It was my father who told me to go to Lhasa. He said it was the best place if you want to be a nun.'

Many of the other women in the nunnery were in their twenties or thirties. I wanted to know what had persuaded them to take up the religious life.

'Each woman has her own reason,' answered Nyima, 'but in my case it was because I wished to make a religious commitment and to study, but also because I love Tibet and thought that as a single person I would be able to take risks for the good of Tibet. From my earliest years I had heard stories about what the Communists had done to our country, and about the Cultural Revolution. It soaked into me from childhood. Also, the way that we were treated by the local Chinese was very bad. They would say that we were beggars or that we were dirty. They would insult us. I suppose that for many Tibetans of my age, it feels as if there's no future.

'I also feel very resentful about what happened to my cousin. I can't tell you his name; that would be too dangerous. He put up twenty posters in Nagchu town, saying that people should support the peace march that the exiles were doing. He had heard about it on the radio, on the Tibetan service of the Voice of America. They planned to march from India right into Tibet to help us. It never happened, in the end. I don't know why.

'My cousin was suspected and he was taken in for ten days of police interrogation. He was given a two-year sentence by the court. It could have been much worse. Some of the officials were Tibetan, and they persuaded the local head of the Gong An Ju, the PSB, to ask for a lenient sentence. When he was in prison he was beaten by the soldiers who guarded the compound. There was a monthly inspection. The prisoners would wait for it, antici-pating it. One of the senior warders would let the soldiers in and they would kick open the door, throw everything around, kick people, pinch them, slap them. They would even kick over the bucket that the prisoners used as a toilet. The prisoners stood facing the wall during the inspection, so they never knew when they were going to get a blow or a kick. If you looked angry, the soldiers would really beat you. My cousin's health got worse and worse. He was unable to urinate. They had no heating in the cells. He got an illness that made him feel cold. He started to cough up blood. They released him and he returned to his family.

'He wasn't allowed back to his monastery. He was deprived of his political rights. Now he just sits around all day. He doesn't know what to do with himself. I feel very angry about the way he was treated.'

I asked Nyima if she had ever been involved in political protest herself.

'I have done a few things so far, when I've had the chance, like putting up posters and distributing poems, Tibetan flags and other information. I have some photographs of His Holiness. I have never taken part in a demonstration. If you do that, you might die. Even inside the nunnery you have to be very careful what you say to people. I never tell anyone when I do anything. I just do it, by my own choice, alone.

'The time I put up the posters was in Lhasa. It was at night. I felt very afraid. You think about the risk all the time. You say to yourself, "I will be arrested, I will be arrested, I am going to be caught." You can't stop thinking about what will happen to you if you get caught.'

Two hours had passed. I slipped out of the apartment block and walked back along the river to my hotel through the pushing crowds, feeling drained. The next day, I returned. The guard was not there, and I moved quickly through the courtyard to the apartment. Nyima was waiting, ready to tell me more. She was in tears sometimes, momentarily, screwing up her eyes but continuing to talk in her soft, intense voice, as if she was reciting a text or whispering prayers. She was frightened to be speaking to me; I was frightened to be listening to her, but I knew that if we were caught, she would be the one who paid the price. I was aware that the worst that would be likely to happen to me, if I was arrested, would be a long interrogation followed by a trip to the airport. Nyima, though, would be taken to prison and charged with 'endangering state security', 'instigating to split the country and undermine national unification', or 'attempting to subvert the political power of the state and overthrow the socialist system', as other monks and nuns had been before her.

Her extreme beauty made my fear more acute, made me feel that the price was greater. Nyima was resolute that she wanted to go on talking. It was part of her vocation, she explained, taking this risk, bearing witness. I felt an overwhelming weight of responsibility, alone there in Xining.

I began by asking her how much religious freedom they really had in the nunnery.

'In 1988, before I joined, several nuns rebelled and were expelled. We are still not allowed to contact them. I know that in their hearts, many of them are still nuns and go on doing their spiritual practice. The difficulty for us now is that we have to do what the Democratic Management Committee says, or we risk being expelled. The Committee comes back at the end of next month. I'm frightened. They gave us propaganda books last time and told us to keep them in good condition. But after the last visit, I threw mine away. They'll want to inspect them. I've had enough. There will only be three or four members of the Committee this time, so maybe it won't be too bad. It won't be as bad as last year.

'They control us very closely, and stop us from practising our religion. Last year, some of the nuns took a vow to go on a long retreat and recite one of the great scriptures, but they were told it was not allowed. The Committee set up controls. They made all the nuns attend study sessions, every day. They say their job is "patriotic education", which means they make us watch television from China and say we support Jiang Zemin and the Communist Party.

'The Committee is made up of people from work units in different government departments. They are all Tibetans. Many of them don't want to be on the Committee. They don't like the work. Some of them told us that, secretly. The leaders are very strict. They look down on us. Last year, because we were believed to be politically suspect, they stayed in the nunnery for three months, day and night, a dozen of them. They took over the whole nunnery.

'They teach us propaganda against His Holiness the Dalai Lama and then test us on it, to make sure we know the phrases. We have to say things like,

We will resolutely oppose the scheming activities of
the tiny number of Tibetan pro-independence elements!

We will strengthen national solidarity and oppose small
minority splittism!

We will safeguard the four basic principles and oppose
bourgeois liberalisation!

'Sometimes your head starts to spin and you don't know what
you really believe.'

Nyima said she had heard that in the past, political prisoners
would be shot, but now they were given a lethal injection.
Although she did not know if this rumour was true, she was
terrified by the thought of it.

'You know the saying, "*Yarlang na go dap, marde na kup dap,
ghang dug dug re shak*"? "If you stand up, you bump your head,
if you sit down, you bang your arse. It's really awful"? That's
what it's like. Day after day, the Committee makes us repeat
slogans, and they stop us from doing important ceremonies. It's
terrible. We get very frightened, especially the older nuns.

'This time, they will probably stay for a few days and issue
documents with the latest Party line. Last year, one of the nuns
refused to read their propaganda books and she was expelled. I
have a feeling that things are getting worse and worse. It's only
my generation that can tell the truth. It's better that the older
nuns don't speak out. They've passed through such painful times
that we don't want them to have any more suffering or political
problems. The old nuns say things like, "It's not as bad as it was
when we were young, sister, it could go back to how it was
during the Cultural Revolution, please be careful, sister, please
be careful."

'I know that I must act according to the teachings of Lord
Buddha, but as an individual I can do little, and have to keep it
all stored up. I don't feel free in my heart. I have no freedom on
the inside.'

It was time for me to go. I felt fairly sure that I had not been
seen going in and out of the apartment block, and that Nyima
would be safe. I was dispirited by her situation, by the idea of
a Buddhist being so restricted that she felt she had no internal

freedom. It was only later, looking back, that I wondered whether her courage – the very act of dissent in a totalitarian society – might be her means of psychological survival. Nadezhda Mandelstam had written that people living in a dictatorship 'are soon filled with a sense of their helplessness, in which they find an excuse for their own passivity'. Nyima, and others of her generation, were far from passive as they worked to keep the idea of Tibet alive.

EIGHT

I took a trip to Kumbum monastery, built at the birthplace of Tsongkhapa, an hour's drive from Xining through suburbs and bleak countryside. Several Dalai Lamas had spent time there, including the 'Great Fifth', the Thirteenth and the Fourteenth, who stayed briefly as a child in 1939 before setting off to Lhasa for his enthronement. According to one account, he was only allowed to leave when the Tibetan government agreed to pay the monks a ransom of one hundred thousand Chinese dollars.

I had been to Kumbum in the 1980s. The air of desolation was unchanged. Stalls selling Tibetan trinkets – hats, purses, postcards – were staffed by Chinese. I walked up to the temples. A guide was obligatory before I could enter the grounds. I settled for Gang, a skinny, lopsided man with a plastic identity badge looped round his neck. It was his first job since leaving college in Shanghai.

'We are at the monastery of Taersi,' he told me, 'known as Kumbum by the local Tibetan people. There are many monks here, studying Buddhology and astrology. In Buddhism, they wear different hats. These monks are the yellow hats. Since the Qing dynasty, China has been a land of many minorities.

'This here,' he said, motioning to a prayer wheel which was being spun in alternate directions by laughing Chinese children, 'we call a *mani* prayer wheel. Inside it is full of Buddhism *sutras*. It is for the illiterate people. This is their superstition. They turn the *mani* prayer wheel instead of reading prayers. It is traditional Tibetan culture.'

Outside, by the Jamkhang, the temple to Maitreya, the Buddha who is yet to come, two old Tibetan women were prostrating themselves at full sweep, back and forth, grey plaits looped over the back of their heads. I asked Gang why they were doing prostrations.

'They do it to make a wish come true,' he said with a smile.

Gang took me through the temples, speedily. Outside the Serdong Chenmo, built six centuries ago by Tsongkhapa's mother on the spot where his placenta fell and a sandalwood tree sprouted, an old monk stood holding a pair of scissors. His job was to cut the corners from tickets. Tourists shoved past him. His eyes were dead.

One temple had three photographs propped up on an altar: portraits of Agya Rinpoche, the old Panchen Rinpoche and the 'fake' Panchen. I asked Gang who they were.

'That is Master Panchen,' he said, 'and that is Young Panchen.'

'Where is he?'

'Young Panchen is eight years old. He is staying in Beijing.'

'Why doesn't he live in Tibet?'

'That is not possible. He must stay in Beijing and keep his mind on learning Buddhism *sutras*,' came the answer.

Agya Rinpoche, abbot of Kumbum and former Deputy Chairman of the Chinese Buddhist Association, who had recently escaped into political exile in the USA, was passed over by Gang. I tried again in the next temple, where there was another photograph of him. Gang looked uneasy.

'He is Agya Living Buddha.'

'Does he live in Kumbum?'

'No. He has gone to another lamasery.'

'Where?'

'To another lamasery nearby, to practise Buddhology and astrology. I cannot say which one.'

We went outside. Two policemen stared at me, Sam Brownes buckled over their dark green uniforms. I avoided their eyes. There were no other foreigners at Kumbum that day.

'You must have a photograph,' said Gang cheerily.

A photographer was at work down in a courtyard, with a big old-fashioned camera on a tripod. He had accessories: hats with ear flaps, hats with embroidery, fur-lined Tibetan costumes. I watched him take pictures of the Chinese visitors: a portly man and his portly son, dressed in *chubas*, beaming; a young couple hugging, wearing Tibetan hats, the woman holding a black plastic yak; a pair of rowdy soldiers, making faces.

I had had enough. I walked down to the car park, which was a web of puddles. A policeman in sunglasses was hosing down a Toyota four-wheel drive. I asked Gang, who was still hovering, why he had come all the way from Shanghai to work at Kumbum. He said it was because his mother was Tibetan. I looked at him, surprised. He had slightly Tibetan features, but his clothes and the spare, folded way in which he moved had made him seem wholly Chinese.

'I wished to see the Tibetan plateau,' he told me, 'because I had never been here before. My life was spent in the east of China. I accepted the Chinese education.'

I felt a sudden concern for him, a man who had gone in search of his own history and believed that this warped, petrified theme park represented Tibetan culture. I was reminded of something the Panchen Rinpoche had written in his petition to Zhou Enlai. I found the lines, later. 'For example,' the Panchen wrote, 'a person whose ancestors were Tibetan but who himself does not understand the Tibetan language, and who does not have a single Tibetan characteristic, and who is indistinguishable from people of another nationality, although he might say he is a Tibetan, is Tibetan in name only.'

I went back to Xining in a taxi, the driver caged in at the front by a heavy metal grille. The city was draped in fumes. At the hotel I tried making a few telephone calls. The lines were bad. I got through to Chen Hongdong, a contact in a nearby town. 'It would not be possible to meet,' he said. 'It is very cold here at the moment.' The line went dead.

Cold. The word worried me. What did he mean? I stopped making calls, and went down to the Muslim food stalls on the main road to see if I could pick up some gossip.

Everything seemed to be fine. Nobody knew of any problems.

The next day I collected my e-mails. There was one which warned me of an incident: two foreigners had been arrested near

Xining. I needed to find out more, but did not want to risk contacting anyone locally. I visited a few websites. As usual, China's internet police had blocked access, but I had been shown by a friend how to break through using a proxy server and mirrored sites. More details reached me later in the day, in web pages forwarded as e-mail attachments.

A pair of freelance researchers, one Australian, the other American, had gone to a closed area in western Qinghai to investigate a contentious World Bank resettlement project, in which thousands of Chinese and Hui farmers were set to migrate to a remote Tibetan area. On the way, the researchers had been put under surveillance. The PSB swooped early one morning. The two men were now being held in a hotel in Xining. A Tibetan man from Rebkong who was travelling with them had been taken to a police station. I felt shaken. Were they in this hotel?

The next morning, more information came through. One of the men, the American, had jumped or been pushed from a third-storey window during prolonged police interrogation. He was alive, but his spine was damaged, his heels were shattered and his liver was lacerated. A team of US Embassy officials had just flown into Xining to see him. According to the Chinese Foreign Ministry he had been 'severely injured when he jumped from a building attempting to escape'.

I sat tight, spending the next few days in my hotel room, reading books and thinking about the past, knowing that it was too dangerous, for the moment, to deal with the present.

NINE

Tibet's history falls into two stages: the early and the late, the martial and the controlled, with disorder in the middle. According to one of Tibet's many competing creation myths, a monkey mated with an amorous ogress in a mountain cave in Tsetang at the beginning of time. The monkey was an emanation of Chenrezig, the deity of compassion, while the ogress was primeval, a creature of the rocks, symbolising strength. Their children created the six tribes of Tibet, who fanned out across the high plateau and became the Tibetans.

Meanwhile, the first humans appeared in India, having descended from the gods miraculously. According to an early chronicle, *The Mirror Illuminating the Royal Genealogies*, 'At that time they partook of the food called "ambrosial-terrestrial essence", being of a white colour and having the taste of honey, and thereby they lost their spacewalking ability.' Later, they ate 'unsown and uncultivated rice . . . but some slothful people took today the ration intended for the following day and ate it . . . Subsequently, they commenced taking up agriculture, but the fields that were tilled by one were harvested and partaken by others, and being at variance with one another, they quarrelled.'

Then, a king descended from heaven on a sky-rope and married a queen. They had a son, and when the son was old enough to ride a horse, the king climbed back up to heaven on the sky-rope. This was repeated for seven generations until a king, under the influence of a wizard from the far west, cut his sky-rope while whirling a sword above his head during a duel. His opponent shot him dead with an arrow, and he became Tibet's first, late, mortal ruler, giving rise to the Yarlung dynasty.

Otherwise, if you follow Tibet's indigenous pre-Buddhist religion, Bon, the great father released fire, air and water to form mountains and a lake, and an egg appeared in the lake which hatched to reveal two eagles. They mated to produce three more eggs, one black, one white and one dappled, and out of the dappled one stepped the first man.

Or, if you prefer the view of the head-measurers, the first Tibetans were hardy types of similar ethnic stock to the Qiang, who advanced from the eastern edges of the Tibetan plateau into central Tibet millennia ago, displacing or assimilating the nomads, farmers and hunter-gatherers from the north and west who had arrived there before them.

Certainly by about the fourth century, as Constantinople rose, linked clans of Tibetans had established forts and walled cities along the banks of the Tsangpo river. Burials and death rites were scrupulously recorded by the Yarlung dynasty, and dead rulers had their hair braided and their faces painted with vermilion by priests, and preserved bodies were offered food and drink. It was noted that 'birds' feathers, coloured wool, sacrificial barley, a wish-granting cow, a feathery fowl, a white monkey and a white badger . . . an offering of green barley, the three milk-products and the three sweet offerings' were needed for the performance of sacred rites.

Over time, the Tibetans united into a military power. They dressed in chain-mail and were feared across Asia for the superior quality of their swords and spears. According to an old Arab source, the ruler of Tibet 'pretends that he has come from heaven and has a cuirass of light'. When a chieftain died from poisoning, he was succeeded by his son, Songtsen Gampo, whose name still resonates in Tibet.

King Songtsen Gampo came to power in the early seventh century, at the same time as the Prophet Mohammed. He was a seminal figure in Tibetan history, who began the expansion that created the Tibetan empire, converted the country to Buddhism and promoted a written language. It was based on the Ranjana script of northern India; unlike Chinese, Tibetan writing has never used ideograms. He propagated law codes, which stipulated among other things that 'if a married woman sets on a dog and causes death, whatever was given as dowry by the original paternal family of that woman shall be given as compensation for the killing'. Above all, Songtsen Gampo was a warrior, conquering territory to east and west, including Nepal and parts of Burma and northern India, and installing governors to maintain the unity of his kingdom. His methods were ruthless, as was to be expected in an era when victorious armies would often massacre the vanquished. He married his sister to the neighbouring king of Zhangzhung, and when the opportunity arose, she led her husband into an ambush where he was killed and his army defeated.

After raiding Zungchu in 638, Songtsen Gampo demanded a bride from the emperor of China as a mark of respect. The emperor finally acquiesced, following Gar's victorious escapades with the colts and the logs, sending his daughter Wencheng Kungchu – which Communist propagandists have since used as evidence of the longevity of Chinese influence in Tibet. Songtsen Gampo also married a Tibetan wife and a Nepalese princess, who built the Jokhang, Lhasa's holiest shrine, and laid the foundations of the Potala. After his death, political power remained in the hands of astute and experienced ministers, who used successive kings as figureheads while they ran the empire, competing with the other great powers of the age: the Franks, Greeks, Arabs, Turks and Chinese. Further victories were achieved to the north, in what is now Xinjiang and the Pamirs, and as far west as Gilgit, Hunza, Swat and Wakhan, on the edge of Afghanistan. Martial brilliance was incorporated into Tibetan culture as a desirable virtue, with horsemen learning to fire arrows at speed and to wrestle wild yaks.

Written records show that the Chinese, with their ancient and sophisticated civilisation, were amazed and disturbed by the sudden spread of Tibetan influence, and unsure how to respond, alternating between efforts at conciliation and a strategy of aggression. In 670, the emperor of China sent the Great Protecting General of the Right, Hsieh Jen-kuei, to command an expeditionary force against the Tibetans. After an initial advance, while still planning his attack, Hsieh Jen-kuei was surprised by Tibetan footsoldiers and cavalry armed with lances, swords and bows. His forces retreated in chaos. Many were killed, crushed by an army of, according to one optimistic source, four hundred thousand Tibetan soldiers.

By the late seventh century, Tibet dominated a wide swathe of territory, and had effective control over the trade routes of Central Asia, leaving China's Tang dynasty in a vulnerable position. The Arab caliphate was the only power capable of challenging the Tibetans at this time, but, as often happens at a moment of glory, Tibet became weakened by internal feuding. The country's powerful families came into conflict, and the boundaries of the empire receded. In 715 the Tibetans allied with Arab forces against the Central Asian kingdom of Ferghana, but were routed the same year by Tang troops, with the Chinese commander decapitating the losers.

The Tang dynasty was annoyed that the Tibetans used 'enemy-country protocol' in their diplomatic discourse, meaning that they referred to the Chinese as equals, rather than as superiors, a slight that the Middle Kingdom has always taken seriously. China's President of the Board of War, Chang Yueh, declared, 'The Tibetans are discourteous; we really ought to punish the aliens,' a troubled cry that could as easily have been heard 1250 years later.

The problem for the Chinese was that the Tibetans were too strong to be easily quelled, and previous military forays against them had ended in disaster. Matters were resolved temporarily when, after almost sixty years of intermittent fighting, an experienced Tibetan envoy, Ming-hsi-lieh, was sent to China to negotiate peace.

Neither side was in a commanding strategic position, and both were exhausted by war. The Chinese emperor agreed to the demand for a halt. In an effort at pacification, he held a banquet at which he awarded a fish-bag, to be attached to the belt of a ceremonial robe, to Ming-hsi-lieh. This bag had great significance. It contained half a golden fish, the other half remaining, symbolically, at the Tang court. When he next returned to China, Ming-hsi-lieh would present his piece of the fish, to be married up with its other half, enabling him to be received with suitable dignity and protocol. This was a characteristic Chinese ploy, designed to show political superiority; it had worked with many of China's neighbours, including the powerful Turgis.

The Tibetans, however, were aware of the symbolism of the fish-bag, and had no intention of accepting the implied suggestion of tributary status. The lateral nature of their response illuminates the historically uneasy relationship between the two nations. Ming-hsi-lieh, with an obliquity that is still practised by Tibetans (in formalised debate, the ability to defend the weaker intellectual position is much admired), 'politely declined the fish-bag, saying that such ornaments were not used in his country and he did not dare to accept so rare a gift'.

In 755, another great figure in Tibetan history took the throne: Trisong Detsen, the great-great-great grandson of Songtsen Gampo. His achievements would be both religious and military. The new ruler promoted Buddhism, inviting Indian teachers such as Santarakshita and Padmasambhava to visit Tibet. They subdued demons, spread the teachings of the Buddha and established the country's first monasteries. A two-year debate was held at Samye, at the end of which it was declared that the Three Jewels, meaning the Buddha, the Dharma and the Sangha (the religious community), would always be respected in Tibet. Buddhism became the state religion, and practitioners of Bon, Tibet's old faith, were harassed. Despite the emphasis in many historical texts on the persecution of Bon at this time, it is apparent that Buddhists in fact incorporated many of its rituals and symbols into their own developing religion. Bon remains an important and sophisticated tradition in Tibet today, and is far from the primitive, animist cult it is often made out to be.

Pacifism was not, at this stage, part of the Tibetan Buddhist philosophy. Trisong Detsen's son ordered the translation of important Sanskrit scriptures, and saw no conflict between the demands of religion and imperialism:

The old armies of east and west had been rotated and the brigands quelled. The messengers of the Karluk offered homage. The Great Ministers ... and others brought much tribute from the territories, and offered camels, horses and cattle to His Majesty ... He gave his command that ... those who had become master translators ... should write a catalogue of the Tibetan translations and coinages deriving from the Sanskrit of the Greater and Lesser Vehicles.

During the second half of the eighth century, coinciding with the rise of Charlemagne and the Caliph Harun al-Rashid, King Trisong Detsen pushed Tibet through another phase of military expansion, at the expense of the Chinese. His empire spread into parts of what is now Qinghai, Gansu and Mongolia, cutting off China from the western regions. The great Bon kingdom of Zhangzhung was finally overthrown. Trisong Detsen's armies took Dunhuang, and their occupation led to the preservation there of countless Buddhist manuscripts, including the world's first printed book, the *Diamond Sutra*, which was to be redis-covered by the raiding Hungarian archaeologist Aurel Stein in 1907. At one point Trisong Detsen's armies pushed so far east towards the Yellow Sea that there was a risk of the Chinese empire being encircled. The Tang dynasty's capital, Changan (now Xian), was briefly captured and the emperor deposed, a substitute being installed in his place.

There were further peace negotiations, and a common border was agreed between Tibet and China. The treaty ceremony was only undermined when the Tibetans kidnapped several Chinese officials and generals. Sporadic fighting continued until 821, when a lasting settlement was agreed, its terms being inscribed on three stone pillars, at Changan, Lhasa and on the Sino–Tibetan border. The tradition of Chinese overlordship in western Central Asia was ending, and China no longer appeared unassailable to local rulers. For many years, diplomatic skill had concealed this fact; China had played a weak hand well, and not made its weak-ness apparent, a traditional feature of Chinese diplomacy. The Chinese reaction to the Tibetans at this time was still one of fear, apprehension and disapproval at their barbarian ways. The Tang annals record an ambassador visiting the Tibetan court and noting that 'priests with feathered headdresses and girdles of tiger-skin beat drums'.

As before, Tibet's rise prefigured a fall, although this time it would last for centuries, rather than for decades. After Trisong Detsen's death around 800 there was squabbling within the royal family and between the royals and the powerful monasteries. When Lang Darma, who was rumoured to have horns and a black tongue, came to the throne, he moved against the Buddhists and, according to the conventional but now largely discredited view, promoted Bon. In 842 a Buddhist monk shot Lang Darma through the heart with an arrow, escaping on a black horse. The horse had been covered in charcoal, and when the monk reversed his cloak and rode through a river, he and his mount changed colour, escaping detection. Lang Darma's assassination is a crucial moment in Tibetan popular history, marking the point at which Buddhism was driven underground in central Tibet. The empire dissolved, and internal conflict divided the country into small, often warring, states run by local chieftains, their territory marked with defensive fortresses.

For the next four hundred years, Tibetans turned to memory and religion, often in secret, with sages such as Atisha, Naropa, Gampopa, Marpa and Milarepa travelling to and from India and spreading a new wave of the Buddha's teachings across Tibet and the Himalayan region.

Milarepa, an eleventh-century religious practitioner whose body had turned green as a result of eating nothing but wild nettles, was one of several yogis who inspired a new wave of popular devotion in Buddhism. After his death his disciples disseminated stories of his selfless deeds, and he became one of Tibet's most popular saints. 'Life is short and the time of death is uncertain, so apply yourself to meditation,' he instructed. 'Avoid doing evil, and acquire merit to the best of your ability, even at the cost of life itself. In short: act so that you have no cause to be ashamed of yourself.'

Military brilliance gave way to expansion of the mind. Dressed only in cotton, Milarepa meditated high in the mountains, at the time of the Battle of Hastings, and wrote songs that would one day be loved by Sven-Goran Eriksson, another England football manager.

> I renounced all affairs of this life;
> And, no longer lazy, devoted myself to Dharma,
> Thus have I reached the state of eternal bliss.
> Such is the story of my life.

Tibet's days of martial glory were over. The country was now controlled by conflicting chieftains and religious sects, and the intervention of outside forces was looking inevitable. In the mid-thirteenth century, Tibet submitted to the formidable new power of the Mongol empire.

When a country becomes weak, its neighbours start to covet its more doubtful appendages. Things happen stealthily. The arrival of an unwelcome diplomatic mission, a small border incursion, the sponsoring of internal dissent – any of these will serve to test the water.

So, when China's government began to falter at the start of the twentieth century, the British were not alone in swivelling a covetous eye towards the land of snows. As the rulers of India, the British needed to keep their northern border secure, and were nervous that Tibet was becoming vulnerable. Anxious that the Russians might try to get to Lhasa first, they sent an army in 1904 led by the explorer Francis Younghusband to negotiate with the Thirteenth Dalai Lama, Thubten Gyatso. After a long and bloody campaign in which several thousand Tibetan soldiers were killed, British and Indian troops rode into Lhasa in full-dress uniform with a noisy Gurkha band. They were greeted by claps and shouts, which they took to be applause, but were in fact the Tibetan practice of *dogpa*. As a local official wrote in his memoirs:

> When the British officers marched to the Jokhang and other places, the inhabitants of Lhasa were displeased.

They shouted and chanted to bring down rain, and made clapping gestures to repulse them. In the foreigner's custom these are seen as signs of welcome, so they took off their hats and said thank you.

As the army approached, the Dalai Lama fled to Mongolia, hoping forlornly that the invaders might be encouraged 'not to nibble up our country'. Biding their time while alternative negotiators were sought, British officers took up wrestling, polo and horse-racing, and on 19 August 1904, played Lhasa's first documented game of football. Then they imposed a treaty, allowing British India to keep a pair of trade agents and a telegraph wire inside Tibet's borders.

In 1912, having made peace with the British, the Dalai Lama moved to assert his authority by expelling all Chinese troops and officials from his country. He made what was effectively a declaration of independence, announcing that 'the Chinese intention of colonising Tibet under the priest–patron relationship has faded like a rainbow in the sky'. When the Dalai Lama died in 1933, British India became nervous about the prospect of renewed Chinese influence, and another mission was dispatched to Tibet, this time with only a light military escort.

With the Dalai Lama's reincarnation yet to be found, it proved hard to determine where real political power was located, and for the British, football became a way of passing the days. They were challenged to a match by a home side called 'Lhasa United', composed of three bearded Ladakhis wearing red fezzes, a Chinese tailor, a Nepalese soldier and five of Tibet's leading young aristocrats, including Yuthok and Taring, both former commanders of the Trongdra or 'Better Families' Regiment, who 'still had their charm-boxes on top of their heads, so were precluded from heading the ball'. The 'Mission Marmots' included four *sahibs*, their Sikkimese clerks and a handful of Tibetan servants, including the star player, who wore gym shoes and a long plait.

The mission's secretary, Freddy Spencer Chapman, thought the pitch, framed by snow-flecked hills and the Dalai Lama's summer palace, the Norbulingka, had 'as lovely a setting as any ground in the world'.

The field was a sandy grassy clearing in the surrounding thorn thickets, and had been carefully marked out. Together with a crowd of supporters, our opponents were already there, turned out in garish harlequin-coloured silk shirts with L.U. sewn on to the pockets . . . After a good, clean, hard game, the Mission side won by scoring the only goal of the day. The goal was so small that the only hope of scoring was to go through oneself with the ball.

The pace of the game was aided by the long, high kicks that could be achieved in the thin air. Things proceeded happily for several weeks, 'until some wandering rogue stole our goal-posts for firewood, but by that time there were always sand-storms in the afternoons, so we decided the football season was over'.

This was not the end of the matter. The mission was under the charge of Basil Gould, a tall, calm, slightly obsessive British official, who was also the team's goalkeeper. He reported back to his masters in New Delhi that football was proving an effective way of establishing contact with influential Tibetans. Soon there were fourteen teams in Lhasa, and it had become 'a common sight to see street urchins playing football with a ball composed mainly of paper and string'.

In 1944, Reting Rinpoche, the ruler of Tibet during the Fourteenth Dalai Lama's minority, was discovered to be playing football daily. He was a controversial figure, said to be able to perform miracles, but Gould's colleague Hugh Richardson (who had first mentioned 'the mind's Tibet' to me) thought him 'naive and self-centred'. Reting had many enemies, and some senior clerics, seeing a means to attack him, objected to the game on ethical and cultural grounds. Football was declared to be tantamount to 'kicking the Buddha's head', and a ban was introduced in the same year.

So, after forty years of intermittent play, football's career in Tibet was at an end.

Although many Tibetans had renounced all affairs of this life and devoted themselves to Dharma, a prominent monk of the Sakya sect, Sakya Pandita, went to the Mongol court on a political journey in 1244. In a letter home, he reported that 'the armies of this Mongol king are numberless. I think that all the world has submitted to him.'

A *cho-yon* or priest–patron relationship was established between the Sakya hierarchy and Godan, grandson of Genghis Khan. Under this system, the Tibetans gave religious teachings, offered moral guidance and performed divinations, while in return the Mongol empire provided political protection. Each side awarded titles to the other, and a new administrative stability came to Tibet, with the Sakya priests acting as agents or viceroys of the Mongols. It was much more than a functional relationship between ruler and ruled. Tibetan, Mongol and Persian sources testify to the influence of the Tibetan clergy at the courts of successive khans. The great Kublai Khan, who conquered China and established the Yuan dynasty, even sat on a lower throne than his spiritual tutor, Phagpa, the nephew of Sakya Pandita, when receiving teachings.

Rashid al-Din, a thirteenth-century Jewish convert to Islam, noted that a pair of Tibetan priests, one with front teeth 'exceedingly long, so that his lips would not close', were invested by Kublai Khan with 'great authority and importance'. After Kublai's death, his grandson Temur Khan 'continues to believe in them, and those two *bakhshis* [priests] are all powerful'. Tibetan clout at the Mongol court was not limited to religious matters; members of the priests' entourage even acted as official weight-watchers to the emperor.

> They have made their *nokers* [assistants], who have a knowledge of medicine, attendants on the Qa'an in order to prevent Temur Qa'an from taking too much food or drink. They have two sticks bound together, and when the occasion arises they beat them on themselves, and the sticks produce a noise, whereupon Temur Qa'an takes warning and reduces his eating and drinking.

The Sakya administration ruled Tibet until the mid-fourteenth century, when the Mongol empire went into decline and the

Yuan dynasty was ousted from power in China. Sakya was overthrown, and Tibet again broke into warring kingdoms.

Although the emperors of China continued to confer honorific titles during subsequent centuries, they exerted no political control in Tibet. Internal sectarian conflict grew, particularly between the established Nyingma and Kagyu orders and the new reformist, scholastic Gelug sect, established by the disciples of Tsongkhapa. The practice of using identified reincarnations as a means of religious succession, a tradition which had begun in the Kagyu sect, now spread through Tibetan Buddhism, and was also taken up by some followers of Bon. The discovery of the first Karmapa (the head of the Kagyu order) in the early twelfth century is usually seen as the first recognised instance of reincarnation, but the Tibetologist Turrell Wylie suggested that it was the third Karmapa who began it, when in 1333 he prophesied his own rebirth. Wylie showed a linguistic distinction in Tibetan between 'incarnation' and 'reincarnation', calling the latter 'innovative and unorthodox'. In his view, the Karmapa's move was motivated primarily by ambition, since the Mongols were considering transferring their authority to him from the head of the Sakya order. Wylie concluded that reincarnation developed in Tibetan Buddhism 'primarily for political reasons'.

As Tibet descended into three hundred years of minor religious wars, the Mongol tribes to the north vied for regional supremacy. By the sixteenth century the Mongols of the Ordos, based in the great loop of the Yellow River, were in the ascendant. Their ruler, Altan Khan, feeling in need of spiritual sustenance, invited the prominent Tibetan monk Sonam Gyatso to his court.

A symbiotic *cho-yon* relationship began, similar to that between Kublai Khan and Phagpa. This alliance had some useful social and moral influence on the khans: the priest persuaded his patron to issue a proclamation on funerals stating that, 'In the future, it is not permitted to sacrifice animals, wives, or servants for the benefit of the deceased.' Sonam Gyatso also enhanced Altan Khan's status by choosing him as the protector of the Gelug order, calling him 'King of Religion', and in return was awarded the Mongol title of Dalai, meaning ocean. Since Sonam Gyatso was the third reincarnation in the Gelugpa line, he became the Third

Dalai Lama. On his death his consciousness migrated, conveniently, into Altan Khan's great-grandson, and when the boy died in 1616, a Tibetan was chosen as the Fifth Dalai Lama.

During the early seventeenth century, politics in Tibet fragmented, with small clans, large clans, powerful monasteries, visiting warriors and sectarian warlords fighting and intriguing for power. Conflict and brutal reprisals remained central to the Tibetan polity. The Kagyu order was harried and persecuted by a Gelugpa-backed branch of the Mongol cavalry. A civil war developed between the supporting militias of the two sects, with monasteries being sacked and their occupants forcibly converted. In some cases, religious leaders did not fully support the aggressive strategy of their military patrons.

Nervous that the strength of the Gelug order was weakening, a delegation of monks and ministers travelled north in the 1630s to enlist the support of the Mongol tribes. Gushri Khan, chieftain of the Qoshot Mongols, gave them his backing and swept through Kham and U-Tsang with an army, suppressing all opposition. The Fifth Dalai Lama was concerned that Gushri might overreach himself, but the great Mongol warrior was unwilling to halt his advance. In 1642 the victorious Gushri Khan declared in Shigatse that Tibet was now a united country, and vested his authority jointly in the Dalai Lama and a Desi, or chief minister. Gelug dominance was assured.

The 'Great Fifth' Dalai Lama appointed regional governors, proclaimed new laws, chose Lhasa as his capital and began to build a huge palace there, the Potala. He was a powerful leader, and the effective founder of the modern, integrated Tibetan state. According to the Italian historian Luciano Petech: 'The supremacy of the Dalai Lamas over Lamaism, and their temporal power are due to the life work of one of the greatest men Tibet ever produced: the Fifth Dalai Lama ... He reached his goal through sheer diplomatic skill.' He expanded his authority across the Buddhist world, 'presenting himself as Avalokitesvara through the performance of rituals ... and the writing of biographies of his predecessors that stressed the reincarnate lineage'.

The Dalai Lama travelled to China to exchange titles with the emperor. With the Chinese empire weak and Tibet protected by

Gushri Khan, the visit seems to have been somewhere between a meeting of equals and a developing priest–patron relationship; it was not a regular tribute mission. The emperor was from the Qing dynasty, which had recently come to power in China. As Manchus, from the north, the Qing had close historical and cultural links with the Mongols. The Tibetan delegation gave the emperor a supply of holy water from the Ganges, sealed in vases, which he took to keeping near him whether in his palace or on his travels. Tibetan Buddhism was incorporated into Qing courtly life, but not into the lives of the Confucian civil servants, the masters of Chinese continuity, who continued to look down on all foreign religions.

When the Fifth Dalai Lama died in 1682, his demise was kept hidden from the public by the Desi for fifteen long years, enabling the building of the Potala to be completed without interruption. Sometimes he was represented by a lookalike, but usually his absence was explained away by the demands of religious devotion, and a ceremonial gown was used in his place during state occasions, a traditional practice known as 'inviting the clothes'.

By the start of the eighteenth century, with the dominance of the Mongols declining, the Dalai Lama dead and China in an increasingly strong political position, the situation had altered significantly. Tibet was unstable, weakened by internal conflict. The Kangxi emperor, a soldier and scholar, became nervous, watching China's western border. The new Dalai Lama, the Sixth, the poet and aesthete, was unable to exert authority, and in 1706 he died. Tibet declined into civil war, the Dzungar Mongols fighting brutally for influence. The Chinese decided to intervene, and it has been plausibly suggested by the Japanese historian Yumiko Ishihama, on the basis of Manchu sources, that the 'first axiom' of their invasion was 'protection of the doctrine' of Buddhism. The emperor of China's high religious standing was crucial to his acceptance by Tibetans. In a letter to the Qing court, the young Seventh Dalai Lama, the Lithang-born reincarnation, referred to the emperor as 'Superior Manjushri, great Khan, turning the meritorious golden wheel, governing the whole country, [who] from the old time knows the whole people as the sun shines and loves and guides sentient beings to good deeds'.

In 1720 the Seventh Dalai Lama was carried to Lhasa by Qing soldiers, and 'entered with all pomp the pillaged and desolated Potala. His retinue was a splendid assemblage of Mongol chiefs, Manchu and Chinese officers and Tibetan clergymen and nobles.' The Tuscan Jesuit priest Ippolito Desideri, who was busy preparing 'in the Tibetan language a refutation of the errors of [Buddhist] doctrine and a defence of the Catholic religion', wrote that 'the whole vast kingdom was flooded with silver' as the Chinese took control. A military garrison watched over Lhasa.

For the next two centuries, Chinese authority in Tibet fluctuated according to the level of internal stability that the Tibetan government managed to maintain. China's influence was mainly ceremonial, rather than substantive. Two Manchu *ambans*, or representatives of the emperor, had what Luciano Petech called 'rights of control and supervision' over the Lhasa administration, and from the late eighteenth century 'direct participation in the Tibetan government'. In 1793 the 'Twenty-Nine Articles on the Reconstruction of Tibetan Domestic Affairs' gave the *ambans* ostensible authority over foreign affairs, military and religious appointments, taxation and the criminal justice system.

Successive emperors bestowed titles and awards on prominent Tibetans, yet as Petech wrote, the opportunity for easier relations 'was to a great part nullified by the fact that both the Chinese and the Tibetan civilisations had already reached and surpassed their highest point and had to a great extent crystallised along fixed and immovable lines'. One Chinese official in Tibet noted that while Tibetans appeared to be respectful and deferential in public, they were in fact often engaged in 'secret resistance . . . they left orders unattended to for months on the pretext of waiting for the Dalai Lama's return or for decisions yet to be made, simply ignoring urgent requests for answers'.

The main link between the two great civilisations was, ironically, religious. In the late eighteenth century, the Qianlong emperor even learned the Tibetan language in order to improve his dealings with Tibet's nobles and high reincarnations, noting that when they visited, 'to express the idea of conquering by kindness . . . I do not rely on an interpreter'. *Thangkas* were produced depicting the emperor as Manjushri, and his court sponsored elaborate translation projects of Buddhist scriptures. Permission to wear robes decorated with five-clawed dragons was given to the Dalai Lama, the Panchen Rinpoche and the leading Mongolian reincarnation, the Jebtsun Damba Khutuktu – a right which had previously been restricted to the emperor, his sons and senior princes.

For the next two centuries, until the fall of the Qing, Tibet was controlled, but no effort was made to integrate or assimilate it into China; the submission was symbolic.

Basil Gould found that football was not the only way of exerting influence. Games, in various forms, were part of a wider diplomatic strategy, the Great Game by other means. At Dekyilingka, the British mission, ballroom dancing was introduced, and the 'Palais Glide' and 'Boomps-a-Daisy' became briefly popular within the grander spheres of Lhasa society. The surgeon at Dekyilingka took to swimming in the Tsangpo river during the cold weather, which 'did much to enhance the prestige of the British people'. At Christmas, Santa Claus distributed toy tanks to chosen Tibetan children, and film reels of Rin-Tin-Tin, King George V's jubilee procession and Charlie Chaplin (who developed 'a terrific following') were shown to guests. Darts and peggity were promoted, and in 1938 Hugh Richardson noted that 'Mah Jong has completely taken hold of Lhasa since I was last here,' provoking a marginal query from a colleague wondering if this represented 'sinister evidence of Chinese influence'. Five years on, Richardson reported to New Delhi that 'after tea we played croquet – a new introduction to Lhasa, which appeared to be most popular. Later on three war reels were shown. These included "Victory in the Desert" . . . They are excellent propaganda value and were much appreciated.'

Whether these exhibitions of British imperial prestige did anything to strengthen Tibet's own military resolve is doubtful. In the 1920s, the British Indian government had supplied Tibet with machine-guns and mortars and several thousand Lee-Enfield rifles. Gould's 1936 mission, three years after the death of the

Thirteenth Dalai Lama, was charged with investigating the condition of these weapons. A military review was arranged at Drabchi, a barren plain outside Lhasa. Most of the Tibetan government attended, sitting on raised platforms under elaborate tents. Large crowds turned out to watch the action, with traders setting up 'small stalls where they sat beneath umbrellas selling apricots, greasy-looking cakes, tea, and cigarettes. The crowd, which was fairly orderly, was controlled by junior officials and several of the gigantic monks armed with whips.'

Proceedings opened with a Tibetan band using bagpipes, bugles and drums to create such tunes as 'It's a Long Way to Tipperary', 'Highland Laddie' and 'God Save the King'. Brigadier Philip Neame, a First World War hero, recorded in his diary after the inspection that the Lee-Enfields were 'disgracefully dirty' and half of them did not work. The machine-guns jammed on firing. The activity on the parade ground was no better. 'The drill, dressing and marching were bad,' he wrote. 'The standard was far below any Indian territorial battalion, in fact it was crude.'

Target practice, meanwhile, was a disaster.

> No soldiers have fired their rifles at Lhasa for six years and there is no weapon training apparatus. The rifles of course were not zero'd, and doubtless sights have got considerably displaced. Each man fired five rounds at a four-foot target at two hundred yards, and not a man failed to register a miss. The marking was of little use, as no attempt was made to indicate the shot hole. It was altogether a lamentable exhibition of rifle shooting.

The optimistic view of this military incompetence would be that it came from instinctive pacifism. Martin Scorsese's 1997 movie *Kundun*, a beautifully crafted piece of Dalaidolatry, opens with the claim that 'Tibetans have practised non-violence for over a thousand years.' The Jey Tsong Khapa Professor of Indo-Tibetan Buddhist Studies at Columbia University, Robert Thurman, has similarly depicted Tibet as a land of 'psychonauts', where 'the cool-revolutionary counterculture' entered the mainstream. Tibet was 'a laboratory for the enlightenment movement to create its model society', replete with 'pacifist monks and nuns spending their days in learning, meditation, and creativity'. Helped by the teachings of the Buddha, the country had developed 'industrial-strength mass monasteries in which individuals conquered their innermost energies and transformed their world into a buddhaverse'.

The idea is appealing, but unreal. The Dalai Lamas rode to political power on the back of the military might of the Mongols. Tibet's history, like the history of any country, is full of war, gore and male domination, even if revenge slaughter never became as popular as in neighbouring lands. As late as May 1947, the footballer Reting Rinpoche was punished for insurrection by having a silk scarf stuffed down his throat, or his testicles crushed, or being poisoned with yellow pills, depending on which version you prefer. Tibet's lack of initiative in the 1930s came from the loss of focus and ambition caused by extended reliance on the mediation and patronage of outsiders. As the historian Owen Lattimore has written, 'the tributary or feudatory status of Tibet' began when the Sakya sect submitted to Kublai Khan in the thirteenth century: 'Politically, the supreme pontiffs of Tibet have from the beginning acted as the agents of one or another alien overlord.'

So, while the newly discovered Fourteenth Dalai Lama grew to adulthood and Mao's Communist rebels edged closer to victory in China's civil war, the Tibetan government remained rudderless, unsure how to proceed. The three great monasteries – Drepung, Sera and Ganden – continued to be a powerful bulwark of tradition, opposing the very idea of change and progress. As an unnamed British diplomat noted in 1940, 'Tibet's military weakness is a danger to her continued independence, if ever the Chinese should have time and energy to spare to attempt once more to establish their domination over the country.'

Most of the reforms attempted by the Thirteenth Dalai Lama during his lifetime had failed. Ambitious modernising initiatives such as the creation of paramilitary units and secular schools, where football might be played, were overturned by the entrenched conservatism of the monastic establishment. When the army did turn out on parade, it was not for rifle-shooting or machine-gun practice; rather, the soldiers concentrated on the maintenance of decorum, tradition and precedent. Each year, on the penultimate day of the Monlam Chenmo, the Great Prayer Festival, a military review was held at Drabchi.

This was Tibet, alone, reliving its glorious past.

Symbolically, it was the days of empire that counted. During the Monlam Chenmo, a pair of Tibetan aristocrats would be temporarily awarded the Mongol title of Yaso, making them commanders of the two wings of the ancient army. Dressed in stupendous brocade robes trimmed with fur, supported by noble attendants, in the decade in which Salvador Dalí gave a lecture in a diving-suit in London, they would watch the cavalry turn out in scraps of ancient chain-mail and peacock feathers, each horseman carrying a quiver of five plumed arrows. At their head rode two standard bearers holding tall lances and painted banners, wearing cherished helmets, possibly dating to the eighth century, with the name of Allah inscribed on the front in gold filigree.

The Arab influence, from the days long before Tibet became the forbidden land of European invention, was not forgotten by Tibetans. The past lived. During the early ninth century, soldiers of the Tibetan empire had harassed Muslim forces in Central Asia, and laid siege to Samarkand. Correspondingly, Arab troops, stirred by the spread of Islam, had captured parts of Kashmir and Wakhan, and taken the Tibetan general ('the commander of the cavalry of al-Tubbat', they recorded) and his horsemen back to Baghdad where they could be paraded in triumph, like downed airmen during the Gulf War.

Martial influence travelled in all directions, with Chinese and Arab sources reporting the superiority of early Tibetan armour. A Tang historian noted the quality of the weaponry of a joint Turkic-Tibetan army in the early eighth century.

> The men and horses all wear chain-mail armour. Its work-manship is extremely fine. It envelops them completely, leaving openings only for the two eyes. Thus, strong bows and sharp swords cannot injure them. When they do battle, they must dismount and array themselves in ranks. When one dies, another takes his place. To the end, they are not willing to retreat.

So, each Yaso led his wing of the symbolic army past the Potala palace to Drabchi, where they halted near some beautifully decorated tents, occupied by the Kashag, the Tibetan Cabinet. The review began, each wing of the army thundering past in turn. *Katags*, the diaphanous scarves, were presented. Tea was poured, rice was eaten, and a high official bowed to the waist, swept off his hat and announced that the correct number of men and horses were in attendance. Other officials, in plaits and yellow hats, repeated their piece, until it was time for the Kashag to break for a picnic. Later in the afternoon, after presents had been distributed and prostrations made in the direction of the Potala, the temporary, galloping soldiers wheeled round and rode home, back to their everyday lives.

This, then, was old Tibet in new Tibet, the eighth century in the twentieth century, martial Tibet in controlled Tibet; a memory. On the plains of Drabchi, where the machine-guns had jammed and the rifle-shooting was lamentable, military glory was represented by horsemen in ancient armour. The mediator, the agent that had made it this way, was religion. Not the theoretical, philosophical system that brings serenity and causes foreigners to love a mind's Tibet, but the religious inversion that had accompanied the abdication of responsibility centuries before, and allowed authority to pass to foreign rulers.

The Thirteenth Dalai Lama – a stooped man with penetrating eyes and pointed ears who had smallpox marks on his cheeks and loved flowers and generally ate *thukpa* and fried vegetables for his supper – knew that withdrawal had led his nation to its doom. In the *Kachem*, his Last Testament, he wrote:

> Unless we can guard our own country, it will now happen that the Dalai and Panchen Lamas, the Father and the Son, the Holders of the Faith, the Glorious Rebirths, will be broken down and left without a name. As regards the monasteries and the priesthood, their lands and other properties will be destroyed ... High officials, low officials, and peasants must all act in harmony to bring happiness to Tibet: one person alone cannot lift a heavy carpet; several must unite to do so.

The Thirteenth Dalai Lama had tried to make things change, but he was almost alone, and he failed, unable to undo the cultural habits of centuries.

If you go back to the time when the Sixth Dalai Lama was murdered in secret near Lake Kokonor –

> White crane!
> Lend me your wings . . .

– you will remember that his successor, the Lithang boy, was carried to Lhasa by Qing troops, and that in 1720 Tibet's time as a free land came to an end.

The Potala had been burned and looted by the Dzungar Mongols in the accompanying civil war. They had stripped it of its gold and precious stones, of its silver and sacred wall-hangings. The Fifth Dalai Lama's palace had to be restored, slowly, in all its glory; the rooms rebuilt, the frescoes repainted, the sculptures remoulded, the embroideries resown. When the craftsmen had finished, the Potala looked 'richer and more beautiful than before'. Donations were made towards the cost of this work by Tibetan and Mongol chieftains, by the great monasteries, by Buddhists from as far away as Lake Kokonor and Kalmyks from the banks of the Volga. The sons of the Chinese emperor contributed too, along with members of the Manchu nobility at the Qing court; but there is no escaping the fact that the principal patron of the restoration of the modern Potala, the symbol of Tibetan nationalism that falls from a million campaign leaflets, was the man known as Superior Manjushri, who loved and guided sentient beings to good deeds: the emperor of China.

TEN

They were strange days, there in Xining. I slept during the afternoons, read *Mansfield Park* twice, drank lots of water and watched television. In time, I learned that the American researcher's fall had happened at another hotel, in a different part of town, and that the two detainees had been expelled through Hong Kong, one on a stretcher. I discovered later that they had been co-sponsored on their mission by the International Campaign for Tibet in Washington, and that many activists had considered the pair to be wholly inappropriate for such a delicate task. My daydreams were heavy with the idea of ejection through a third-storey window, and the likely future of the Tibetan man who had been arrested with the two foreigners.

One day, I tried to visit the Dalai Lama's home village of Taktser. I was interested to learn about its current ethnic make-up, and whether there were many Tibetan villagers left. The taxi-driver, a Chinese woman, was not sure how to get there. I had a map. We got stuck in thick traffic in Pingan, a town which Tibetans call Tsongkhakhar, and, emerging, took the wrong road. It was steep. The landscape became a red, sunny emptiness, mountains and rocks looming as the verge fell away. Turning a corner, we almost hit a man who was standing in the middle of the road. He was a roadworker, skinny and toothless, in a Mao suit, holding a red flag. We reversed and waited, while high above us on an escarpment, workers provoked a small landslide to obtain rocks and gravel for the repairs.

At the crest of the hill was a Muslim village. Flayed sheep

hung on poles. An old man with a white beard and lace cap, an umbrella strapped across his back, gave us directions to Taktser. We drove down through a Chinese neighbourhood, past children carrying baskets of melons and peppers, and women winnowing grain on the road, who stepped back to allow us to drive over their grain. The next village had tall wooden flagpoles bearing coloured prayer flags. A line of tiny pink pigs ran between two houses. A Tibetan woman in a *chuba* and headscarf redirected us to Taktser, a couple of miles away.

As we drove down the rutted, dusty road, with dusk closing in, I saw a figure in a dark-green uniform standing in front of a striped metal barrier. We stopped. The man was young and nervous. We had to turn back. His boss was expected at any moment. Taktser was closed to foreigners. He could not possibly let us through. It had been decided by the Public Security Bureau in Xining. Nobody could come through the barrier except local people. I could visit any other village in the whole district, but not Taktser. He gave no reason for the exclusion.

I returned to my hotel room in Xining, and fell into a state of inertia. Thinking back over the events of the afternoon, I knew that I should not have been surprised at the village being closed. The Fourteenth Dalai Lama, Tenzin Gyatso, was at the centre of so much, portrayed as inseparable from the existence of the Tibetan nation, making him its purpose and its meaning – a position that he has always rejected, saying that it is the fate of six million Tibetans that matters, not his own future.

The Dalai Lama has become more famous than any Chinese citizen, but is required to cross the world on a yellow identity certificate issued by the Indian government. When he travels, he can attract agnostic crowds in their tens of thousands, an achievement unmatched by any other religious leader. Despite speaking in broken English, interspersed with bursts of Tibetan translated by an interpreter, he has an extraordinary ability to command and move an audience. 'I have never seen any body assume more complete and natural control of great assemblies,' wrote Basil Gould after the Dalai Lama's enthronement in Lhasa in 1940. An official back in London thought this a ridiculous claim to make about a five-year-old boy, writing the words 'a flight of imaginative fancy' in the margin, but Gould was right. He was only echoing the reaction of the British traveller Thomas Manning, who wrote after meeting a previous incarnation of the Dalai Lama in 1811, 'I was extremely affected by this interview with the Lama. I could have wept through strangeness of sensation . . . This day I saluted the Grand Lama! Beautiful youth.'

The Chinese government, excusing its failure to win the hearts and minds of the Tibetan people over the last fifty years, blames the Dalai Lama for all its troubles in Tibet. Beijing has called him an 'arch criminal who splits the motherland', a 'tool of Western anti-China forces', a 'jackal', a 'reactionary feudal serf-owner', a promoter of 'rape, murder and child cannibalism' and a 'wolf in monk's clothing' – a litany of abuse not even surpassed by that heaped on Chris Patten, who when governor of Hong Kong was labelled a 'serpent', a 'strutting prostitute' and a 'tango dancer'.

China's propaganda against the Dalai Lama is remarkably inept. Responding to his popularity around the world, the government mouthpiece the *People's Daily* reported in 2001: 'The support rate for Dalai Lama among Tibetan Buddhists recorded a drastic drop, according to a sample survey released Friday. Responding to a question of "what kind of a person the Dalai is?" 86 per cent of the respondents think that he is a separatist.' The same report also found that when asked, 'What do you think has been the most delightful thing since the peaceful liberation of Tibet fifty years ago?', more than 90 per cent of the residents replied, 'The smashing of the shackles of the feudal serf system, which enabled a million serfs to stand up and be masters of their own fate.'

As the tone of China's attack has grown shriller, the Dalai Lama's stature has risen. *Arena* magazine has described him as simply 'the coolest spiritual-leader daddio around' – a global icon, the hero of a generation, renowned for his laughter and for spreading a message of peace and compassion, and for speaking frankly about matters such as global poverty and injustice, as well as being joyful and celibate; a rare combination of qualities. He has tried to unite different religious traditions, only drawing the line at taking part in animal sacrifice – at a religious festival in France in 1997, he refused to join a Buryat shaman on stage for the ritual slaughter of a chicken.

The Dalai Lama's detractors have managed to land remarkably few punches on him over the years. They say that he accepted CIA funding during the 1960s; that he had links with Shoko Asahara, the head of the Aum cult responsible for the 1995 Tokyo gas attack; that he is intolerant of homosexuality; that his followers used violence against devotees of Dorje Shugden, a Buddhist protector deity whose worship the Dalai Lama has discouraged; and that he spends too much time with expendable singers and movie stars. All of these charges are fair, although it is apparent that the Dalai Lama has little genuine interest in the celebrity circus, and is unaware of the identity of many of the Hollywood stars who pursue him. He uses the famous, at times naively, as a tool to promote the Tibetan cause. As he has said, 'I don't bother about a person's background. Beggar, actor, AIDS victim, prince, monk – all fascinate me and I must care for all equally.'

He has a few Western critics. The singer Elton John has complained that he is 'fucking nowhere to be seen . . . in times of war and times of aggravation', and the journalist Christopher Hitchens has charged him with making 'crass and banal' comments about nuclear weapons, and heading 'a Hollywood cult that almost exceeds the power of Scientology'. The media owner Rupert Murdoch, who has extensive business interests in China, famously called him 'a very political old monk shuffling around in Gucci shoes', a statement which caused confused pleasure in Beijing, one newspaper reporting that 'Dalai Lama is an old lama very interested in politics, who is going canvassing among countries in a pair of Italian-made Gucci leather shoes'. Murdoch also claimed the Tibetans' main problem was that 'half the people of Tibet still think that the Dalai Lama is the son of God', which misunderstands the fact that he is seen as an emanation of the *bodhisattva* of compassion, rather than as the son of God. More importantly, it misunderstands his motivation. Although the Dalai Lama may be fêted by the rich and the glamorous, he himself would not know his Guccis from his Nikes, and his failing is that if anything he is insufficiently political. His inclination has always been towards the spiritual and the conciliatory, rather than towards worldly cunning.

From the time he took up temporal power in 1950 at the age

of sixteen, the Dalai Lama's restricted education and the Tibetan cultural emphasis on prevarication meant that he was in an exposed position. Naive and optimistic, faced with the ruthless, battle-hardened Communists who had just won power in China, he floundered. In 1955 he went to see Mao Zedong in Beijing. Towards the end of the meeting, the Chairman leaned over and whispered to him, with a friendly smile, 'Of course, religion is poison.' The Dalai Lama felt 'a violent burning sensation' across his face, and buried his head in his notes, hoping to disguise his discomfort. Yet in the same year, the Dalai Lama told a visiting reporter in Tibet: 'Politically the People's Democratic system with the working class as its leadership and the worker–peasant alliance as its base is a correct system which works above all for the welfare and happiness of the mass of the people . . . Tibet has left the old way that led to darkness and has taken a new way leading to a bright future of development.'

At a previous meeting with the Dalai Lama, I had asked him whether comments such as this attributed to him in the 1950s were genuine. He said they were his true sentiments at the time. Believing that change would lead to progress, he thought that Mao's revolutionary reforms would bring prosperity to Tibet. Only later, as news came through of death and destruction in Kham and Amdo, did he alter his views and make plans to flee into exile. During his time in office between 1950 and 1959, the Tibetan government operated with the same mixture of cupidity and incompetence as it had in the 1930s and forties.

In recent years the Dalai Lama has made several political mis-judgements. His handling of the selection of the new Panchen Rinpoche led to an alternative candidate being put up by Beijing, and to a religious crackdown in Tibet. His reaction to conciliatory overtures from the Chinese government during the early 1980s, when Deng Xiaoping invited Tibetan refugees to return from exile, was short-sighted. The Dalai Lama was offered a symbolic post in Beijing, the right to visit Tibet when he wanted, and freedom to speak to the press. By the standards of the time, this was a remarkable offer to come from Mao's lineal successor. Instead of seizing it and entering into direct negotiations, the Dalai Lama sent numerous fact-finding missions to China and

Tibet, and delegates who demanded trivial concessions, such as the right to meet with two ageing Tibetan quislings who had lost political influence many years before. The historian Tsering Shakya has written that the exiled government in Dharamsala 'badly misjudged' the situation at this time: 'Beijing's commitment had underlined the involvement of Deng Xiaoping, China's paramount leader, and of Hu Yaobang, the most senior Party official. Once the Chinese leaders lost interest in the issue . . . any possibility of reaching a compromise was effectively ended.'

In 1989, the Dalai Lama refused an invitation to take part in the Panchen Rinpoche's funerary ceremonies in Beijing, despite being told it would be an opportunity for high-level discussions. His advisers in Dharamsala, conscious of protocol and precedent (would the Dalai Lama still qualify as a refugee after being allowed back into China?) and mindful of the rapid growth in popular support for Tibet in the richer countries of the world, advised him to turn down the offer. The writer Tom Grunfeld has suggested that the Dalai Lama's failure to go to Beijing in 1989 was 'probably the gravest error of his political life'.

Since then, the prospects of accommodation have receded. As external support for the Tibetan cause has increased, and political ties between the exiled government and its foreign patrons have grown, China has hardened its position against the Dalai Lama. The Chinese government is unlikely to cut a deal with him, except on terms of total surrender, meaning abandonment of dreams of a greater Tibet, and of a democratic, demilitarised autonomous state within China. The Dalai Lama has come to represent too much; his return to Tibet, with the world's media travelling in his wake, hoovering up the biggest story of its kind since Nelson Mandela's release from prison, would be profoundly destabilising to Communist rule.

There were moments, seeing things from inside China, the other way round, when it appeared that foreign lobbying had only served to tighten repression and promote false hopes among Tibetans.

Around the mid-1980s, the Dalai Lama and his exiled government turned for guidance to a number of Western lobbyists, lawyers, levitators and Sinophobes, most of whom had minimal understanding of Chinese history or politics. A variation on the *cho-yon* or priest–patron relationship developed. The Dalai Lama became what *Newsweek* called 'a lama to the globe', and Tibetans gained apparent political backing, and ceaseless advice of varying utility. In the words of the essayist Jamyang Norbu, sympathetic foreign advisers were soon 'battening themselves on the Dalai Lama's court with the tact and sensitivity of lampreys'.

These well-wishers suggested that the Dalai Lama might raise his political profile in the West, and push hard for democratic self-government for Tibet within the People's Republic of China. It was the sort of approach that might have worked well had China been a secure democracy, rather than a xenophobic dictatorship. In practice, it turned out to be a disaster, simultaneously aggravating Beijing and fracturing the exile community, which had built its identity around the optimistic notion of '*Po Cholkha Sum*', a free homeland comprising the historic regions of ethnic Tibet.

The Dalai Lama presented a 'Five Point Peace Proposal' to the US Congressional Human Rights Caucus in September 1987, and another version nine months later at the European Parliament in Strasbourg. He spoke of zones of peace and of the protection of the environment, catching the mood of the time. The location of the speeches might as well have been calculated to outrage the Chinese government, playing on all its old, unreconstructed fears, stretching back to the nineteenth century, about foreign interference and designs on China's national integrity. The Strasbourg proposal was followed by an ill-judged attempt by the exiles to bounce Beijing into negotiations. When they announced that they intended to include a Dutch lawyer on their team – an act of astonishing miscalculation, internationalising the issue still further – it was inevitable that China would refuse to cooperate.

Three days after the Dalai Lama's speech on Capitol Hill, a pair of Tibetan prisoners were publicly executed in Lhasa. This was widely viewed by Tibetans inside Tibet as a political statement, and it exacerbated existing social and religious tension. Three days after the executions, demonstrations and riots broke out in

Lhasa which lasted, on and off, until March 1989, when martial law was declared. The protests during these eighteen months were brutally suppressed by paramilitary police, with hundreds of Tibetans being killed and injured, and others being tortured, sometimes to death, in prison.

The demonstrations were provoked in part by simple misunderstanding. Footage of the Dalai Lama speaking in Washington had been broadcast across China's state media, accompanied by vigorous condemnation. According to Tsering Shakya, 'What struck most Tibetans was the image of the Dalai Lama being enthusiastically received in the parliament of the most powerful nation in the world . . . The vehemence of the Chinese denunciations also strengthened the Tibetans' perception that a US commitment to Tibetan independence really existed and this led them to believe that they too must contribute to hastening the withdrawal of the Chinese from Tibet.' For Tibetans brought up within the Communist system, the distinction between the US Congress and the US government was meaningless. From everything that they knew about how politics worked, an official body of this kind would only have applauded a speech on the orders of the country's leadership. So they rose up, and were killed.

When I discussed the events of 1987–89 with people during my journey through Tibet, I repeatedly had to try to explain the difference in a democracy between the executive, the legislature and a pressure group. Even educated Tibetans found it hard to comprehend. I said that an elected representative may or may not support the ruling party, and that the legislature may oppose the executive, and vice-versa, and that protesters might demonstrate freely on the streets, but that their protests would often be ignored. Living in a political system where there was no legal means of obtaining accurate, neutral information about anything (except, on a good day, through the internet), people found this baffling. One woman, who had spent two years studying in a European country, asked me in all seriousness whether it was true, as she had been told, that in a democracy you could support an opposition party without putting your job at risk or coming under suspicion from the authorities. We came from different political worlds, and the gap between us often felt unbridgeable.

A few months after I had left Tibet, my fears were reinforced by a roundabout television interview with one of the West's most prominent Tibetophile campaigners, Adam Yauch of the pop group the Beastie Boys. 'I think there's still quite a way to go on the Tibetan movement for Tibet to gain its freedom,' Yauch told the viewers of MTV.

I think it'd be a mistake to start counting our blessings before the job is done. But I think it is getting closer. I think the actual environment in Tibet, the political climate, is worse than it's ever been, with the human rights violations and so on. But in a sense, I think that's a sign that the Tibetan movement toward gaining its freedom has been successful, and it's the Chinese government's fear of outside perception that's making the Chinese government crack down on people even more.

So, in Yauch's analysis, the political climate in Tibet being 'worse than it's ever been, with the human rights violations and so on' was evidence that the pro-Tibet lobby was being successful.

Although the voters of the Western world might like to see the Dalai Lama back in the Potala, there is no evidence that their views have had any influence over the ageing Communist Party leadership in Beijing. Nor have they changed their own governments' policies towards China. The West will always place commercial and strategic concerns ahead of sympathy for Tibetans. Even if democratic voters were to sway their elected representatives, it is hard to see how any foreign government could persuade the People's Liberation Army to quit Tibet, short of beginning a world war.

When the tanks were sent into Tiananmen Square in 1989, Wang Zhen, a Party elder famed for crushing the Muslims of Xinjiang back in 1949, had this to say to Deng Xiaoping: 'Those goddamn bastards! . . . They're really asking for it! . . . Anybody who tries to overthrow the Communist Party deserves death and no burial!'

If the leaders of the Party view their own citizens with such ruthless cynicism, they are likely to be contemptuous of the opinions of well-intentioned foreigners.

Beijing has little interest in overseas public opinion on the Tibetan issue. It is hard to think of any country which produces such consistently implausible propaganda in its own defence. The Chinese foreign ministry's response to media criticism abroad is invariably formulaic, and often absurd:

> Tibet has been part of China since ancient times. The central government has continuously exercised its sovereignty over Tibet since the thirteenth century. Before 1959, when democratic reform was carried out, the old Tibet ruled by the Fourteenth Dalai Lama was a society of feudal serfdom under despotic religious-political rule, a society darker than the European serfdom of the Middle Ages. For the broad mass of serfs and slaves who comprised 95 per cent of Tibetans, even their basic right of subsistence was not guaranteed, let alone any other human rights.
>
> Today, the people in the Tibetan Autonomous Region enjoy not only civil and political rights like the people of various nationalities in China, but also special rights granted by the law governing regional national autonomy of China . . . The Tibetan people enjoy full freedom of religious belief.

The writers know that this is not true; the readers know that it is not true; it is shoddy work, churned out by low-level officials, for form's sake.

The China specialists Frederick Teiwes and Warren Sun have argued that 'Westerners think of politics in certain ways which make it difficult to accept Chinese realities,' presuming that 'politics is about policy, that a great country has a large policy agenda which naturally preoccupies the politicians', and that 'political power flows to people with certain skills and capabilities'.

In a nationalist dictatorship founded on blood, like the one which gained power in China in October 1949, the assumptions that are taken for granted in a democracy do not hold true. Leaders are selected not for their ability to do a job or to represent the nation, but for their willingness to uphold the Party's authority and suppress dissent. Vocal popular pressure does not cause a change in policy. Institutions do not act as a check on those in power. Only when the Chinese system starts to fracture from within will it be vulnerable to methods of open defiance, such as street protests and non-cooperation. Mohandas Gandhi, often invoked by the Dalai Lama and his supporters as an exemplar, has no message for the Tibetans. (Mao's student years might be contrasted with those of Gandhi's heir, Jawaharlal Nehru: while Mao joined a revolutionary militia in Changsha, where people were hacked to death and a head was paraded outside the governor's residence on a stick, Nehru studied at Cambridge University, where he joined the college boat club and played plenty of tennis.) Gandhi's strategy of mass civil resistance was a tactical response to the British political system; had he tried it against Mao or Stalin, he and his followers would have been rounded up and shot.

The impasse over Tibet's future has increased the volubility of foreign support for the Dalai Lama. When he visited the USA in the summer of 2000, for instance, he had meetings with the National Security Adviser and eminent Washington politicians, and thirty-five minutes with the President. Encased by a huge entourage of State Department security people, he promoted a peaceful solution for Tibet to the American people. His supporters put him on *Larry King Live* on CNN. He had been on the show six months earlier for a Millennium Special, when King had asked the Dalai Lama, as a leading Muslim, what he thought about the new year celebrations.

This time, the host knew that his guest was a Buddhist, but it was a sorry spectacle, the Dalai Lama, the *bodhisattva* of compassion, being forced by the exigencies of global politics and celebrity culture to compete for airtime with the passing flotsam of high-speed television:

LARRY KING: He's the author of a brilliant book called *The Art of Happiness: A Handbook for Living*. Before we talk about that and many other things, we thank you for being with us, Your Holiness, and we'd love your reaction to the announcement today by President Clinton and Prime Minister Blair about the genome. What do you think of the book of human life?

DALAI LAMA: About what?

LARRY KING: About the genome, the book of life, announced today.

DALAI LAMA: Please explain something about that. I do not know what is the meaning.

LARRY KING: Well, they announced today that the discovery that they could put together a book of life on every person, DNA, the genome, et cetera, the book of everyone's genes in life.

DALAI LAMA: I still, I am not very clear, you see, about that.

LARRY KING: You did not hear this today?

DALAI LAMA: No, no . . . I engaged teaching, my teaching today.

LARRY KING: OK, I understand you were busy.

DALAI LAMA: But what is the meaning, then? So, anyway, is it some kind of new life or something?

LARRY KING: Yes. What are your thoughts about DNA in general?

DALAI LAMA: DNA, of course, my knowledge is very, very limited, but it is something I think that each individuals have some sort of sense of DNA, so this may have some kind of common link, that's coming from a Buddhist viewpoint, but otherwise I have no sort of much idea about that . . .

LARRY KING: We'll be right back with more of His Holiness the Dalai Lama . . . Deepak Chopra later. And tomorrow night, a program about reality shows. We'll deal with CBS's hit, *Survivor*. And also, *Big Brother* is coming. Darva Conger and Hugh Hefner will be here on Wednesday . . . We'll be right back.

American Tibetophilia even provoked a two-week happening at the Smithsonian Folklife Festival, including a public speech by the Dalai Lama which drew a crowd of tens of thousands.

The Monlam Chenmo, the great prayer festival founded in 1409 by Tsongkhapa, was plucked from its regular home among the exile community in India and incorporated into the commotion. Dozens of monks from Drepung Loseling and Namgyal monasteries were flown into Washington DC to chant in suitably guttural tones and look impressive in maroon and saffron robes. Nobody seemed to notice that the Monlam Chenmo was a central date in the Tibetan state calendar, which had never been hijacked in this way before, and that its cancellation in Dharamsala that year led to acute religious and financial tribulation for the many Tibetan refugees who depend on it.

Meanwhile, at the Forest Lawn Memorial Park in Los Angeles, the Dalai Lama blessed a new Shi-Tro mandala (a three-dimensional religious sculpture) in front of a large, paying audience. The mandala had been created by a Tibetan monk who ran a local Buddhist centre, assisted by his American wife, who worked in creative marketing for Warner Brothers Records Inc. She had generated volumes of publicity, using the slogan 'Shi-Tro Happens'. The *Los Angeles Times* described this as 'marketing the mandala in a hip and humorous way'. So, there was the Dalai Lama, up on stage, Shi-Tro happening, the ceremony compered by the requisite Hollywood star, in this case the actress Sharon Stone, famous for lacking underwear in the movie *Basic Instinct*, but this time wearing a feather boa and bare feet. After musing aloud for a while about how she might introduce the Dalai Lama, she finally settled for, 'The hardest-working man in spirituality . . . Mr Please, Please, Please let me back into China!' The fact that the Dalai Lama came from Tibet was momentarily lost.

A Muslim leader, a man who wants to get back to China – everyone has their own Dalai Lama, a Dalai Lama of the mind. Deepak Chopra suggested later to Larry King that the Dalai Lama was so widely loved because 'he reminds us very much of who we would all like to be'. In fact, he is who we would like him to be, as we invent distorted versions of him for our own purposes. A bogus chain e-mail purporting to be the Dalai Lama's 'millennium mantra' (containing such unlikely injunctions as 'APPROACH LOVE AND COOKING WITH RECKLESS ABANDON' and 'ONCE A YEAR, GO SOMEPLACE YOU'VE NEVER

BEEN BEFORE') has happily circled the globe, its homely wisdom being photocopied, stuck on fridges and read out at weddings, despite having no connection with him at all. He accepts this process, seeing it as part of his altruistic religious duty. As he has said, 'I am what you want me to be . . . I am a screen saver for computers. I don't mind. People can use me as they want. My main practice is to serve human beings.'

This is what is so curious about the phenomenon of his fame: devoid of egotism, committed to his religious vocation, the Dalai Lama has little interest in the way in which he is recreated by the world. The side-effect of his celebrity, and the way it is projected by his apparent backers, is that the battle over the future of Tibet has become curiously apolitical. We are left with the cry of longing, the repeating slogan of the foreign campaigner, the plaintive call of the refugee, the emphatic claim of the born exile, 'Tibet! Tibet!'

ELEVEN

Escaping the confines of Xining, I travelled south through wheat fields until I reached the fringes of Golog, a Tibetan Autonomous Prefecture punctured by innumerable military checkpoints. The landscape was Amdo, pure Amdo – a high, unpopulated sweep of space and mountains, the sky massive and open, a long, high arc stretching away for ever with no markers on the horizon on which to fix your eyes. The region had once been run by nomadic tribal chieftains, who had occasional contact with embassies from Lhasa. In the early eighteenth century Qing troops had tried, unsuccessfully, to suppress Golog raids on their territory. Only in the 1920s and thirties, after skirmishes with the Hui warlord Ma Qi and his kinsman Ma Bufang, did the area come under anything resembling Chinese influence.

Machen, the provincial capital, was a severe, unexpected, artificial town, built by the Communists in the late 1950s as an instrument of control. The town did not belong there, stuck on the edge of the grassland, below the omniscient snow mountains. It was lifeless, as Zorge had been, a place from which to discipline nomads over the surrounding miles. There was a long, dusty main street where Chinese shops sold noodles and meat. Drunken Tibetans in cheap synthetic clothing swayed past heavy administrative buildings, and bored Chinese migrant workers advanced into a karaoke block called The Art Gallery of the Masses. I was conspicuous, so I moved on quickly, out towards the nomad areas, skirting a large prison on the edge of the town and enduring a night in a fetid village guest house before heading further east, closer to Ngawa prefecture.

The grassland was a wave, rising to green velvet hills and a wild, limitless sky. I was in a place where no crops could grow, where snow fell and wind blew. Such land could only make you durable and resilient, a survivor, and it was this engendered toughness that had enabled Kontso to last into her eighth decade. Her face had the colour and sheen of the roast ducks hanging in restaurant windows in Chengdu. 'Tsampa sou!' she ordered as I sat down by the fire in her tent, her home. 'Eat tsampa! If you are in Tibet, you must eat tsampa.'

Thin black plaits fell from the side of her head, in the local style. She had a big, leather-covered prayer wheel, which she held high and kept spinning as she spoke. There were many things to ask me: how many children I had, what was going on in the rest of the world, where I was heading in Tibet, what the Dalai Lama was doing, whether he was in good health. Each time I mentioned him, she would bang the prayer wheel on her forehead, and when she found out that I had actually spoken with Kundun, the Presence, there was a burst of banging and some of her reverence for the Dalai Lama was transferred to me, which made me feel embarrassed.

She disliked talking about herself, but aspects and moments of her life were slowly revealed: how she had been born into this nomad community and married within it, how life had continued in the timeless way with the coming of the seasons and the accepted moments for migrating, storing, making offerings, having a festival or propitiating a deity, until the People's Liberation Army came. A great battle had been fought on the hillside while the women stayed back in the tents and prayed. Two of Kontso's five brothers had been killed. Her husband and the three remaining brothers were arrested as rebels and taken off to a prison where they all died from starvation and overwork in the early 1960s.

All this was told to me in a matter-of-fact way. Then she took me out, away from the small circle of tents, to some raised ground, and I was astonished to see that the site of the battle which had half-destroyed her life was on the high green hill beyond the river, only a mile or so from where we were now standing.

'All the men in my family were dead,' she explained. 'Only the women were left. It was a problem with the time we were born into this world. All sentient beings alive under the sky were suffering at that time. It was the effect of *karma*. Things were bad even for the Chinese. We were no different.'

She gave two low whistles, which persuaded a wandering yak to move away from her tent.

'I was sent to prison, accused of giving food to the rebels. I was beaten so hard that some of my bones broke, but I'm not going to make a fuss about it. No, even great lamas were killed during this time – they're much more important than me. I'm not going to make a fuss about it.'

Misunderstanding, thinking that she had reached a point of forgiveness or resolution, I asked if this meant that she felt no bitterness about what had happened in the past.

'Oh, I'm still bitter all right. I'm still angry. I'm still very angry. I promise you that if I ever got near to one of those Chinese leaders, someone like Jiang Zemin or Hu Jintao, if they dared to come here to the grassland, I'd bite them. The pain the Communists have given me is so great that even if they said they'd shoot me on the spot, I'd still do it. I really would, I'd take a bite out of them.'

One of Kontso's descendants coaxed me onto the back of his motorbike and drove away, bouncing over the grassland, the yellow and purple flowerland, through soft thistles and swarms of butterflies, through the haze and the streams, laughing happily at my shouts of discomfort as we drove up and down ditches and through a ford, until we reached some square black tents with rising aerials of smoke.

The nomads' encampment was at once the most alien and the most welcoming place I had ever visited. I was an oddity, but nomad hospitality was instinctive. A group of them came to inspect me, dressed in a motley mixture of manufactured clothes and huge, heavy sheepskin *chubas* tied tight below the waist, with the sleeves hanging almost to the ground. One man wore a baseball cap reading 'CHICAGO KULLS'. Women stood in a huddle and laughed at me through their hands, amazed at the sight of me, precious stones around their necks and threaded in their hair. Men with long plaited hair, gold teeth, pierced left ears and wide-brimmed boaters, their faces marked with ferocious scars, did nothing but smile and laugh at me in an open, unaffected way. I was an entertainment, a phenomenon. Later, as the days passed and I removed my contact lenses, or produced a flat torch, or took off my shirt to bathe in the river and revealed a hairy chest, I became a sight which had to be seen by the whole community.

There were maybe two dozen extended families living there, continuing a pattern of nomadism that was at the root of traditional Tibetan society, part of its culture and identity. The world I was seeing represented old Tibet, a way of life stretching back over centuries, which now survived only in remote pockets across the Tibetan plateau.

Each family had its own yak-hair tent, some with smaller satellite tents clustered around. Whenever the group migrated, the relative position of each family's principal tent remained the same, in accordance with tradition. Each principal tent had a yak-dung fire at the centre, so the mild, serene smell of burning dung was always with us.

A strip of light shone down through the slit at the top of the tent, and the position of that strip of light was the clock, the sundial, telling you when the dris, the female yaks, needed milking or the milk had to be churned. Once a year a new length of matted yak hair would be added to the centre and another would be removed from the edge, so a tent would last for generations, renewing itself like a river. Sacks of rice, plastic water containers and piles of dried dung patties were stacked against its sides. There was a little altar, with wrapped scriptures, pictures of high lamas and bowls of water as an offering. Little bunches of animal parts hung all over the roof, and along the slit of the chimney there were shiny skinned legs of yaks and sheep, dangling like ornaments, which did make me wonder how my Brahmin friends would have coped with life in Amdo.

The families lived close, all the generations together, and there were boundaries that could not be transgressed. People rarely touched each other, although an upset child would be instantly coddled, the grandmother opening the top of her *chuba* to suckle a five-year-old on her slack breast as a comfort. The women and children lived on one side of the tent, the men on the other, although children could move between the two sides with some freedom. Walking inside the tent, you avoided crossing in front of anyone. People were to be respected, and a show of disrespect would be punished roughly.

Early each morning the father, the patriarch, would go out and light an incense offering on a low mound and chant prayers. The younger women would advance into the embracing mist and milk the dris, each animal yielding a minuscule amount of milk, and then sieve the milk to get rid of hair and grit before churning it to make butter and cheese. The older children, supervised by a mother or an aunt, would collect the yak and dri dung and spread it by hand to dry in the sun for fuel, and later jump into the river, often fully dressed, to rinse their hands in the freezing water. Work was constant. If you failed to milk a dri, or prepare the butter, or collect the dung, or locate a missing animal, there was nothing to fall back on. Every task was essential: making a horse-hobbler, turning a spindle, plaiting a rope, sewing a *chuba* or whittling wood, a precious commodity since we were above the treeline.

At dusk I would see the sheep and yaks coming in from the mountain, and in the distance, a little later, the men on horseback, tough and self-possessed, their *chubas* trimmed with leopard fur, weaving and galloping, twirling lassoes. The yaks were tied to fixed ropes near the tents at night, and the horses were hobbled, three together. Thick-haired, hulking dogs circled, tails curling up onto their backs, guarding the flock and the tents.

In the evening, with the animals tethered and darkness closing in, barley flour would be kneaded into dough, stretched into lengths and tossed into a big saucepan of water on the fire. Hunks of meat would be unhooked from the roof of the tent and chopped and boiled. This was the meal, the same every night, yet the eaters looked healthier than the vitamin-poppers and diet addicts of the world beyond. After dark, the tent, lit by a single bulb that drew its power from a boxed battery, charged by a single solar panel, was a theatre, a place of stories, religious homilies and games. The children, three to a big sheepskin sleeping bag, with their flat faces and red cheeks chapped from the wind and sun, would laugh and play until they fell asleep.

And the new day would begin with the chant of the incense offering and the sight of the dris, unhappy at being milked, waiting to be untied and left to wander into the hills to graze.

One day soon ran into another.

I had come to a place where people lived as they expected to live, defiant of external authority. There were restrictions on movement, on where the community could go and when it could migrate, on the size of the herds and the number of horses you could own. There was a limit of two children per family, intermittently enforced. The grassland was being bounded, fenced with wire, and the nomads were having to pay for the fencing. Life was regulated, and yet, providing you avoided involvement with the authorities, and could cope with the harshness of the work and the routine and the climate, and could put to the back of your mind the things that had happened during the bad times, daily life for these Amdo nomads was good.

Looking back, some months later, it seemed to be the only place I had been to that was something like an idyll, near my old dream of the mind's Tibet.

'We believe that humans came from the union of a monkey and a god. What do you believe?'

'We believe that humans come from monkeys too.'

'I think Westerners may be descended from birds. If you look carefully at the shape of the face and the way you move, you are more like birds than monkeys.'

This was unanswerable.

Ngawang Namdrub was a man of great dignity, who thought carefully before he spoke and said no more than was necessary. The lenses of his dark glasses were made of polished stone. I had noticed him watching me closely in the days before he formulated his avian theory of evolution.

Namdrub was an intermediary between the nomad community and the authorities. In the past, the Chinese had invented their own nomad leaders (usually turncoats or people from very poor families), but their standing had become so low that they had now been dispensed with. Mediators like Namdrub helped the authorities avoid daily dealings with the nomads, who frightened and confused them. For instance, if there was a feud between nomads and someone was killed, the killer would never be exposed. The traditional leaders like Namdrub, having been chosen by consensus for their wisdom and authority, could be relied on to deal with the crime. He mediated in personal and tribal disputes, and if necessary awarded a punishment; the worst fate for a nomad was banishment from the tribe.

I had two long conversations with him. We sat on either side of the fire at the centre of his sparse, neat tent, while his niece bustled about in the shadows, churning butter and offering me first *tsampa*, then lumps of dried cheese, and finally, after I had refused, a boiled bone. Namdrub was calm but intense, examining each question thoughtfully before answering. As he talked he used his hands like a debating monk; clenching, opening, emphasising, rebutting.

'When did you first see a Chinese?' I asked.

'In around 1951. We never knew about the civil war in China until it was over. It was of no concern to us. The first Communists we met were friendly, giving out medicine and cigarettes in the town, very polite. They looked strange. It was only in about 1955 that things became uncomfortable, when soldiers from the PLA arrived here. They suggested to us that we join the Communist revolution, so we held a big meeting of all the surrounding tribes and after a discussion we agreed to say no, we wouldn't join. We thought that would be the end of it, but then more soldiers came and put up buildings in the town. They set up an encampment on the hills. Finally all the local nomad chiefs decided we had to take them on. There was no idea of strategy; we just thought it was better to make a direct challenge, and to fight them. On the day before the battle, my wife went down to the river and a soldier on the far bank shot her. So on the day of the battle I stayed back in my tent with the women, the children and the monks, and tended her. We all said prayers and the monks did *pujas* as the men rode off to fight. My wife died the next day.'

'What happened in the battle?'

'There were about four hundred of our horsemen from the different communities in the region, with swords and rifles, against several thousand Chinese soldiers, some of them with machine-guns. They were dug into the hillside. We never had any chance of victory. About eighty of our men died. Others were wounded. Some escaped into the hills. The bodies were left on the hillside. We couldn't even get near them to perform the funeral rites.'

Namdrub began to weep when he said this, but indicated that I should go on with my questions.

'How many Communists died?'

'Not many.'

'Why did you fight?'

'We fought from pride, because people were trying to take our land. We had no choice but to fight. The same thing happened across Amdo with the other nomad tribes. After that, Amdo was gone. All this happened on one day.'

He was silent for a while.

All this had happened on one day.

'I was thirty-six years old,' he continued. 'We escaped into the hills. I lived like a wild animal. We had to let our livestock run free. Sometimes we would go without food for days. There were about forty of us in our group, trying to attack the PLA when we could. We were ruthless because we knew that if we were caught we would be shot. There were other bands of Amdo men, mainly nomads, and a few younger women, trying to do the same. We would work together when we could, but we weren't able to operate in large groups. It was after about one year that we ran into an ambush, over in the west on the slopes of Machen Gangri. We had a shoot-out. I got a bullet through the hip which came out through my abdomen and tore a big hole. Warriors traditionally fought on an empty stomach to reduce the risk from abdominal wounds, which were thought lethal. My intestines started to fall out so I just wrapped the belt of my *chuba* round them and pulled it tight to keep them in. Then I fell off my horse. My "brother", my spiritual friend, managed to drag me away and up onto his horse but then he could go no further. I told him to leave me to die. When I woke up I was in a Chinese prison.'

To his amazement, Namdrub was tended in a prison hospital until he recovered. A respected nomad chief arrived from a nearby monastery, and told him a deal had been made with the Communists. If Namdrub could persuade his fellow rebels to surrender, they would be given an amnesty. Trusting the chief, he returned to the hills and told his comrades they were beaten. Most of them surrendered, and the Communists kept their word, although when the Cultural Revolution started, many were imprisoned for being ex-rebels. It was only when Namdrub came out of prison that he learned what had happened to his community after the great battle.

'It was mainly monks, women, children and old men who were left. Life was unbearable for them. Their tents were taken and they were made to live in cement sheds. Can you imagine it, having your tent taken away? Hair ornaments and coral jewellery were not allowed at that time, and they all had to wear Mao suits instead of *chubas*. Everyone, men and women, had their hair cut short. Most had never had their hair cut before. They weren't allowed to make their own food. Twice a day they would be served a thin *tsampa* soup in a big communal tent. They had to work very hard. They weren't allowed to keep animals, although some people secretly kept sheep. The authorities even had an idea of turning us into farmers, because of what Mao had said about the need to boost wheat production. They tried ploughing up the grassland and planting crops, but of course nothing grew.'

'That was during the Great Leap?'

'It was in 1959 and 1960, the worst years of the famine. A lot of people died. Many of my old friends died. My father's brother, my mother's mother, my mother's brother's wife, my paternal cousins – all of these people starved to death.'

'Did things get better after that?'

'In some ways they got even worse. It was in the mid-1960s that the *sejor* began, the reclassification according to class background. Because my family had been leading figures in the community, I was judged to have a bad class background. We were labelled as *shanakpo*, which meant that we were given, figuratively, a "black hat". Each month there would be a procession and public beating of the people who had the black hat. At first it was very violent. At these sessions, which we called *kapso*, your hands would be tied behind your back and they would slap, push and abuse you. They might pull your hair or tear your clothes. It was organised.'

'Who did the beating?'

'People from here. They had no choice but to take part.'

'What do you mean?'

'If they held back, the Party officials would say, "Do you love the black hat families? Are you an enemy of the state?" So they had to do it. But you knew who was doing it with conviction and who wasn't. The authorities found that members of our own community were not willing to persecute us properly, so we were moved to land occupied by another group of nomads, closer to the town, where our persecution could be supervised. At first it was terrible, you would get great bruises on your body and clumps of your hair would be pulled out. But as the years went by it became part of a routine. It might sound strange, but that was how it seemed. I knew after a while that I would only be beaten and not killed, so I stopped being afraid. It was only in 1978 that the black hat was formally "lifted" from our family, and we could return to our community.'

Namdrub was stoical about where his life had taken him.

'Things are easier for us now, but we are like insects lying on an open palm. In a matter of seconds we can be crushed. We have no choice but to cooperate with the Chinese, however much we may want our freedom. I have done what I can with my life, like the rest of my generation, and now I am waiting to die. In the meantime, I want to hold on to my present happiness. The only wish I have left is to see His Holiness the Dalai Lama again.'

'You saw him before?'

'I saw him when I was nine years old, when my father took me to Lhasa. It is my most precious memory.'

'Do you think that the Chinese will ever leave here?'

'They are not going to leave. Fighting for our freedom would make no difference to them. Tibet is too important to the Communists for them even to discuss independence. The exiled Tibetans in India and Nepal who talk about freedom are wasting their time. I say to them, if you want independence for Tibet, why don't you come here and make a protest and see how far it gets you? It may make them feel good, but for us, it makes life worse. It makes the Chinese create more controls over us.'

His words were harsh, but undeniable, and they rang in my ears for months to come.

'I say to them,' he repeated, 'if you want independence, why don't you come here and make a protest and see how far it gets you?'

One afternoon we walked through the grass and flowers to the cement sheds where the remnants of his community had lived during the later phase of rural collectivisation. Insects buzzed and rodents scurried. The sky was high above us, blue and pure. There was a smell of herbs. I always felt as if I was floating when I walked across the grassland.

The sheds lay in a long, crumbling row about a mile away, in the lee of a hill. Each one was two metres high, an arch of rough brick and cement, open at either end to the wind and the rain. It was hardly imaginable that people had lived there, ten to a shed in the burning winter cold. The sheds reminded me of the hutches used to keep pigs in England.

Namdrub's grandson, who had walked with us, said the nomads disliked going anywhere near the sheds. Being younger, having travelled and learned something of the world, of large injustices and the possibility of human rights, he was more angry than his grandfather at what had happened to his community, and he wanted to show me his fury.

'This was a concentration camp,' he said. 'A place of great suffering. When a nomad looks at these sheds, it is like a Jew looking at a concentration camp.'

We stayed there for a while, not speaking, before returning slowly towards the tents. Distances on the grassland were hard to judge; a journey that you thought would take ten minutes would end up taking thirty.

Later, Namdrub said to me, 'What happened to us here was because of Communism and because of Mao. He only wanted to have power so that he could control people. I will tell you frankly, young people like my grandson are happy enough now. Their life is not hard. But old people have a wound. We have a wound to the heart.'

I asked him what he thought Mao's legacy was. He answered immediately, '*Mao Zedong gi shiji dhuknye kona re.* Mao Zedong's legacy was misery.'

TWELVE

The train was slow and long, packed with soldiers returning to duty. The only way for me to reach central Tibet was by going back to Xining, taking the truncated railway line across the edge of the Tibetan plateau to the city of Kermo, then descending to Lhasa by bus. The soldiers, some accompanied by their families, drank gaseous beer and ate instant noodles from plastic bowls. One man wore a pair of pirated trousers with the label 'MARLBOLAO' on the pocket. Another had a sports bag saying 'NIKE: NON CHONINE BEACH AS NEED'.

There were no Tibetans. We were a world away from the vast emptiness of the Golog grassland. This was the old China, far from the glamour of Shanghai and Shenzhen, the alluring land of consumers loved by Western economic forecasters. I had forgotten the squalor, the rhythmic nose-blowing, the screeching announcements, the theatrical ejection of phlegm, the elbowing, staring, shouting and poking, the sheer numbers that managed to crowd into each carriage and onto each bunk, the sense you had on China's railways that you were in a land of people – 1.27 billion at the last time of counting. There were tables smeared with food and grease, pools of liquid on the floor, children with slit trousers, urinating casually, and reams of attendants in blue uniforms and peaked caps sweeping bones and peanut shells angrily along the corridor with bristly brushes.

Opposite me sat a young, timid woman with stacked shoes and flesh-coloured socks. She was an English teacher at the Military Secondary School in Kermo, but was unable to speak any coherent

English. Beside her, wedged in, a man in a black leather jacket swilled a jar of green tea. He was sweaty and intrusive, the sort of person you would travel to Tibet to avoid. He worked for an oil company, and was returning to work after an annual holiday in Wuhan. He wanted to practise his English, and I was his target.

The oil man said that we should have a discussion, for reasons of international fraternal solidarity. His chosen subject was, unremarkably, the Opium Wars. The iniquity and inequity of the Opium Wars have long been presented in Chinese schools as the apex of human suffering, so the script was familiar. The oil man talked of the theft of manuscripts and treasures by foreign predators, and asserted that the European powers had taken advantage of China's weakness in the nineteenth century, exploited the people, ravaged the land and imposed unequal treaties. It was a reasonable position. I had no wish to defend the Opium Wars. My thoughts, though, were still on the tens of millions of deaths inflicted on China during the twentieth century, but we did not speak of this. The Great Leap, China's internal wound, was not mentioned; the Opium Wars were preferred, as a refrain.

The oil man said that no country had endured such suffering as China at the hands of the colonial powers. He mentioned the injustice of the Treaty of Nanking, when China ceded Hong Kong island to the British and gave them preferential trading rights. I mentioned other aspects of the colonial experience: mass exterminations in Tasmania, revenge slaughter in India after the 1857 mutiny, King Leopold's Force Publique chopping off the hands of rubber-collectors in the Congo. The oil man went on, long into the night. His country was the victim of imperial aggression and unequal treaties. China would not be humiliated again.

In the morning it was cold. I pushed down a corridor to the toilet. It had a filthy washbasin and a little sign reading 'PLEASE DON'T THROW ANY ODDS AND ENDS INTO THE POND'. The tap was dry. In the corridor, sitting on their luggage, a family ate cold, greasy meat from a yellow plastic bag. I stood by the window, thinking of my time in the grassland. We were advancing steadily now across an empty sandscape, grey hills in the distance. There were no buildings, only sand and more sand. On each side of the railway line were criss-crossed patterns of stones and little bamboo fences to stop the swirling sand from swamping the track. Many of the bamboo fences had been blown away. We passed through tiny stations. They were just platforms, caught in the middle of the cold desert, surrounded by a few nearly derelict buildings, little mining factories, a squashed basketball hoop on a smashed board, heaps of stone. There were almost no people, only maintenance workers and lone soldiers.

Finally, that afternoon, the train neared its destination, passing through a vast, winking, expanding salt flat, with huge pipes and trucks by the side of the railway line. There were workers, tiny in the distance, shovelling. The sun beat down. We reached Kermo, the end of the line, where dozens of expectant policemen in green hats and uniforms were lined up along the station platform, waiting for the daily event, the arrival of the train from Xining, with its cargo of migrant workers and soldiers, hookers and profiteers.

There was nothing to be said in favour of Kermo, a city officially known as Golmud. At one time it had been a tiny settlement used by pilgrims and traders on their way to Dunhuang, but since 1984, when it became Tibet's railhead, it had grown into a snarl of construction. Plans were now being made to extend the railway line down to Lhasa, in a massive, hazardous feat of engineering. Oil and mining gave Kermo the impermanent feel of a frontier town, where wealth could be made quickly. There were bars, brothels and even a supermarket. Army officers cruised the dust-blown streets in implausibly flashy foreign cars.

I knew that one hotel in Kermo accepted aliens. I got a lift there on a mini-tractor.

'GUESTS SUPREME AND QUALITY FIRST' was painted above the entrance. A receptionist was lying on a desk, snoring, her face in an open packet of crisps. I walked across the lobby to a kiosk which had a notice saying 'THERE ARE KINDS OF BEVERAGE'. There were no beverages. I went back and woke up the receptionist, who set off in search of keys.

I got a room, finally. There was no water. I lay down on the bed and read the brochure, an elaborate production full of rules and promises, prohibiting the destruction of hotel furniture and the carrying of radioactive material.

1. NO DANCING IN THE ROOM
2. FAVOURATE ANIMALS AND BIRDS NOT ALLOWED IN THE HOTOL
3. THE RESTAURANTS WILL PROVIDE YOR WITH BUNQUET, OR IN THE DINNING HALL WHERE INDIVIDUALS ARE SERVED

Across China, English came in this form. Signwriters and printers relied on electronic pocket translating machines, where they typed words or phrases in Chinese and received an English response. Great trust was placed in these machines, although their translations were never accurate. Often, the creators of signs and brochures could not read Roman characters, which made their copying haphazard.

I went downstairs. The receptionist was gazing into space.

'Do you have a laundry service?'

'We have laundry service.'

'How long does it take?'

'We have laundry service.'

'One day, two days?'

'One week.'

I went back upstairs. I had only come to Kermo in order to reach Lhasa, and I did not want to stay for a week.

The Tourism Bureau in Lhasa had a scam going with the local branch of the China International Travel Service, CITS, to fleece foreign tourists. It was a typically inventive piece of capitalism, and I hoped it would let me gain unrestricted time in Tibet. The scam worked like this. The long, rattling bus ride from Kermo to Lhasa cost US$24. For an additional US$170, you could join a tour group. When you reached Lhasa, the tour group disintegrated and you were able to remain there until you ran into trouble with the authorities. There was a catch: you were not allowed to buy a bus ticket unless you joined a tour group. With Kermo to Lhasa being the only land route open to foreigners, there were plenty of customers shelling out dollars to line official pockets.

I went in search of others to join a tour group. It took several days to find enough people. By the end, there were around a dozen of us. It was the first time I had seen aliens since Labrang, and their presence was strangely reassuring. The CITS office issued us with travel tickets and a cheerful brochure titled 'GOLMUD: A THROAT FOR LHASA BY BUS'. We were told to assemble early the next morning at a potholed area of wasteland near the hotel.

The bus looked like a shed, and the tyres were bald. Regular Chinese, Tibetan and Muslim travellers sat at the front. The tour group sat at the back, on two levels of reclining seats. We were an uneven collection: a hefty German woman with a tiny Hong Kong Chinese man attached to her like an incubus; three heavily-prepared Japanese businessmen with GPS satellite navigation equipment and oxygen cylinders; a dreary, amiable couple from France, in the international backpackers' uniform of grimy T-shirts, baggy printed cotton trousers, hiking boots and exploding rucksacks; several nervous South Koreans, who were already suffering from terrible headaches although we were only three thousand metres above sea level; a sort of hippie from the Czech Republic, who merely grinned; two Israeli men, long-haired but martial; and an Indonesian-Chinese husband and wife, dressed in shorts and sandals, who were about to become very, very cold.

Before we had reached the outskirts of Kermo, the German was off.

'Since I was in Pakistan,' she began, 'I have stopped using the toilet paper I had some stomach problems I just use the water now it's about inner balancing and when I am back in Essen I think I will not use the toilet paper in Europe we must learn to use less from the planet it's a lesson you learn when you are travelling take only photographs and leave only footprints or no footprints I should say I had some eggs in an omelette at my breakfast and now I have a little gas it is not too bad my body is feeling fine.'

The first twelve hours were uneventful, passing through formless high-altitude desert with hazy brown mountains on the horizon and nothing to accompany you but a constant dry wind, soft dust and the glare of the sun. We passed a little mining settlement with slavering chained dogs, an outdoor pool table, plenty of smashed bottles and a deranged storekeeper who sold beer, instant noodles and cigarettes. Ideally, we should have been travelling only by night, when the wind was down. In past times, in the days when yak and camel caravans travelled slowly to Lhasa, getting the timing wrong could be fatal. The traditional way to cross the high Tibetan desert was in short bursts, at set times. Between midnight and daybreak the wind would fall and a caravan would push on fast, but in the morning the wind would blow fiercely until midday, and the caravan would have to halt, with only boulders and sand dunes for protection. It was possible to travel for a short while during the afternoon, and then to rest up and sleep until midnight.

Leaving Chumarhe, we came across a line of stationary vehicles. Up ahead, a military lorry was slewed across a small concrete bridge, its cargo of watermelons lying in the gully below. There were dozens of PLA soldiers, and army trucks with taut metal towing cables. We all stood around, watching. One of the Japanese men took a photograph, which was a mistake. A soldier shouted; more soldiers came; the man was frogmarched to a senior officer who wore mirrored sunglasses. The camera was opened and the film exposed. More senior officers were summoned by radio. We all had our passports inspected. The Japanese man had to sign a document of contrition. This took several hours. When he was finally allowed back on the bus with us he was shaking with fear.

Night fell, and it grew very cold. I could not sleep. Every so often there would be a bang as someone's packet of crisps or sweets exploded with the rising altitude. I lapsed into a state of interminable, fitful, wakeful dozing. The minutes pushed by, until at last they turned into hours and the sun came up. Everyone had headaches by now, but at least it was morning. The German woman was vomiting regularly into plastic bags, which her Chinese helper carried to the front of the bus and ejected through the one good window. He was kind and considerate, keeping her warm and giving her sips of water. I asked him how long they had been together.

'Two days,' he said. 'We made friends waiting for the bus.'

It was a phenomenon I had noticed before in Asia: solicitous young men, usually students, acting as baggage-handlers and fixers to lone foreign women in the hope of winning sexual or financial favours, or just an opportunity to practise their English. They were often successful.

We reached Marchudram Babtsuk, a small administrative centre consisting of a cluster of low buildings. The driver stopped the bus, disappeared into a hut to have breakfast, and then began to disembowel the engine. This lasted for much of the morning.

In the afternoon we reached the summit of the Tangu La, a pass between two high mountains. It was bitingly cold, and the air had become very thin. My heart was racing. The bus pulled over. There were strings of prayer flags snapping in the wind. A big stone monument depicted Chinese soldiers doing useful things. A painted marker said we had reached a height of 5220 metres. The air had become hard to breathe. The Tibetans threw scraps of paper, block-printed with prayers, into the wind, shouting the invocation 'Lha gyalo', 'Victory to the gods'. The Chinese urinated. The Muslims stayed in the bus. The Koreans vomited. The Japanese emerged wired up to their oxygen cylinders and took photographs of themselves, rather daringly under the circumstances, in front of the military monument.

A few hours later we crossed another high pass, and started the descent towards Nagchu. By now the road had given up, and we were skating across a plain of rock, ice and mud. I had had enough of the journey, with the desolate landscape, the stink of the bus and the cramp of sitting in the same position for so long. Night was falling again, and it was getting desperately cold.

We reached Nagchu. A young Tibetan woman with shiny red cheeks boarded the bus and climbed to the upper-level seats, huffing and puffing. She was followed by a glowing man of a similar age, with braids in his hair. An older woman passed up two small bundles. The family bowed their heads to each other and the older woman got down from the bus. It was only about an hour later, when I heard crying and snuffling, that I realised the two bundles were babies, tightly swaddled.

They were perfect, beautiful six-day-old twin boys. The

woman and her husband lived in Lhasa, but had gone back to her home town of Nagchu so that she could have the babies, her first, with her mother. She had not known that she was expecting twins: two babies had been a surprise, she said, a happy surprise.

I had a thump of pain, seeing them there, thinking of my own children, imagining their faces, so many miles away, and knowing how much longer it would be before I saw them. It was a joyful, epiphanic moment, watching the Tibetan couple, so young and elated and overwhelmed by the change in their life, each hugging a baby close as the bus rattled on towards Lhasa through the night. It was a moment that lived with me, like the cadre eating chickens' feet, or the nomads fighting on the bus to Zorge, or the young nun Nyima saying she did not feel free in her heart, or Namdrub out in the Golog grassland telling of an unequal battle that had destroyed all he knew and loved, and saying, almost in amazement, that it had happened on a single day.

As I ate my last packet of biscuits, the bus descending through the darkness, I thought of Lhasa, the emblem of Tibetan nationhood, home to the Potala and the Jokhang. I had never been there before, and it was strange to think of the city soon becoming a physical reality for me, a home of real people, rather than an anticipation, or a location of past events. My mind drifted to a passage from Fosco Maraini:

> The fascinating thing about Tibet is its delightful, disastrous, irrepressible humanity. Perhaps one day I shall write a book and call it *Secret Tibet*. The secret will be, not the strange things that it will reveal, but the normal things in it – real people, flesh and blood, love, desire, repentance, pride and cowardice.

Maraini wrote the first modern book on Tibet, *Secret Tibet*, published in 1951, to depict Tibetans as people rather than as ascetics or ciphers, and their society as a setting for universal passions. Before him – and since – books on Tibet tend to drop into categories: scholarly tomes like the works of Aurel Stein or Sven Hedin, whose *Southern Tibet* arrived in twelve hefty volumes; Lamaist inventions such as *The Third Eye* by the all-seeing T. Lobsang Rampa, who was in truth an English surgical-truss manufacturer named Cyril Hoskin, or by the tiny but massively resilient Alexandra David-Neel with her descriptions of flying monks in *Magic and Mystery in Tibet*, although her sightings may have been (according to Hugh Richardson, whose arcane knowledge died with him) no more than hallucinations caused by her attempted self-immunisation against cyanide, for she took minute dosages of the poison daily; manly adventures, usually involving British stagers crossing frozen mountains in order to locate the source of a river or shoot rare animals in a very remote place; Lamaphobic rants, such as Austine Waddell's seminal 1895 *The Buddhism of Tibet or Lamaism*, which concludes, 'it will be a happy day, indeed, for Tibet when its sturdy over-credulous people are freed from the intolerable tyranny of the Lamas, and delivered from the devils whose ferocity and exacting worship weigh like a nightmare upon all'; or the heavy religious tracts of Desideri, the berating eighteenth-century Jesuit, or Geoffrey Bull, who tried to convert to Christianity a Tibetan soldier who had been shot in the arms and legs by the Red Army. 'The wounds were already festering terribly and the flies sucking at the pus. He seemed to be in great pain,' wrote Bull. 'I tried then to speak to him of the Lord Jesus Christ. Poor man, he was so demented he could hardly listen.'

Since Maraini published *Secret Tibet*, the categories have expanded to take in a Tibetan edition of *Tintin in Tibet*, with Captain Haddock's 'billions of blue blistering barnacles' rendered as 'may your head dry up you old dog from hell'; primitivist fiction by Chinese and Tibetan writers, working within the strictures of Marxist-Leninist theory; tragic, romantic accounts of old Tibet written by displaced aristocrats who had learned good English at boarding schools in India; detailed academic creations by those who prefer to spell Tashi 'bkra-shis' and Taktra 'stag-brag'; works of shameless propaganda by European and American fellow travellers of the Chinese Communist Party; fine photographic productions, showing Tibet's remoter splendours to the world; books of atrocity and special pleading, campaigning for idealistic political alteration; analytical introspection looking at the phenomenon of the phenomenon, with titles like *Demystifying Tibet*, *Imagining Tibet* and *Virtual Tibet*; and countless guides to the Dharma, of varying utility, many of them nominally authored by Tibetans, their aim being to bring Buddhism to a wider, wealthier audience. The religious books tended to have a curious detachment. The writer Dawa Norbu has suggested that the Panchen Rinpoche's report on the Great Leap famine remains 'far more relevant to Tibet's future' than the collected works of the exiled clergy, 'whose targeted audience comprises the disenchanted sections of the middle class in post-industrial societies, who are far removed from the problems and the reality of Tibet'.

The reality of Tibet. Was it there, around me, as I descended through the Tibet Autonomous Region in a mobile shed contemplating Walter Benjamin's claim that history decomposes into images, not into narratives? Princess Kula of Sikkim, speaking to Fosco Maraini, called Tibet a land of 'greed, magic spells, passion, revenge, crimes, love, envy, torture', to add to his suggestion of 'real people, flesh and blood, love, desire, repentance, pride and cowardice'. So far, there had been no sign of magic spells, although there was the case of the senior politician Lungshar, a contemporary of Reting Rinpoche, who put evil jottings in his boots in an effort to kill a rival, and was found out, and sentenced to removal of the eyeballs. That was in Lhasa, in 1934.

We had reached a Chinese city. There were bright lights and big buildings, topped with neon. The journey was over, in just under forty-eight hours. Half a century ago it would have taken four months with a yak and camel caravan. The time seemed to be late at night, or early in the morning, but Land Cruisers were still driving through the streets. The bus swung into a walled courtyard, and the engine coughed and died.

We scrambled down from the bus, rubbing our legs and walking like jockeys. There was shouting and commotion as the luggage was untied and hurled down from the roof into the night. It was time to move. Grabbing my bags, I pushed through a scrum by the gate of the bus station, noticing for the first time that one of the Korean men had the word 'TAMPON' embroidered on the back of his jacket. At the far end of the road there was a taxi rank. A driver agreed to take me to the Tibetan ghetto at the other end of the city.

As we drove through the wakeful, sleeping streets, past the

shops and restaurants with their Chinese signs, I thought how strange it was to be arriving by night. I had always thought that my first glimpse of the city would be by day, with the golden roof pavilions of the temples shining in the sun like tongues of fire. As it was, there was traffic, and drizzle, and police posts at every intersection. It was all so distant from my imagined memory, and I recognised nothing until, suddenly, driving through an arch, the Potala – the Potala! – reared up to my left. It looked much smaller than I had expected, like a flat of scenery suspended in the distance. Much stronger, and more real, was the sight of three truckloads of Chinese soldiers parked in front of it, watching over a vast, flat, empty square.

Then the Potala was gone, and I caught a glimpse of Tibetan shop signs, and the road turned muddy, and the size of the squads of police on each corner grew. The Hotel Legchog was full, but the gatekeeper suggested I try the Hotel Raidi, further down the road. The taxi drove on, past more Tibetan shops and some howling street dogs. The Raidi had a room. I sat in the lobby and filled out registration forms, my hand still juddering from the bus journey. The receptionist, a smiling Tibetan woman, barely out of her teens, brought me a cup of tea. The sun was coming up, and I was in Lhasa, at last.

II

THIRTEEN

A white crane flying in from the marshlands of northern Lhasa would see a wide, modern sprawl of a city, nearly twenty times the size it was in 1950, stretching from east to west, running down to the watery boundaries of the Kyichu river. The great monasteries of Ganden, Drepung and Sera are not the city's only sentinels: at its quick lies the Jokhang, built during the reign of King Songtsen Gampo and protected by geomantic power points stretching over hundreds of miles, some as far away as Kongbo and Bhutan. The Jokhang, Tibet's most sacred shrine, is built on the heart of a giant, supine ogress whose shoulders, hips, elbows, knees, hands and feet all have to be kept pinned down by strategically built temples. The other landmarks, Chakpori, the iron hill, and Marpori, the red hill, still rise over the city, but Tibetan architecture has diminished. Chakpori is no longer topped by the ancient medical college, which was shelled by the PLA in 1959, but by tall radio masts. While Marpori still provides a home to the Potala, the Potala, in all its glory, seems to have shrunk as Lhasa has grown.

The city had been looking forward to the National Minority Games for weeks. Sporty Uighurs, Tibetans and Mongolians were interviewed nightly on the television news, and filmed practising archery, tug-of-war, wrestling and equestrian acrobatics. Cheerleaders in bright ethnic costumes were shown dancing, singing, banging drums and strumming musical instruments. Skittish young Chinese women presenters tried to get taciturn Tibetan men in tracksuits to talk. The tone of the commentary was enthusiastic but patronising, like a 1950s BBC documentary on enchanting tribal customs.

It was the first time that the games had been held in Lhasa. This was presented as a great coup, marking the fortieth anniversary of the introduction of Democratic Reforms in central Tibet. The stability of the Tibet Autonomous Region and the cheerful harmony between China's fifty-six plucky national minorities was a running theme. Lhasa was strewn with advertisements for the games, which showed a jaunty cartoon yak. Everywhere you went, the yak would be there, grinning, stuck in a shop window or strung across the street on printed prayer flags, doing the sort of things you might expect from a minority mascot: throwing a spinning top, waving *katags* merrily, whispering in a horse's ear, shooting a pop-gun or capering in a colourful *chuba*.

From the volume of coverage on China's national media, I was expecting a regional version of the Olympics. Would it be hard to get a ticket, I asked a friend. She smiled, and said that she didn't think so. I should just turn up, and I would certainly get in. Tibetans were boycotting the games.

The stadium was near Drabchi, where the Yaso commanders had led their symbolic armies and Brigadier Neame found the rifle-shooting lamentable in the 1930s. Drabchi was now famous as the home of Tibet Autonomous Region Prison Number One, the most feared detention centre in Tibet, where political prisoners were prone to die. In July 1996, Jampal Khedrub, a respected monk serving an eighteen-year sentence for printing woodblock leaflets about democracy and human rights, had apparently been beaten to death by a prison official. Two summers later, five young nuns died. A European Union delegation had visited the prison, coinciding with a demonstration by inmates. Instead of singing the required patriotic songs, they had shouted pro-independence slogans. The People's Armed Police were called in, and beat the prisoners so severely that in the words of one survivor, 'It looked like an abattoir. They beat us with their belts, until their belts broke. Then they used electric batons.' After several days of beating, and further tortures involving sand-filled hoses, stripping, electric shocks and sexual humiliation, the five nuns were dead, possibly after suffocating themselves with *katags*.

From the stands in the stadium, which was also used for mass-sentencing rallies, I could see the outline of the low buildings of Drabchi prison. It looked calm and innocuous, like an empty army barracks. Below me, a dozen horsemen were racing round a muddy track, snatching *katags* off the ground at speed, twisting down from their saddles, their feet still looped in the stirrups. It was impressive, but less impressive than it had been when I saw it done by nomads in the Amdo grassland, for pleasure rather than for China Central Television. Dignitaries sat in a covered box above the camera crews. I understood now why the footage on the nightly news showed a backdrop of officials in blue blazers and white baseball caps wandering across the arena. The cameras could not film the crowd, because there was no crowd. I had come to a fantasy National Minority Games.

Approaching the stadium, with its big, tethered balloons and yards of flags, everything had looked right. As I entered the main gate, I realised that the place was filled with young men and women in the dark-green uniform of the People's Liberation Army. They ringed the arena: a warning. By the time I reached the stands, I had passed through six security checks. Men in suits and dark glasses were barking into radios, their eyes scanning the new arrivals.

Standing there, watching the forlorn athletes doing their duty, enduring the commentary, which was in Chinese rather than Tibetan, I guessed that there were five hundred soldiers and police in the stadium, and about the same number of spectators, of whom a clear majority were Chinese. I walked over to a group of Tibetans who were chatting in the sun, eating pumpkin seeds. They had been told to come by their work unit.

The television news declared that night that the National Minority Games were proving a success, and were very popular with the Tibetan people.

A white crane, rising from the Drabchi plain and flying over the stadium and Prison Number One and the Potala (which was first photographed in 1901 by a wandering Kalmyk named Narzounov) and the Lhasa television station (where the British diplomatic mission, Dekyilingka, once was) would see the iron hill, Chakpori, and below it the Dalai Lama's summer palace, the

Norbulingka. I had expected the entrance to the Norbulingka to look as it did in old photographs, a solid gate flanked by two pointed wooden sentry-boxes. The traditional Tibetan gate was still there, but in place of the sentry-boxes sat a pair of big, rough Chinese dragons and a bulbous fibreglass panda, which doubled as a dustbin. There was a large sign, prepared with the usual indifference to truth or accuracy.

The Brife Introduction of Norbulingka.
The original p alace ou-yas was built in the eighth ce ntury by the Seventh Dalaiplama in ass ociation with Amsan. The representative of thepching Imperor . . . also in the park summer cottages. Ma n made mountains and a stone tablet. I nnnnaddition, are precious trees animals such as lynx and deer, fragrante flowers and green grass.

At one end of the park was a squalid, desolate zoo, where ferocious, red-arsed monkeys were fighting in a concrete pit. Some had been badly lacerated by glass bottles and tin cans which had been thrown into their enclosure. Brown bears were held in tiny cells, and one was banging its head against the bars, making a terrible, plaintive sound. A dusty black-necked crane stood lifelessly in a nearby cage. The place was a warped reminder of the days of the Thirteenth Dalai Lama, who had loved animals and kept geese, camels, deer and a tiger there. He spent a lot of his time at the Norbulingka, and drove around it in a Baby Austin, licence-plate TIBET 1, which had been presented to him in the 1920s by the British mission, after being carried over the Himalayas in pieces, strapped to long bamboo poles.

The little palaces in the Norbulingka, the Jewel Park, were once the most secluded buildings in Tibet, more inaccessible even than the Potala, which housed government offices. Walking through the private rooms of the Fourteenth Dalai Lama, where he had disguised himself as a soldier before beginning his famous escape to India, felt like an intrusion. He had described leaving the Norbulingka for exile as the saddest moment of his life. The rooms were unmarked and run down. Since he is a non-person and cannot be mentioned in Tibet, except to be condemned from time to time as a splittist and a serf-owner, there was nothing to indicate that the Dalai Lama had lived there.

I climbed the threadbare carpeted stairs to his simple bedroom, with its religious paintings and old-style radiogram. In the bathroom was a Primus stove which kept him warm on the cold days, all those years ago. I stood in the doorway and watched as a group of rural pilgrims, muttering prayers, each holding a guttering butter lamp, approached the Shanks Vitreous China washbasin with great reverence and, having checked that no guards or spies were watching, filled it with banknotes and handfuls of barley, brought forth from the folds of their *chubas*. It was the closest they were likely to get to the Dalai Lama.

Away from historic buildings, which offer a reminder of the Tibetan days, Lhasa is like any other Chinese city; but disjointed. You go from a department store with computers and escalators to a street off the Barkhor where big yellow balls of butter are sold in a yak-skin, scrawny monks beg for cash and Tibetan children defecate in the open gutter. The city is made up of shoddy, faceless, concrete office and apartment blocks, which have turned the old Tibetan heart, centred on the Jokhang, into a ghetto and a tourist attraction.

Entering the shrine at the centre of the Jokhang after two hours of queuing, I had an instant feeling of the past as I reached a ledge, touched my forehead against the most sacred spot and was immediately pulled back by a large monk, who pushed me towards another monk, who in turn gave me a handful of wet crab apples. Although it was partially destroyed during the Cultural Revolution, the Jokhang has again become a place of religious fervour, and was filled with pilgrims from all over Tibet.

Dozens of monks sat in the courtyard, chanting, striking drums, carrying vats of slopping butter to refill the lamps. It was only outside that the depressing absurdity of the present became apparent. China's state news agency, Xinhua, evoked the scene, despite its best intentions.

Located near the Potala Palace, Jokhang lamasery was established 1,000 years ago and is a major arena for holding Buddhist religious activities . . . The central government and Tibet Autonomous Region government have poured US$1.3 million into dismantling 530 buildings and paving new roads around the historical site . . . Moreover, the government has built twenty-four state-of-the-art public toilets for tourists and renovated twenty-seven ancient-style houses near the lamasery.

Sangkar Dargye, known as Sangdar, a *chimo dobso*, or master-mason-cum-architect, explained how Lhasa had been undone. He had a handful of short white whiskers, holes in his earlobes from the old days and three stumps of teeth, with which he was chewing *tsampa* balls laced with yak cheese and sugar. Sangdar's parents had been farmers in the south, with tax duties to a local noble family. In the economy of old Tibet, most taxes were paid by *ulag* or human labour rather than in cash. It was this system that the Communists termed serfdom or slavery. In practice, it was a form of bonded labour, by which an extended family was obliged to supply a certain number of worker-hours to their 'lord' each year. In Sangdar's case, this meant working as a labourer until he was twenty-three, when his younger brother took over the family tax duties.

Although he found the dialect difficult to understand, Sangdar had moved to Lhasa and worked as a stonemason, specialising in building walls, and qualified as a *chimo dobso*, entitling him to join an influential trade guild. Like most parts of Tibetan life, construction was closely regulated by custom. Each worker had an area of expertise, such as making floors, ceilings, corners or doorways. In 1961 these grades and distinctions were abolished. Contractors who were known to skim money or pay workers badly were denounced and insulted at public meetings as part of a formal political movement to undermine the rich, which was popular with many construction workers. In the mid-1960s, reform was taken a step further. Tibetan builders were required to 'clear the four old ways of thinking' and build according to Communist principles, which meant abandoning all they knew. Indigenous materials such as brick, stone and mud were judged to be outmoded. Thick walls, with a wide base to guard against earth tremors, were forbidden. Despite Lhasa's rapid changes of temperature, buildings had to have thin cement walls and no indoor wooden supports, or flat roofs, or corner pillars on the roof for holding *darjog*, the prayer flags on sticks, or even a decorative cloth across a room's rough ceiling.

Sangdar had been sent to put up houses near the Potala, where he had to take orders from a Chinese site foreman, despite sharing no common language. During meal breaks, builders were no longer permitted to mix butter tea and *tsampa* in a leather bag, as they had always done, since it was a sign of having a 'green brain'. The rules on eating and the rules on building were relaxed in the 1980s, but if a civilisation can be judged by its architecture, Chinese Communism has not done well in Tibet.

Such massive physical change has destroyed the mental map that made the old Tibetan culture possible. Lhasa is no longer Lhasa. Builders no longer use geomantic techniques, or position the rooms of a house in accordance with the lunar calendar. In a society which took sacred geography so seriously, as shown by the Jokhang's apparent power to pin down a far-reaching ogress, it became hard to pursue the ancient arts of divination and prophecy. Only outside the city, in certain parts of the ghetto, was there a feeling of the Tibetan religious past. The credibility of visions – even perhaps the ability to have them – depended on a prevailing social and spiritual order which had made dreams conceivable.

In old Tibet, a belief in the supernatural was implicit in all aspects of life, and was not restricted to the religious. Even in 1901, the Thirteenth Dalai Lama issued a proclamation that 'for the sake of happiness in this country, prosperity of livestock and the alleviation of strife and illness etc., all Tibetans must carry out the following religious activities: to read and study the Kanjur, the great collection of the Buddhist writings; 100,000-verse Prajnaparamita; various Transcendent Wisdom Scriptures; the 1,000 Buddhas of Bhadra Kalpa; the ten-volume Suvarnaprabhasa . . .' The Fifth Dalai Lama, the creator of the Potala and a politician of exceptional ability, was as steeped in the spiritual life as the most abstruse, cave-bound hermit. He lived in a world in which there was no gap between the quotidian and the esoteric.

In *Secret Visions of the Fifth Dalai Lama* (the only illustrated secret autobiography of a Tibetan lama known to exist, which was written in the late seventeenth century and discovered and published in the 1980s), mental experiences are recorded that would test the mind of any modern psychiatrist. The Fifth Dalai Lama heard sounds and saw multi-armed deities, humans emitting fire, a lotus bathed in an egg-shaped white light, syllables of words and people riding buffaloes. In the year 1672, 'In the evening of the 19th of the ninth month, the Dalai Lama is aware that his body has transformed itself into an unknown dark brown bird, bigger than a normal raven.' In 1654, the year in which the first Jews arrived in the New World, he saw a rainbow. His chief sacristan spotted it too, but only the Dalai Lama noticed a figure within the colours, 'Padmasambhava in the middle of the rainbow in the style of Zahor, holding a *vajra* in his right hand and a vase in the left'.

Visionary experiences of this sort were expected of Tibetan Buddhist masters. The Dalai Lama's visions – recorded in beautiful detail in illuminated manuscripts – may lie somewhere between projections, dreams and daydreams. Some hint at sleep. During a ceremony in the hall of the palace at Ganden, 'When the chanting of the prayer to Avalokitesvara begins, the Dalai Lama enters into a deep meditation which prevents him from sounding the bell which he is expected to continue doing. During this meditation, he feels a white cloud suddenly emerge: from behind it the Sakyapa master Tsarchen Losel Gyatso appears with a pale but slightly brown complexion and bearded . . . Later the Dalai Lama feels very pleased on account of the experience.'

At other times, a vision could foretell the future. While on a visit to the Chinese emperor, the Dalai Lama 'performs the atonement rite in honour of Palden Lhamo. During the performance he sees Yangsang Drakmo coming towards him carrying three human heads. When he renews the "support" (*rten*) of the goddess, she appears together with her four attendants in full attire. He then realises the fact that there is no longer any danger to his life in spite of his own fears and a prophecy of danger threatening him during the coming year.' The Tibetologist Heather Stoddard has pointed out that these visions are 'mental projections . . . destined for inner eyes and for the manipulation of the powerful forces of the human psyche'. A Tibetan who came across a Tantric text of this sort would read no more than the title, believing that it was unwise to approach a 'secret' religious document without initiation. The present Dalai Lama, in a rather nervous Foreword to his predecessor's *Secret Visions*, cautions against the dangers of making religious use of the material it contains, writing, 'I simply wish to say that it is of the utmost importance that Tantra is not abused.' In the Western world, where secret knowledge of any kind is considered extraordinary, such thinking is hard to comprehend.

In contemporary terms, the Fifth Dalai Lama's visions bear a resemblance to the hallucinations of serious drug-takers, although narcotics are not used in Tibetan Buddhist ritual. This was no hindrance to Timothy Leary and his associates Ralph Metzner and Richard Alpert (otherwise known as Baba Ram Dass), who in 1964, the year in which brutal public 'struggle' sessions began in Tibet as part of the Socialist Education Movement, published *The Psychedelic Experience: A Manual Based on the Tibetan Book of the Dead*. Leary's view was that 'consciousness-expansion' was the purpose of Tibetan Buddhism, and this could be attained through taking acid.

An obscure Nyingmapa mortuary text, which had obtained unexpected popularity in the West in the 1920s when it appeared under the title *The Tibetan Book of the Dead*, was Leary's starting point. He explained, as best he could, how it should be read with the aid of psychotropic drugs. A dose of either LSD-25, mescaline or psilocybin was advised. 'In group sessions, the arrangement of the room is quite important. People usually will not feel like walking or moving very much for a long period, and either beds or mattresses should be provided.' Most of the instructions in the 'manual' make little sense:

The Wave-Vibration Structure of External Forms: Eyes open or rapt involvement with external stimuli; intellectual aspects. The pure, content-free light of the First Bardo probably involves basic electrical wave energy. This is nameless, indescribable, because it is far beyond any concepts which we now possess. Some future atomic physicist may be able to classify this energy.

Allen Ginsberg was another romantic with an eye on imagined Eastern mysticism. In *The Dream of Tibet* in 1976 he recorded a dream of a visit to 'the Tibet of his imagination', where he learned that William Burroughs was 'secretly a Buddhist agent'. The revelations are oddly familiar; this was another journey to a distant mental space, projected up to the white paradise in the Himalayas: 'The depth is by now increased to where the Dream within Dream takes on cosmic proportions and I am aware I am really visiting secret Tibet, secret because it is a place for real in the Mind, universal, populated by ghost Samsaric lamas . . . I eat anyway – a small plate of hash and some strange sliced raw fish or rare bird meat.'

To a Tibetan in actual Lhasa, rather than Ginsberg's secret Tibet, the scope for such projections is restricted by a new land-scape. The Dalai Lama, in his present form, away in exile, may have visions, and his state oracle can still perform divinations. But the city's buildings are now linked by straight, dusty roads and cold-hearted landmarks, like the pair of giant, kitsch, golden yaks that were given to the Tibetan people by the Chinese govern-ment to mark the fortieth anniversary of the Seventeen Point Agreement for the Peaceful Liberation of Tibet. Imagination has been blocked by unfeeling development and inappropriate archi-tecture. A sacred lake behind the Potala has been filled with electric boats for the benefit of Chinese tourists, and beside it are fairground rides with little police cars and pandas dressed in the uniform of the Lhasa police. A famous picnic site, down by the Kyichu river, has been replaced by a large shopping and entertainment complex. To the north of the city, a leisure village has been created with shrubs, walkways and cement awnings which have been shaped and painted with dark-blue designs to look like parodies of traditional Tibetan tents.

I was invited to the leisure village by a quirk of fate, for a party for members of a state body. Celebrations of this sort were usually held in grand restaurants and involved prolonged glut-tony at the taxpayer's expense, sometimes followed by a trip to one of Lhasa's many brothels. This was a larger, more informal affair. Many of the guests sat on the grass, chatting away, using strips of torn cardboard as seats. When I arrived they had all been drinking beer and spirits for several hours, and the Chinese and Tibetans had gravitated into separate groups, although there was some crossover between them.

I had met government officials in the borderlands, but these were the first I had spoken to in the Tibet Autonomous Region. The younger ones were professional, sharply dressed, proud of the mobile technology they carried in their pockets. They looked less like bureaucrats than business people, which was what many of them were, taking advantage of the openings that power gave. Lhasa was rife with tales of fortunes being made from the awarding of construction, haulage and military contracts. I felt that there was envy and exaggeration in some of these stories, but it was certain that public life in the People's Republic of China had become riddled with corruption over the last decade, and that Lhasa, a frontier town, was a place of alluring commercial opportunities.

There were songs, drinking games and conversations. Many of the Chinese said they were on three-year postings to Tibet, and in some cases were separated from their wives or husbands, whose work obliged them to remain behind in their home province. They regarded their annual long leave as the high point of the year, and were desperate to leave Tibet. The days when a Chinese official would devote a lifetime of selfless service to the Tibetan people (what the exiles in Dharamsala scornfully called 'the Yellow Man's Burden') were long gone. The political idealism that inspired the early Communists had been replaced by managerial jargon and aggressive nationalism. Tibet was now no more than a hardship posting. The determinant of politics in the Tibet Autonomous Region was not local needs, but the fallout of internal power struggles in Beijing, namely the bartering between the Standing Committee of the Politburo, the State Council and the People's Liberation Army.

Although most exiles would consider Tibetan members of the Party to be merely collaborators, I felt that their position was more complex. Some, at least, were working within the system as a way of defending the interests of Tibet. They were not altruists; it was a pragmatic and sometimes cynical decision, a career choice that brought them material benefits. But in the course of doing their job, they tried to develop and defend their homeland. Many were openly resentful that the key decisions about the running of Tibet were taken in Beijing, and that the Party Secretaryship, the top job, had never been held by a Tibetan.

The younger Tibetans who worked in the government did not seem very different from their Chinese counterparts in education or ambition. The generation that intrigued me was the next one up, people aged around fifty or sixty, who had been elevated on Mao's instructions in the aftermath of the Cultural Revolution, solely on the basis of having a good 'serf' background. Little was known about these officials, except that they would usually have been active Red Guards, and were installed in positions of authority in the late 1960s for ideological reasons, as part of the backlash against the old aristocracy. They were sometimes seen on state television, walking in and out of meeting rooms, but were rarely heard to speak. They had no popular power base, and no profile as individuals. Their importance lay in what they represented: impeccable, old-style proletarian credentials and open reliance on Beijing. Among Tibetans in Lhasa, this generation of cadres was perceived as ruthless, aggressive and stupid, and viewed with scorn and fear.

They were to be avoided, but I found myself among them, by chance, without realising what was happening. The men were paunchy bureaucrats in brown suits, v-neck jerseys, ties and soft shoes, and the women were dressed in skirts or *chubas*. Many of them wore dark glasses. They all looked drunk. These officials disliked the idea of me, a stranger and a foreigner, in their midst. I was not drinking alcohol, but they decided that I should have a glass of *chang*, or barley beer. I refused politely. They said it was the custom. I was caught in a crowd. One of the men grabbed the back of my head and shoved it forward, while another pushed a glass against my lips and poured liquid down my face and clothes. I wriggled free. They grabbed me and began again, this time with a glass of fruit spirit, angry now at being opposed. Some Chinese cadres intervened and extricated me, and we moved to another part of the park.

The Chinese were acutely embarrassed by what had happened,

and apologetic about the disrespectful behaviour of their colleagues. I was shocked, but they were not. 'Our Tibetan brothers
always behave in this way, it is part of their culture,' they said
with a smile – the Chinese smile of awkwardness and shame. I
had never come across Tibetans like this before. Boisterous drinking and singing are popular Tibetan hobbies, part of the culture,
but the difference here was the aggression, expressed towards a
guest. The Chinese, from a younger generation than my Tibetan
coercers, wore a look of pained apology, as if they were caught
in a social trap from which there was no escape. They seemed to
see the Tibetan cadres – who were tied to Mao and the damage
he had done, with their immobile political position stemming
from the chaotic aftermath of the Cultural Revolution – as
Frankenstein's monsters who had to be tolerated.

The Tibetan cadres reminded me of the 'living dead' of pre-
Buddhist Tibet. In the old times, when a king died, his loyal
ministers and servants would move to a secluded place near his
tomb. They were not permitted to be seen or spoken to by outsiders. Food and offerings would be left for them at the tomb,
with a horn being blown by the living to warn of their arrival.
If a wandering yak or sheep happened to reach them, the living
dead would brand it with a special mark, and it would be slaughtered and returned to them, unseen. Their separation from normal
society continued until all of them had died.

These men and women were Mao's living dead. For them, the
past was the same country; the bridges to the present had been
burned. For the Habaling Khache, the Muslims from the Place
by the Riverbank, whom I met a few days later, the past had
stopped with people like Mariam, a great-grandmother with
empty gums and muddled, partial recollections of what her uncle,
the imam, had told her.

At first, the idea of a Tibetan Muslim had surprised me; a
Tibetan seemed, almost by definition, to be a Buddhist, a follower
of the Dharma, although on consideration the notion was no
odder than a Tibetan being a Christian, which had happened, or
an Italian being a Buddhist, a prevalent conversion. The Habaling
Khache were part of traditional Lhasa society and the economic life
of the city, a minority in an outwardly uniform land. According

to one writer, 'Unmolested by natives to initiate whatever trade they desired, and inspired by incentive, the Muslims became commonplace features in the major cities of Lhasa, Shigatse, Gyantse and Tsethang.' They were renowned for speaking in chaste, courtly Lhasa dialect, even if they did sometimes eat dishes from Central Asia, which gave rise to the Tibetan warning not to be taken in by sweet words: 'Do not listen to a Muslim's voice, look at what he is eating.'

Most of the Habaling Khache were indistinguishable, physically, from other Tibetans. Only the names were different: Hamid, Abu Bakr, Salima, Fatima. In the past, most of them were merchants, but some had been given posts in the Dalai Lama's government as writers or translators, and been allowed to wear a special court uniform. A second group of Lhasa Muslims lived beyond the Potala, having been given a plot of land by the Fifth Dalai Lama. Their imam, Abdul Ghalib, told me that most of his small community had fled in the 1950s, and there were now only a few dozen of them left. Abdul Ghalib, with his Central Asian face, lived by an orchard with chickens and cows and apple trees and an old water-pump. It was an idyll, but he knew his world would soon disappear.

Mariam's uncle, the imam of the Habaling Khache, had known the history. He was responsible for the documents, going back to the twelfth century, which recorded the important marriages in their community, how the traditions had begun, what lands and privileges were granted to them in Lhasa by previous Dalai Lamas, and how their ancestors, merchants and traders, had made their way up from coastal China through the mountains to Tibet. There were about two thousand indigenous Tibetan Muslims left in Lhasa now, trying to preserve something that had been nearly washed away, their position undermined by the arrival of ambitious new Hui and Chinese Muslims from the east.

When the Red Guards – all of them Tibetan – came to purge Lhasa's main Muslim quarter, Thelpung Khang, in 1969, there was a moment of bafflement. The Habaling Khache, being Muslims, had no idols or statues that could be smashed, no painted frescoes that could be defaced, no sacred pictures that could be ripped. There was nothing to destroy. So, after retreating to discuss this problem, the Red Guards sought out the ledgers, the old legal papers, the name-books, the *dustar* or ceremonial prayer caps, the maps, an ancient decree granting Muslims an exclusive graveyard on the edge of the city (Buddhists do not bury their dead), and every copy of the Holy Quran, including the imam's own, which was several centuries old, and made them into a great bonfire in the courtyard in front of the mosque. The history of the Habaling Khache went up in flames.

The mosque was made into a cinema, for the watching of propaganda films; farmers and their animals were sent to live in the precincts and in the *madrasa*. The imam, Yahya, aged about eighty, was paraded through the streets to the east of the Barkhor wearing a conical white paper hat with the word 'ghost' written across it. Later he was slapped and pushed and told that he was an exploiter of the people.

'But he was a purely religious man,' Mariam kept repeating, tugging at the straps of her black lace headdress, 'a purely religious man.' He died soon afterwards, she said, of grief.

Mariam tried to describe the effects of this destruction. There were no words for it. For much of the Cultural Revolution, she had 'just felt like dying'. Finally, she compared the Habaling Khache to a person who has eyes but is unable to see. There was a problem translating exactly what she meant. She seemed to be saying, miming, that they were like someone whose vision was blocked by a cataract. They had the capacity for sight, but they could not see.

The Habaling Khache were deracinated. They no longer had any way of knowing what had made them what they were. And so, in this way, another part of Lhasa was destroyed.

FOURTEEN

In 1934, the eminent Tibetan politician Lungshar Dorje Tsegyal made plans to reconstitute the government. Tibet, he felt, was in urgent need of modernisation and reform. His opponents were unnerved by this idea, and while on a visit to the Potala, he was informed that he was being put under arrest.

Knowing that he had a servant waiting outside with a pistol and a horse, Lungshar resolved to make a dash for it. He would escape to Sera monastery, and try to raise support. Running out of the door, he found that the servant had disappeared. There was a moment of uncertainty. Frantically, he charged down the steep stone steps of the Potala. The servant, returning from a hurried trip to a latrine, ran up the steps towards him, holding the pistol in his outstretched hand, but as they met Lungshar was grabbed from behind by a huge monk guard, and his head brought smashing down on the steps.

The monk picked up Lungshar and carried him to the regent's office. His top-knot box and ceremonial robe were removed as a mark of dishonour. As Lungshar's boots were pulled off, a piece of paper fluttered from one of them. He grabbed and swallowed it, despite efforts to restrain him. A second piece of paper was found in the other boot. His interrogators examined it, and found to their horror that it bore a black mantra: '*Trimon Norbu Wangyal Nyan*', the full name of a senior minister, linked to the word '*nyan*', meaning bad or harm, to be trampled underfoot. It confirmed the rumours: Lungshar was a practitioner of the arts of evil. He was taken to a dungeon to await his fate.

His political supporters, hearing the news that he had been using sorcery, fell away. Culturally, what he had done amounted to attempted murder. Two monk officials and two lay officials formed an investigating committee. During his lifetime, the Thirteenth Dalai Lama had outlawed the use of execution and mutilation as criminal penalties, overturning a system of switching between corporal and capital punishment in alternate years, so that murderers would be either executed or lashed and made to wear a wooden collar, depending on the date of their crime. Lungshar's case was close to treason. Giving him the death penalty, however, might cause danger to Tibet; if he could perform the black arts, his malevolent spirit might roam the world and interfere with the discovery of the new Dalai Lama, the unlocated child in whose body the Thirteenth had chosen to reincarnate.

After deliberating, the committee decided that Lungshar would be sentenced to removal of the eyeballs. His two sons would each have a hand amputated, and his descendants would be banned from holding public office in perpetuity. Lungshar, a cool customer, said nothing as the sentence of blinding was read out to him, but lowered his head to indicate displeasure when he heard of the ban on future generations.

His punishment was carried out in the eighth month of the Year of the Wood Dog, the same month that Bonnie and Clyde were shot dead. The act was done by the hereditary performer of mutilations, a member of the low-caste Ragyaba community. First, Lungshar was given a drink called *langchen nyochu*, the water that sends an elephant mad, and then the smooth roundness of a yak's knucklebone was placed on either temple and compressed with the aid of a leather strap, which was constricted, tighter and tighter, around his head. Since this was Tibet in the 1930s, when all things seemed to go wrong, only one eyeball popped out, and the other had to be removed with a knife. The eye sockets were cauterised with hot oil.

Following representations for clemency from senior monks, the government decided that Lungshar's sons, Chapase and Lhalu Tsewang Dorje, would not have to endure amputation, although the ban on the family holding public office would remain.

You could see the history of Tibet through a family, by looking at the way its influence unfolded and retracted over two hundred years. Reincarnation has long been intertwined with heredity in the exercise of power in Tibet. Take the house of Lhalu, which first found its way into the records in the mid-eighteenth century, with the rise of three brothers – the forebears, although not the blood ancestors, of Lhalu Tsewang Dorje.

The first brother had three sons: Sonam Tashi, Lobsang Dorje and the Eighth Dalai Lama. Sonam Tashi was influential enough to be noticed visiting the Panchen Rinpoche in 1771, and a decade later was made a *kung* or duke by the emperor of China. His elder son was selected as the Fourth Jebtsun Damba, the Mongolian reincarnation, and his younger son succeeded to his title, being granted the rank of the peacock feather by the emperor. Lobsang Dorje was a leading monk official who represented the Dalai Lama at the installation of the new Seventh Panchen Rinpoche in Tashilhunpo in 1783. The Eighth Dalai Lama, Jampal Gyatso, was a mild, spiritual man who was happy to leave power in the hands of a regent, and only made a brief and unsuccessful attempt to rule. He built the Norbulingka, the summer palace of the Dalai Lamas, and died at the age of forty-five.

The second of the three prominent brothers, whose name is not known, had a son named Palden Dhondup. This boy became a political envoy, and was sent on two missions to the Sixth Panchen Rinpoche in Tashilhunpo. When the Panchen died from smallpox in Beijing in 1780, Palden Dhondup's son Palden Tempa Nyima was recognised as his reincarnation, the Seventh Panchen Rinpoche. As a result, the emperor of China made Palden Dhondup a *kung*, and awarded him the coral button and the peacock feather.

The third prominent brother was Lobsang Phuntsog, who was a close associate of the Sixth Panchen Rinpoche, visiting him on four recorded occasions. He sent an envoy to retrieve his smallpox-ridden corpse when he died, and was granted an official seal by the emperor. He attended the enthronement of the new

Panchen, his nephew's son. His own son, Lobsang Gendun Drakpa, was made an abbot by his first cousin the Eighth Dalai Lama. In 1790, Lobsang Gendun Drakpa and another cousin, the monk official Lobsang Dorje, were sent under arrest to Beijing, having fallen out with Chinese officials in Tibet. They were accused of 'unlawful extortion of money, unruly behaviour and strong Nyingmapa leanings'. After questioning, they were pardoned and awarded high ecclesiastical titles. On his return to Lhasa, Lobsang Gendun Drakpa was sent to negotiate with the Nepalese, who had recently invaded southern Tibet, but he died before taking up the post.

Members of the Lhalu family continue to be mentioned occasionally in official records until 1832, when they disappear from view. They were probably sent into abeyance by a failure to produce male heirs, but their decline may have stemmed from political machinations. The Lhalu dynasty had enjoyed an exceptional surge of influence in Tibet at the end of the eighteenth century, largely because of the discovery in the family of three eminent *tulkus*, whether by manoeuvring or destiny.

When the Twelfth Dalai Lama, Trinley Gyatso, was located in 1856, the Tibetan government was short of money. His three predecessors had died suspiciously young, and substantial estates and wealth had been distributed to their families, in accordance with protocol. To restrict the outlay of further assets, the government instructed Trinley Gyatso's family to move in with the remnants of the Lhalu family, and the two clans intermarried.

The Twelfth Dalai Lama's father was made a *kung*, and on his death the title passed to his eldest son, Lhalu Yeshe Norbu Wangchuk, who can be found fighting against rebels and erecting a tomb for his late brother on the roof of the Potala. By the 1870s this man was a leading figure in Tibetan politics, and in 1880 he was appointed a *kalon*, or cabinet minister. He travelled to Shigatse to investigate a riot caused by the Manchu *amban* extorting money, and tried to defuse a conflict with the Nepalese government over a disputed debt.

In 1888 he was ordered to the Sikkim border as commander of Tibetan forces during a dispute with the British over India's boundary demarcations. Ignorant of the military might of the

British Empire, his soldiers were soon routed, which gave rise to the Lhasa street song:

> Lhalu has returned,
> But, he's lost the border.
> Lhalu has returned,
> But, he's lost his cannons.

He died soon afterwards, and his son inherited the title.

When British and Indian troops led by Colonel Francis Young-husband reached Lhasa in 1904, the Lhalu family's residence was commandeered as their headquarters. They found it to be 'a very large commodious house' on three storeys, with glass in the windows rather than the usual thin air, built on the wealth of country estates. The correspondents of the London illustrated papers soon renamed it 'Younghusband House', with the Potala becoming 'Windsor Castle' and the Barkhor, the sacred walk around the Jokhang, being nicknamed 'Piccadilly Circus'.

In 1918 the new *kung* or duke died without leaving an heir, seriously weakening the Lhalu dynasty. His widow, the *lhacham* or duchess, fell in love with Lungshar, then one of the most influential politicians in Tibet. Under the kind of irregular dom-estic arrangement that was common among the nobility in such situations, it was agreed that Lungshar's son, Tsewang Dorje, would be subsumed into the house of Lhalu as the *lhacham*'s adopted son, in order to carry on the line.

So in 1924, the nine-year-old Tsewang Dorje took the name of Lhalu.

The fluctuating fortunes of the Lhalu family give a sense of the conduct of the Tibetan aristocracy in the period after the Chinese takeover of 1720. The production of male heirs, the seren-dipity of a useful reincarnation and skilful interaction with the Qing court were all essential for the maintenance of prestige. What is more remarkable, and equally revealing of the developing direction of Tibetan politics, is the fate of the house of Lhalu during the twentieth century.

Lungshar was one of the more intriguing political figures of the time. He had a political vision for Tibet, but it would lead him to lose his sight. Although he came from a traditional, if penurious, aristocratic background, he was a mercurial man, adept at business, medicine, music and obscure religious divination. He worked both as a military commander and as a senior official in the government's accounting and taxation department. His knowledge of the world was broad by Tibetan standards, and he understood the urgent need for his country to reform if it were to maintain its identity and integrity. Unlike most of his progressively-minded contemporaries, he was not pro-British, believing it was necessary to search more widely, as well as to go back into Tibetan history, for fresh ideas.

In 1912, Lungshar was sent to Europe by the Thirteenth Dalai Lama as a roving ambassador. His formal purpose was to accompany four Tibetan boys to school at Rugby, Harry Flashman's old stamping ground, in a curious sociological experiment. The idea was that the boys would become imbued with the British boarding-school ethos, return to Tibet and propagate this new Occidental faith. The boy Kyibuk, for one, was not a success, with his tutor-in-charge, Mr F.W. Odgers, reporting that 'he has no manners unfortunately and is a perfect idiot at a simple game of cards'. In later life Kyibuk helped control the Lhasa police force, and brought electricity to the city's smarter houses. Lungshar used his time in Britain to learn about democracy and constitutional monarchy. He refused to be orchestrated by British officials, and insisted on meeting King George V and senior ministers to present gifts from the Dalai Lama. His travels across the continent of Europe and his contacts with Indian, Japanese and Chinese activists disturbed his hosts, who put him under surveillance by police detectives.

In 1914, Lungshar's wife became pregnant. Terrified by a suggestion that a baby born in England would have sandy hair, blue eyes and a long nose, they immediately set sail for India. The child – the boy who was to take the name of Lhalu – was sent to a school for the children of high officials at the Jokhang, before entering government service and becoming a personal bodyguard to the Thirteenth Dalai Lama. Back in Tibet, Lungshar instituted reforms to the taxation system, which made him unpopular with his fellow nobles. Although he was a reformer, he avoided joining forces with other modernisers, relying instead on the personal patronage of the Dalai Lama to maintain his position.

When His Holiness left for the Heavenly Field in 1933, there was, as ever, a period of uncertainty in Tibet. A reincarnating head of state creates a chronic lack of policy continuity between administrations while the replacement is located. The Dalai Lama's death gave Lungshar and other eminent politicians an opportunity to increase their own influence, but they also ran the risk of being ousted, perhaps brutally, from power.

Lungshar was intelligent and highly competent, but he was also arrogant and headstrong. Rather than biding his time and playing a careful game, he encouraged the Trongdra, or 'Better Families' Regiment, run by his monk rival Kumphela, a good-looking favourite of the late Dalai Lama, to mutiny. This was a success. Kumphela, who owned the second of Tibet's two private cars, a blue Austin A–40, licence-plate TIBET 2, now fell from grace, lacking a protector. Next, Lungshar raised a petition, which many mid-level officials were persuaded to sign, demanding reform to the structure of the government and an end to nepotism. He wanted power to shift away from the inner clique of aristocrats towards the Tsongdu, or National Assembly, which he hoped would boost his own position and ensure stability until the next Dalai Lama was discovered and came of age.

On the day that his supporters presented the petition to the Kashag or Cabinet, Lungshar was summoned to the Potala and told that he was being placed under arrest; an opponent had spread a story that he planned to assassinate a senior government minister, Trimon, and to install a Bolshevik government in Tibet. This story exaggerated his true intentions, but Lungshar panicked, and tried to flee. The monk guard caught him. His boots were removed. The incriminating piece of paper fluttered out. The yak bones and the knife were prepared. Lungshar's eyes were removed.

After four years in prison, Lungshar was released into the custody of Lhalu Lhacham, his mistress or junior wife, the plump daughter-in-law of old Yeshe Norbu Wangchuk, whose troops were routed on the Sikkim border back in 1888. Blinded but unbowed, he advised his children to abandon thoughts of revenge, and not to let their generation be consumed by feuds and intrigues, as his had been. As the Second World War broke out and the young Fourteenth Dalai Lama was brought to Lhasa from his home in Amdo, Lungshar died.

Lungshar Dorje Tsegyal was a resolute, imaginative man, and a dedicated Tibetan patriot. His place between the modern and the traditional, promoting vital political reform while keeping black mantras in his boots, marks the hiatus in the Tibetan polity in the first half of the twentieth century. His terrifying downfall became a warning to other modernisers, blocking the chances of reform or innovation in the crucial decade leading up to the Chinese invasion of 1950.

In one of the curious, lateral paradoxes that can often be found in Tibetan affairs, Lungshar's son Lhalu Tsewang Dorje, by now a bright, ambitious man in his early twenties, quickly managed to get himself reinstated as a government official, despite the ban on members of the family holding public office – his siblings were sent into internal exile in eastern Tibet. Lhalu's success was achieved not by reversing the ban, but by paying a large bribe and maintaining the fiction that he was not Lungshar's child. By pretending that he was someone else's son, although everyone knew that he was not, he got his job back, while the prevailing legal and cultural order was not disturbed. It was the perfect Tibetan solution, like the practice of sending your hat on ahead of you if you had to go on a journey on an inauspicious day, hoping that the gods would mistake your hat for you.

Lhalu became a secretary to the Kashag, then an official in the accounting and taxation department, as his father had been, and in 1945 was made a *kalon*. The following year, he was the victim of an assassination attempt. On his way home one night, his horse was shot from under him. He later told friends that several bullets had passed through his body, but had caused no damage since he was wearing amulets blessed by the Dalai Lama.

When in 1947 the former regent Reting Rinpoche was discovered to be plotting against the government, Lhalu was one of two senior officials sent to arrest him. Arriving at his monastery, they prostrated in front of the Rinpoche, despite Lhalu being nervous that the eminent reincarnation might pull out a pistol and shoot him in the head. Fortunately, he did not anticipate arrest, and gave Lhalu a blessing instead. A member of the military escort then grabbed Reting's leg, presumably while prostrating in front of him, and told him that he would have to come with them to Lhasa. Reting acquiesced, and was charged with secretly requesting troops and weapons from China's Guomindang regime, and with sending a parcel bomb to the current regent, Taktra.

The news of Reting's arrest put the monks of his old college at Sera monastery in a riotous mood. When their superiors refused to lobby the government in Reting's favour, a gang of *dob-dob*, or warrior monks, began to rampage. Several people were killed, and the abbot of the college was chased across the rooftops and stabbed to death by his own monks. The Tibetan army was mobilised and set up cannons on the hills overlooking the monastery. Reg Fox, the English radio officer at Dekyilingka, who had served as a gunner during the First World War and was now married to a Tibetan wife, helped the troops to load the cannons. In the battle that followed, around three hundred monks and fifteen soldiers died before Sera capitulated.

Reting Rinpoche was incarcerated in a tiny prison cell where he died, you will recall, in gruesome and mysterious circumstances in May 1947. The twelve-year-old Fourteenth Dalai Lama was particularly upset by his death, since his own discovery had depended on a vision that Reting had at Lake Lhamolatso, when he saw a house with turquoise tiles and strangely shaped guttering near a monastery with a jade and gold roof, matching the home of the Dalai Lama's parents in Taktser.

Lhalu, meanwhile, was sent east by the Tibetan government to become the Domed Chikyab, the governor of Kham. With the Chinese civil war reaching a climax, it was a critical posting. Much of the region was under no clear control, with Khampa tribal chiefs holding sway. Having only a few thousand poorly trained soldiers under his command, Lhalu did his best to recruit local people to help defend the border. Much of his energy was devoted to preventing skirmishes between his avaricious troops and the Khampa levies, who were notoriously pugnacious, and renowned for never taking prisoners in battle.

Robert Ford, a British radio operator who was working for the Tibetan government in Chamdo, Kham's principal city, went to see Lhalu on New Year's Day 1950, after hearing an announcement on Chinese radio that the People's Liberation Army's tasks for that year were 'to liberate Taiwan, Hainan, and Tibet'. In his memoirs, Ford described this meeting with Lhalu.

> He was wearing a bright yellow robe with a red sash. His plaited hair was tied in a double top-knot with a golden amulet or charm-box in the middle, and a long gold-and-turquoise ear-ring dangled from his left ear . . .
> 'There is news?' he asked.
> I told him the news.

Lhalu knew the situation was grave, but his options were few. A handful of automatic rifles had been promised by Lhasa, but had yet to arrive. He had no serious weapons, and no explosives with which to detonate bridges. He told Robert Ford that the Chinese Communists were more dangerous than the Guomindang, but that as long as he was governor of Kham, there would be no surrender.

'They have no gods, and they would destroy our religion. We shall never let them in,' declared Lhalu. 'The Chinese never keep their word.'

To boost the strength of the army, he decided to recruit five hundred monks as soldiers. The monks disliked the idea, and offered to increase the volume of their prayers instead. The matter was referred to the young Dalai Lama's tutor, Trijang Rinpoche, who was hundreds of miles away in Lhasa. Ford and his counterpart in the capital, Reg Fox, had to set up a voice (rather than a Morse) link to enable the governor to speak directly to the Rinpoche.

Lhalu arrived at the little radio station, 'preceded as usual by his equerry, standard-bearer, steward, and servants', wrote Robert Ford.

> I asked Lhalu to speak, and he approached the microphone reverently and placed a ceremonial white scarf and a package of paper money on the table in front of it. Then he bowed his head as if to receive a blessing.
> 'What's holding you up, Bob?' Fox and I had separate

microphones, and his voice sounded almost blasphemous.

'His Excellency is offering a white scarf and a present,' I said in a hushed voice, feeling like a BBC commentator in Westminster Abbey. 'His Excellency is awaiting Trijang Rinpoche's blessing.'

'Trijang Rinpoche accepts the white scarf and the present,' Fox replied after a few moments, also almost intoning the words. 'He is giving Lhalu Shapé his blessing.'

Trijang, who would one day write the words of the Tibetan national anthem, agreed that the monks should become soldiers rather than continuing with their prayers, but it was not enough to dent the advance of the PLA, five million strong, well-equipped and fresh from victory over Chiang Kai-shek's forces.

On 7 October 1950, as United Nations troops under General Douglas MacArthur crossed the 38th parallel in Korea, forty thousand Chinese soldiers invaded Kham, advancing rapidly, following a military plan laid down by, among others, Deng Xiaoping. The Tibetan forces engaged in several skirmishes, but were soon encircled. Lhalu Tsewang Dorje had by now been replaced by another rising young aristocrat, Ngabo Ngawang Jigme, who reported the invasion to Lhasa and urgently sought orders.

Four days passed, but there was no response. Panic was breaking out in Chamdo. In desperation, one of Ngabo's aides contacted a Kashag official, and had this celebrated radio exchange:

CHAMDO: Look, we have sent three urgent messages and haven't received a single reply. What is going on? As far as we are concerned we see ourselves as virtually caught and every second is important to us. If you don't give us a reply we don't know what to do.

LHASA: Right now it is the period of the Kashag's picnic and they are all participating in this. Your telegrams are being decoded and then we will send you a reply.

CHAMDO: Shit on their picnic! Though we are blocked here, and the nation is threatened and every minute may make a difference to our fate, you talk about that shit picnic.

This was the last radio contact between Chamdo and Lhasa; Robert Ford removed the crystals from his transmitters, burned his files and prepared to leave. Tibetan soldiers were deserting. Families were escaping. Khampa levies were looting. Monks were performing propitiatory rituals. Ngabo, who had lost his nerve, was trying to flee, but was intercepted by Chinese soldiers, who filmed him as he signed a document of surrender.

The invasion had taken twelve days.

Tibet was falling.

When I arrived at the headquarters of the Tibet Regional Committee of the Chinese People's Political Consultative Conference in Lhasa, a big building made of white tiles and blue glass, the soldiers at the gate told me to go away. The CPPCC in Tibet is a non-Party body comprised mainly of former nobles and prestigious reincarnations, designed to show the broad range of support that the Chinese government enjoys. Its members are obliged to appear from time to time on television or in the press, endorsing the wise policies of Comrade Jiang Zemin, denouncing 'the Dalai clique' and meeting foreign dignitaries. I persisted, and a junior official was summoned from within, who also told me to go away. I explained that I wanted to see Lhalu Tsewang Dorje, one of the CPPCC's distinguished vice-chairmen. I might as well have asked to see the Great Helmsman himself. The official stared at me in amazement. It was out of the question. I asked to talk to someone more senior. The man continued staring, and told me to come back in an hour.

I walked down Lingkor Chang Lam to the Yeti Bar, Lhasa's coolest hangout, which by a quirk of history is run by one of Ngabo's sons. Outside the bar stood a large, lime-green, one-eyed plaster yeti with a bulging groin, standing on a rockery, draped in *katags*. I went in and ordered a drink; the music was pumping, welcoming us to the Hotel California. There were Tibetan waitresses wearing denim jackets and baseball caps. The bar's theme was unclear, but involved chains, prayer flags, suspended metal, luminous yetis and fir trees. On the walls there were paintings influenced, very badly, by Picasso. You can check out any time you like, said the music, but you can never leave. I finished my drink and went back to the CPPCC office.

Another nervous official emerged and told me that it would not be possible to see Lhalu, since he was in hospital convalescing after an allergic reaction. If I wanted to see him, I should write a letter to the head office of the CPPCC in Beijing and my request would be considered.

Chancing it, I went down the road to the People's Hospital. There was a wing for VIPs at the back. I had come to see Mr Lhalu. A doctor pointed me in the right direction. Once I had advanced up a few steps and down several corridors, I almost felt that I was supposed to be there. The hospital became increasingly sumptuous, with chandeliers and panelling. This must be where the senior Party leaders came to die. Two doors. I chose the one on the left, and knocked. A young woman, a nurse, opened it. Behind her was a large, formal reception room, with heavy wooden furniture, low seating and rich carpets, the sort of place you saw each evening on state television.

Lhalu? No, Lhalu was next door. These were the rooms of Phagpala.

Phagpala! He was the chairman of the CPPCC in Tibet, an important reincarnate lama but a notorious thug, womaniser and gambler, whose son was a convicted murderer. Phagpala was a hate figure for many Tibetans. Famous for beating the old Panchen Rinpoche at a public struggle session in the 1960s, he had also frequently denounced the Dalai Lama. Was he in poor health, I asked. Yes, he was very ill. His son had just arrived to see him. I reversed sharply and tried the next door, which opened to reveal a similar room and a similar attendant. She ushered me in uncertainly, baffled by my presence. Through an arch I could see a tall, frail figure in trousers and an open-necked shirt sitting by a window, backlit, his feet up on a stool, a rug over his knees, with a flat face and lank hair pasted down over his head. It was Lhalu, now in his mid-eighties.

I explained why I had come. He listened, startled, and said that he would like to talk to me, but that it was quite impossible without the permission of the secretary of his committee. I should make a written request. We both knew that a request would be referred to Beijing, and that it would go nowhere unless I had an endorser within the hierarchy. Could we have a brief chat about his father and the events of the 1930s and forties, I wondered? He was sorry, but it was not possible; I must understand his position; he was constrained. I withdrew.

On the way out, passing Phagpala's door, I remembered that he too had been in Kham during the invasion. I found a reference to him in the memoirs of Robert Ford. Ford had written that during a Losar celebration, at which Lhalu was the guest of honour, Phagpala had 'looked across at me curiously as I sat cross-legged in a European suit with a wooden tea-bowl on my lap. He was only nine.'

Half a century had gone by, and there they were, two figures from history, ailing in adjacent rooms in the People's Hospital in Lhasa.

In the years following the fall of Tibet in 1950, Lhalu had been through extraordinary experiences, like other members of the nobility. At first he tried to defend his country by working within the system, and had led a delegation of optimistic Tibetans to Shanghai and Beijing. They were received by Mao Zedong and Zhou Enlai and treated courteously, but their views were ignored. It became clear that officials of the old Tibetan government were being used merely as stooges.

In 1959, Lhalu took part in the uprising against Communist rule, and was caught and charged as one of its leaders. He was subjected to public struggle sessions and paraded through the streets of Lhasa as a class enemy. After a public trial, during which he thought he was going to be executed, he was sent to prison for six years, where he worked as a washerman and a clerk. When he was released, at the start of the Cultural Revolution, Lhalu's life was so circumscribed that he might as well have still been in gaol. He came from the worst possible class background, and he was a convicted rebel. Although some of his family had escaped to Nepal, he and one of his two wives were sent to live in the north of Lhasa, to work under close police supervision as farm labourers. If they passed their grandchildren in the street, they were not allowed to acknowledge them.

In the late 1970s, Lhalu made a deal with the Communists. Its exact terms are unknown, but in essence he made the same Faustian pact as several other members of 'the patriotic upper strata'. In exchange for backing Chinese rule, he was rehabilitated and given a sinecure on the Tibet Regional Committee of the CPPCC. Perks came with the post: a salary, good accommodation, travel opportunities, access to power and a chance to reunite his family. Despite this turnaround, Lhalu avoided giving his support to China's rewriting of Tibetan history. In his autobiography, published in 1993 under the auspices of the CPPCC, he boldly contradicted several aspects of the authorised version of events, denying, for example, that the enthronement of the Fourteenth Dalai Lama in 1940 took place under the authority of China's central government.

Lhalu gave an interview to the magazine *China's Tibet* in 1999 in which he said that he had once 'owned a score of large and small manors and thousands of slaves', and had 'even tried to rely on imperialist forces to defend the prerogatives of serf-owners'. He was quoted as saying:

> I saw with my own eyes that old Tibet was very poor, with people suffering greatly . . . The Tibetans, under the leadership of the CCP [Chinese Communist Party] and with the support of the Chinese people as a whole, have driven the imperialist forces out of the region and China at large, overthrown feudal serfdom and made continuous progress in socialist construction.

Here, Lhalu was following a formula, playing a game to satisfy the Party propaganda chiefs in Beijing. Whether he believed a word of it – this man who was conceived in England before the First World War and whose hand was nearly removed in 1934 – was open to question. In the same interview, he deviated from the Party line by saying that he missed his old colleagues who were still in exile, and wanted the Dalai Lama to come back. 'There is a Tibetan saying: "Old bird misses forests and old people miss hometown." I sincerely wish the Fourteenth Dalai Lama will return, in the interests of the motherland, at an early date and join us in socialist construction.' In the climate of 1999, this was a brave statement to make.

A few weeks after my visit to the hospital, I spoke to an associate of Lhalu, who tried to explain his position. She said that he wanted the best for Tibet, and had joined the CPPCC committee to try to moderate the excesses of the ideologues, and for the sake of his family. His standing had enabled his grandchildren to obtain the necessary permits to set up a successful restaurant and hotel business in Lhasa. Lhalu would not do or say anything that might jeopardise their future. 'If the authorities ask him to read a speech,' she told me, 'Lhalu can answer "yes" or "no". He can't say anything else. He has no alternatives.'

Others expressed similar views about Lhalu and his generation of aristocrats. Their position was laced with irony. Tibet's former ruling class, persecuted during the Cultural Revolution and routinely derided in China's state media, had been embalmed and co-opted in an effort to prop up Communist rule. I suspected that Lhalu, like Lungshar in old age, was concerned primarily for his own family, hoping that the next generation would not be consumed by suffering and ideology, as his had been.

Tibetan intellectuals in Lhasa drew a clear distinction between the likes of Phagpala, who was seen as a committed traitor, and Lhalu, whose treachery was believed to be conditional and pragmatic. When members of the 'patriotic upper strata' appeared on Tibet Television condemning feudal serfdom or the NATO bombing of Kosovo, nobody took much notice, but if they denounced the Dalai Lama in person or endorsed the 'fake' Panchen Rinpoche, they were derided on Lhasa's covert grapevine. As in the old Soviet Union, media coverage was formulaic. The number of minutes allocated to a leader on the TV news was more significant than the content of the report. You had to analyse each word in the context of the political climate, and try to guess its symbolism. Everything was in code, and you could never be sure whether you had the right cipher.

Later, after I had left Tibet, I heard that Lhalu had recovered and taken to attending CPPCC meetings in dark glasses, so that he could doze without being noticed. It was in 1934, the year in which the Long March began, that his father lost his sight.

FIFTEEN

Lhasa's strangely oppressive atmosphere came, in part, from the strong physical presence of the security forces. You had to cope with the regular police, found on every street corner; the traffic police, who tended to be Tibetan and portly, dressed in shiny white jackets, like wine waiters; the Barkhor police, exclusive to the Tibetan ghetto, wearing scruffy dark-blue uniforms, high-peaked caps and knee-length black rubber boots, which made them look like low-grade Nazis; PLA soldiers, who would appear whenever a large public event was taking place; the People's Armed Police or PAP, a grander, paramilitary outfit, who rode in four-wheel drives and trucks, flashing automatic weapons; the Public Security Bureau or PSB, who could be found in uniform or in plainclothes; and the State Security Bureau or SSB, China's feared security and intelligence agency. Only in Shanghai, it was said, were there more SSB officers than in Lhasa.

As the weeks passed, I came to see some of the experiences that lay behind the abnormality of everyday life in Tibet. In such a restricted society, it was the details – obscure and obscured – that offered glimpses of understanding.

Footnotes to history were always intriguing. There was a man named Mahmud Isa, who had been on my mind for some time. He might be ranked as one of the great explorers of the nineteenth century, except that being a paid servant, who wrote no books for printing in European capitals to be traded a century on for magnificent sums, he can be found only in the asides of others. Mahmud Isa was the caravan *bashi* – the producer – of successive expeditions to Tibet and Central Asia, including the adventures of Andrew Dalgleish (who was hacked to death by a giant Afghan on a remote mountain pass), Captains Ryder and Rawling (who surveyed the emptiness of western Tibet), Sven Hedin (the eminent Swedish explorer), Jules Dutreuil de Rhins (the French naval officer) and Francis Younghusband (the invader of Tibet). I had once thought of putting him into a film script, pulling him in from the margins and placing him at the centre of the historic expeditions he had made happen, enabling him to reveal the quirks of these intrepid European heroes from his unique, reverse perspective. I realised in time that this view would be no more than fiction; I would be asking him to present a contemporary take on a culture that was not his own.

There was too much about Mahmud Isa that could never be known. Did he admire his foreign masters, or think them lax and self-important? What made him, most unusually for his age and time, renounce the Buddhism of his childhood and convert to Islam? Was it a spiritual, economic or perhaps a marital decision? What was the truth about the murder of Dutreuil de Rhins near the source of the Mekong river in 1894? The French traveller was trying to reach Lhasa, without the permission of the Tibetan government, when he was shot in the stomach with a matchlock rifle during a dispute over horses, but there were disputed stories about his death. What was the small, irascible but phenomenally determined Hedin really like, as a person? Why did Mahmud Isa refuse to follow Younghusband on an expedition down the Mustagh Pass in 1887, but agree to join him for the invasion of Tibet in 1904? Crucially, what made Mahmud Isa risk his life again and again to cross impossible, uncharted landscape, including some of the most dangerous high-altitude territory in Asia, enduring sand storms, ice storms, mortal thirst and the death of his companions? At the height of his career he earned forty rupees a month, nearly three times as much as a regular porter, but fifteen times less than a middle-ranking civil servant in British India. The answers to all these questions were unknown, yet without him, the fate of several valiant European explorers might have been radically different.

When he first crops up in the margins of history, Mahmud Isa is in his early thirties, a tall, strong man known simply as Drogpa, or 'nomad'. Another camp servant, Ghulam Rassul Galwan, made a note in broken English in 1890 that 'He been long in service of travelling-sahibs, who went Chinese Turkistan.' Over the next two decades, Mahmud Isa can be glimpsed, if you look carefully, in almost every corner of High Asia, calling a muster roll of porters, purchasing horses and mules by the dozen, disciplining troublemakers in three languages (Turki, Hindustani and Tibetan), checking loads, inspecting a questionable map, ensuring a supply of potted meat and tobacco for his *sahib*, scanning the horizon through a pair of field glasses, and arranging cooking pots, packsaddles, copper cans, ropes, frieze rugs, horseshoes, hats, axes, spades, crowbars, rafts, signalling wire, tents, rifles, bellows, trunks, ammunition boxes and folding chairs.

Despite knowing only fragments of his life, it was possible for me to see Mahmud Isa clearly on one precise date, the day of his death, 1 June 1907, his 'stately form upright on his grey horse, his pipe in his mouth, his green velvet cap on his head, and the black sheepskin loose on his shoulder, trotting quickly in the track of the caravan'. By the banks of the Tsangpo river, near Saga in southern Tibet, he had a stroke which paralysed his left side. He murmured, 'I was a Lamaist but went over to Islam; help me now, oh Allah, out of this severe illness.' As he died, a Tibetan Buddhist friend named Tsering cradled him, but was pushed aside, 'for a Mohammedan must hold the lower jaw and close the mouth after the last breath'.

The next morning Mahmud Isa was buried, and in a graveside oration Sven Hedin, who would one day be stripped of his British knighthood and fellowship of the Royal Geographical Society for supporting Germany in the First World War, declared that he had 'earned a great name in the exploration of Asia, for during thirty years he had served other Sahibs as faithfully and honestly as myself'. Mahmud Isa's friends and comrades wailed and beat their heads by the graveside. One man wept 'like a child', and later they sat together and ate a memorial feast of *halva*, mutton and tea.

If you look at a country's history through individuals, you are tied to the ones who made it into the records. In Tibet, this usually means nobles, warriors or reincarnations. But if you want to look at the present, or at the recent past, you could choose anybody, or anybody who was willing to talk. You could even seek inspiration in the note made by the young Mao – 'I am the universe, life is death and death is life, the present is the past and the future, the past and the future are the present, small is big, the *yang* is the *yin*, up is down, dirty is clean, male is female, and thick is thin' – in the margins of a copy of Friedrich Paulsen's *System of Ethics*, in an exact foreshadowing of the chaos of the Cultural Revolution, and go in search of the aristocrats of those days of inversion, the outcaste Ragyabas.

There were said to be about a dozen left.

After long negotiation, a Ragyaba named Ugyen agreed to speak to me. His head was a skull with a fuzz of short white hair, and his skin was worn and blackened. He looked at least eighty, but said he was in his mid-sixties. I had seen many faces in Tibet that had passed through suffering, but Ugyen's was uniquely disturbing. He had none of the ebullience that goes with being Tibetan. He flinched, he cowered, and he kept his distance, as if he expected to be struck at any moment, and was ready to strike back. He was, I thought later, like one of the older generation of Dalits, the Hindu caste once called Untouchables, who had endured so many years of mistreatment that they were discomfited when you spoke to them courteously.

Ugyen's room was in the Tibetan ghetto, near the Barkhor. Contrary to custom, he did not offer me tea, I think because he did not expect anybody from outside his own community to want to share food or drink with him. His room was simply decorated, with pots and pans and thermoses of hot water. A badly cured animal skin hung by the door, being chewed by a small grey dog, and it gave off a meaty smell. Ugyen wore several greasy cotton shirts under a brown cardigan, and sat on the floor. I sat on his low bed. He had a throaty cough, and every so often he would lick his lips and wipe his neck and face with a damp flannel. His back pocket held a long knife, which he whipped out occasionally to trim his fingernails.

'We were different from the rest of Tibetan society. Everyone looked down on us. They saw us as beggars. We had our own laws and our own master, the hereditary lord of the Ragyabas, the Dhaye. His name was Phurbu Tsering. We lived in a special place that was set aside for us, called Tsopa Kangsar. There were about twenty families. Many of them were intermarried. My wife came from within the community. Nobody would want to marry a Ragyaba if they could help it, because if you did you would have to join our community.'

Ugyen explained that the Ragyabas had various tax duties, which they had to perform at different times of the year. There were set tasks, such as begging at the big aristocratic weddings. They begged loudly, using special chants and songs, and presented *katags* to certain guests. Legally, you only became a full Ragyaba when you were twenty-five. They also had to collect money – three *sang* – from any outsiders who were in Lhasa. They would spot newcomers in the streets and ask them for payment, then take the money to the Dhaye, who distributed it within the community.

'The Dhaye would keep a lot of the money for himself. We had to do exactly what he said, or his assistant, the Ponpo, would give us a beating. The Dhaye didn't have to pass on any money to the government, because the Ragyabas performed their tax duties in other ways, by doing compulsory jobs such as clearing the Barkhor drains. Disposing of unclaimed corpses was one of our main duties. If somebody had been murdered or committed suicide, or if they had died in an unnatural way, the Ragyabas would be called in. We would go and collect the body and carry it to a special building in our compound, and then take it to a place over at Drabchi where we would bury it in the ground. It was believed that if someone had been murdered, it was necessary to store their body in the ground rather than let their spirit escape in the normal way, through sky burial or cremation.'

Once a year, during the Monlam Chenmo, the Great Prayer Festival, the Ragyabas would go to Drabchi and disinter skeletons for use in religious rituals. Sometimes it was a whole skeleton, sometimes just particular bones. The monks would let them know beforehand what was needed. They would bring the bones to a site just in front of the Jokhang, at sunset. The monks would put the skeletons on a bonfire and chant prayers. Ugyen believed this was done to ensure that the Tibetan people were free of bad spirits during the year ahead. Another of their official duties was to erect the big prayer mast known as the Ganden Darchen at the start of the Monlam Chenmo, on a corner of the Barkhor.

'It was hard work putting it up,' Ugyen told me. 'We were all involved. Everything had to be done correctly. It was an important job. When we had got the mast up, an official would go and report to the government that it was in place, and the festival could begin. The Ragyabas also had to do a *cham*, a ritual dance, at the end of the Shoton, the Yoghurt Festival. It was one of our annual tax duties to the government. It was also a religious duty. We would have to learn the steps of the dance, and all the movements and hand gestures that went with it. I remember it was very difficult, and if you made even a single mistake, you would be beaten afterwards by the Ponpo. There were lots of musical dances during Shoton, done by troupes from all over Lhasa. The one that we did was unique to the Ragyabas. We wore masks that made us into demons. Afterwards, we would be given food and blocks of butter or bags of grain. The food you got depended on your status.

'There were other types of Ragyaba in Lhasa, like the Sholpa Ragyabas, who had their own duties. Social groups like butchers and blacksmiths, and others who had impure bones, were not Ragyabas. People sometimes thought that they were, or that ordinary beggars were part of our community, but they weren't. The Ragyabas wore *chubas* and had long plaited hair, which we tucked up into the yellow woollen cap worn by all government servants. The men were required to wear the cap when they went about their duties. We weren't allowed to have an earring, though, because of our low status.

'Our lord, the Dhaye, wore a different type of hat and had expensive clothes from India. He thought very highly of himself, but for most people in Lhasa he stood for nothing, he was just the leader of the outcastes. Our community was originally formed from those who could not pay their taxes, or had committed a serious crime such as murder. I know that my family has been

185

in the community for at least four generations, but I can't tell you any further back than that.

'We had our own justice system, which was administered by the Dhaye. We weren't allowed to go to the Lhasa court if there was a dispute. I suppose that if we had done something really serious, like a killing, we might be handed over to the government. We just had to put up with whatever the Dhaye decided. If he told the Ponpo or anyone else to punish us, it would be done. His power was only in our community, but nobody challenged him because it was his hereditary position. If we failed to raise enough money at a public event, or we did something wrong, or if we just got a bit cheeky, we would be flogged. Usually it was the men who were beaten, but sometimes the women were too. The Ponpo would use a long bamboo stick that had been cut open slightly at one end in order to tear the skin. I'm not saying we were the only ones who suffered. I remember a habitual thief who had been ordered by the court to have salt bound to his hand with leather. After a time, the salt corroded away most of his hand. That was his punishment.

'I really can't begin to count the number of times I was beaten. One time I was unable to sit down for fifteen days. You would usually be bleeding after a beating, and sometimes bits of flesh would come off on the bamboo.'

Ugyen stood up and undid his layers of greasy clothing at this point, with no embarrassment, and showed me a deep red welt that ran across his chest. As he tucked himself back in, scratching his chest vigorously, he went on talking.

'Usually we would be beaten on the buttocks or on the back of the legs. One time, the Ponpo had given me such a bad whipping that I was stopped in the street by an Indian man. He worked in the hospital that was part of the British mission at Dekyilingka. I'd heard of the hospital but had never thought to go there. They took me into the hospital and treated me, for free. I was amazed at what was happening. They just treated me like any other patient and didn't seem to be concerned where I came from. I tell you, if I got ill today I would just stay here and wait to die, I would never be able to pay the money to go to hospital.

'When the Chinese first came to Lhasa, it didn't make any

difference to us, so far as I was concerned. But a few years later, our whole life changed. It was at the time of the Lhasa uprising, when Yeshe Norbu, our Precious Protector the Dalai Lama, escaped into exile in India. I took my chance. The whole of the city was in chaos at that time. The Chinese were bombing the Norbulingka and the Potala and there were fires and explosions everywhere. I thought, this is it. Lhasa is in revolt, and I am going to take my revenge on the Dhaye.

'I had a knife, just like the one here in my pocket, and I walked over to his house. It was dark. I was going to stab him. I crept up the stairs. He lived on the second floor. There was silence. I pushed open the door, and found the whole place deserted. He had gone. He must have known that it was the end for him and his family. He had taken all of his possessions and his money, his silver and jewellery, and fled. Later, I heard that he had been hit by a shell on the outskirts of Lhasa, near the Norbulingka where the Chinese were bombing. He died immediately. I was very happy when I heard that news. His son died around that time too, so that was the end of his family.'

When Ugyen had finished telling me the story about the Dhaye, I asked why he had wanted to kill him.

'Because of what he'd done to my father,' he answered. 'He had beaten my father to death. I had been waiting for my chance to get even.

'During the uprising, I went and joined the resistance fighters. His Holiness had gone into exile, and we felt that we'd been abandoned. There were all sorts of rumours: that he'd been captured and taken to Beijing, or that he'd been abducted by counter-revolutionaries and taken to India, or that he was dead. At that time, nobody cared that I was a Ragyaba. It was just Tibetans against Chinese, because they were trying to take away our country. I went to fight near Nagchu. It was a desperate time. I was only there for a few months. We were outgunned. We didn't have enough weapons. At the end of a ten-day gun battle with the PLA troops, our side ran out of ammunition and the survivors were captured.

'My motivation for fighting was not political. I never knew much about politics. I joined the resistance to protect our religion, and out of loyalty to His Holiness. The Communists wanted to take away our monasteries and temples. They wanted to destroy our gods.'

Ugyen's words were nearly identical to those of Raduk Ngawang, an ex-monk and hardened fighter whom I had met in Old Delhi. He was an elderly man with a soft mouth and a prominent chin, who had in the 1950s been a founder of the main Tibetan resistance force, the Chushi Gangdrug (Four Rivers, Six Mountain Ranges). Raduk Ngawang lived in a hot, cramped refugee camp surrounded by signs saying 'BOYCOTT CHINESE GOODS BUY INDIAN GOODS'. He had spoken to me of the arrival of the Communists in his home town, Lithang, and of his anger when they publicly called monks 'thieves'.

Raduk Ngawang told me of the first and worst battle, at Dukhak Sumdo in 1958, when the Chushi Gangdrug had run out of ammunition and charged the PLA on horseback, swords drawn.

'I took eighteen bullets,' he remembered. 'I felt angry. As a Buddhist, the invocation "om mani padme hum" comes to my lips when I kill an insect, but I didn't feel sad during that battle. I felt happy. The Red Chinese had killed monks and destroyed monasteries, so we killed them. I felt nothing when I saw them dead. They had no religion.'

This was Raduk Ngawang's way of animating the worthlessness of his dead enemies: they had no religion. For Ugyen, who came from a different social background and a different part of Tibet (they would scarcely have been able to understand each other's dialect), the sentiments were the same. It was a way of thinking, an instinctive, conditioned devotion to Tibetan Buddhism. Crucially, the Chushi Gangdrug, an organisation now often depicted as a symbol of militant Tibetan nationalism, was at its inception a movement for the preservation of religion. Its military badge carried the legend 'Guardians of Religion in the Land of Snows'.

'We had done what we could,' Ugyen went on. 'I was brought back to Lhasa and put in prison, together with other resistance fighters and even a number of aristocrats. We were kept there for a while before I was sent away to a labour camp in the north, where I had to break stones and do hard manual work. I was under a death sentence throughout that time. I had killed Chinese soldiers in Nagchu. They knew I'd done it. I was due to be shot. I was expecting it every day. Then the Chinese leader, the commandant of the camp, split up the prisoners. Some were taken away and executed, and others were kept in the camp. I stayed there until around 1968, when I was released.

'Because the Ragyabas were poor and the Communists believed we had been exploited by the feudal serf system, the members of our community were given many special privileges. People were given jobs or pensions, and some were asked to join the Communist Party. Most of them suffered great sickness from drinking too much alcohol, and many of them died. When I returned to Lhasa, lots of my contemporaries were already dead from alcohol. They didn't know what to do with themselves when they were put in this new position, getting a pension and being told that they were from the best class background.

'We were invited to go to struggle sessions and beat members of the former ruling class. To be honest, I disliked the idea of doing that. I thought there was no use in bothering other people. What was done was done. It was the past. The nobility and the merchant class didn't have anything to do with the Ragyabas. It was the Dhaye and the Ponpo who used to beat us, not the ruling class.

'The Communists had a lot of problems deciding what to do with me when I came back to Lhasa. I'd been given the label "counter-revolutionary", because I fought in the resistance. They kept on telling me that His Holiness was a serf-owner, and I was now free under the Socialist system, but I never believed them. I refused to say that I agreed with what they were saying, and I refused to go to the struggle sessions. They said that my brain was green, that I was thinking old thoughts, and that I loved *chitsog nyingpa*, the old society.

'There wasn't much they could do with me though, since I came from a good class background. They gave me a room to live in and a pension of around US$25 a month, and then left me alone. My wife and I never had any children. We just had to get by on our own, with nobody to look after us. The younger generation of Ragyabas are part of regular society now. A few of them still have some connection with the old duties. I know of a family who took the concession on operating the public toilets near the Jokhang. They pay the authorities a small rent, and in return they can charge a fee to people visiting the toilets. The younger ones don't really think of themselves as Ragyabas, though, they wouldn't use that word. There aren't any more of us left now. Most people in Lhasa these days have probably never heard of a Ragyaba. They wouldn't know who we were. We are the last of the Ragyabas.'

Towards the end of our conversation, hesitantly, I turned to the blinding of Lungshar. I was unsure how Ugyen would take this, and whether he would be offended by talk of his community performing mutilations.

'That wasn't one of us,' he said. 'We weren't allowed to do things like that. I remember my father telling me what had happened to Tsipon Lungshar when I was a child. It was said that he was a favourite of the old Dalai Lama, and had tried to kill another government minister. They took a pair of yak bones and squeezed them against the side of his head until his eyeballs came out. That wasn't one of our duties. People looked down on the Ragyabas. We wouldn't have been allowed to do something as important as a state mutilation. That would be the job of a Kochak.'

I asked him who the Kochaks were.

'They were officers of the court, like policemen. The Kochakpas worked at the main city court by the Jokhang, called the Nangtse-shak. They had to carry out whatever sentence or penalty was handed down. They wore the same yellow cap as we did because they were government officials, but were allowed to wear a long earring in the left ear to show their status. If someone had to be flogged, or put in fetters, or have his Achilles tendon slit, or have his hand cut off, it was the Kochaks' job to do it. I should tell you, though, that in my lifetime, mutilations were rare. The worst punishment most people ever got was a whipping. The Kochakpas weren't bad men, they were just doing their job. I knew some of them. They weren't sadists, not like the Ponpo. No, the Ragyabas didn't blind Lungshar. I'd have known if that had happened. Who told you that we'd done it?'

'I read it in a book,' I answered, lamely.

'Well I wouldn't know about that, I can't read, myself. As I say, the Kochakpas were in charge of things like that. They were all right. They did a *cham* dance at the Shoton, just before us, and at the end they would always get better food than us. I mean, if it had been a common criminal being mutilated and the Kochakpas had asked us for assistance, I suppose we might have helped. But the idea that a Ragyaba would have been allowed to perform a blinding on a high official like Tsipon Lungshar, well that's totally out of the question.'

'So it was a Kochak who blinded Lungshar?'

'Well, strangely enough, it wasn't. My father told me the Kochakpas had some trouble doing it. I think that none of them knew the correct technique, because nobody had been blinded for such a long time. Apparently, in the end they asked a Nyerpa, one of the official government storekeepers in Shol, to come and help them. For some reason, this Nyerpa knew what to do. I heard though that it didn't go too well, and they had to use a knife as well as the yakbones to get his eyes out. Don't get me wrong, I'm not saying we would have refused to help with a blinding if we'd been asked to, but it just wasn't our job, certainly not on a government minister.'

All this was said in an entirely unaffected, matter-of-fact way. As I was leaving, I went forward to shake Ugyen's hand, but he recoiled, as if I was going to hit him. Walking back towards the Hotel Raidi through the light, clear rain, a half-forgotten line came to me, that part of the taboo of being an Untouchable was expecting not to be touched.

SIXTEEN

Some historical events have a great, looming, epic inevitability about them. Others, like the Cultural Revolution, spring up, alter history, and leave you looking over your shoulder. Even Mao Zedong's closest associates did not foresee it, were bashed and buffeted by it, and tried to put it out of their minds when it was over, if they were alive. Although it lies at the heart of Mao's legacy, it is, finally, unfathomable. The historian Jonathan Spence has pointed out that 'Mao himself never wrote a single, comprehensive analysis of what he intended to achieve by the Cultural Revolution, or of how he expected it to proceed.' Even Roderick MacFarquhar, who has provided extraordinary detail on its origins, offers no conclusive explanation of its purpose.

Spence has characterised Mao Zedong as a 'lord of misrule', who enjoyed promoting the upset of stability and order. In 1937, three decades ahead of Jacques Derrida, Mao wrote in 'On Contradiction':

> All contrary things are interconnected; not only do they coexist in a single entity in given conditions, but in other given conditions they also transform themselves into each other. This is the full meaning of the unity of opposites.

A love of reversal remained with him throughout his life. As he told his doctor, Li Zhisui, when the Cultural Revolution began, 'Everything is turning upside down. *Wo xihuan tianxia da luan.* I love great upheavals.'

By the 1960s, Mao cut a grotesque figure. He retained the

earthy speech of his rural Hunanese upbringing, using images of farting, shitting and motherfucking even when speaking at public meetings. As he entered his seventies, he was overweight and unhealthy, with a mouthful of rotting teeth and a variety of medical complaints. He refused to wash, except for a cursory wipe with a hot flannel, or to clean his teeth, content to rinse them with a swig of green tea, peasant-style. A trail of young women, mainly chosen from military dance troupes, was provided for him to have sex with, sometimes in twos and threes. When Li Zhisui told the Chairman that his poor hygiene was giving them vaginal infections, Mao responded with one of his favourite aphorisms, which never found its way into the Little Red Book, 'I wash my cock in their cunts.'

The ageing Mao thought that the Communist revolution was stagnating, and was nostalgic for the thrill of the civil war. He held grudges against old enemies, and enjoyed the idea of promoting disruption and watching chaos unfurl, just as he liked to swim in the dangerous currents of the Yangtse river and watch his security officers panic. Carefully, he manipulated his apprehensive colleagues until he could achieve his ambition to purge and purify China. 'Never before,' wrote MacFarquhar, 'had a dictator unleashed the forces of society against the state which he himself had created. This was indeed the mother of all mass movements.'

In August 1966, Mao released a 'big character' wall poster, written in his own hand. The message was limpid: 'BOMBARD THE HEADQUARTERS'. The masses were to liberate themselves, and Party bureaucrats would be their target. A million Red Guards, the juvenile shock troops of Mao's proletarian revolt, travelled to Beijing for the first of several huge rallies. The 'red sun' appeared in person on the balcony at Tiananmen, dressed for the first time since 1950 in a PLA uniform. A female devotee was permitted to fix a Red Guard armband to his sleeve, provoking hysteria. Once the action began, nobody was safe, except for the ringmaster, secure, inviolable, cosseted in his rooms in Zhongnanhai in the Forbidden City.

The rapid spread of disorder and unrest was provoked above all by the earlier cruelties and failings of the Communist system.

Many idealistic young people believed that they were being offered a genuine chance for change. The writer Zheng Yi has recalled the exhilarating sense of 'emancipation' when the movement started. Since 1949, Party bureaucrats had controlled even the smallest aspects of daily life, engaging in constant petty persecutions. Now it was possible to take revenge. Zheng Yi wrote that 'cruelty during the Cultural Revolution ... was an expression of rebellion and wrath in response to the violent politics of the [previous] seventeen years ... The deeper the exploitation, the more violent the rebellion.' Mao knew this, but believed, rightly, that the rebellion could be manipulated for his own purposes. Although the movement was too diffuse and chaotic ever to be orchestrated in detail from the centre, he never let go of the reins of power. Through his entourage, he made it clear who was to be targeted and who was to be protected. Once he had achieved his disruptive aims, the army was sent in to reassert control.

For many of Mao's old comrades, the Cultural Revolution marked the end. Liu Shaoqi, China's head of state, was 'struggled' by Red Guards, and discovered to be 'a lackey of imperialism, modern revisionism and the Guomindang reactionaries'. His death came passively, as Mao preferred. He was left naked, his hair uncut for years, on the cement floor of an unheated prison cell, before he died from pneumonia in 1969.

In Tibet, where religion and tradition were integral to personal and social identity, the Cultural Revolution was doubly catastrophic. Red Guards arrived from China. Some were Tibetans, fresh from college, buoyed up with ideology and determined to eliminate 'old' habits and practices. They recruited other young people, mainly from poor backgrounds, to join the crusade.

The making of *khabse*, a biscuit cooked during religious festivals, was denounced as a feudal practice. Amulets had to be destroyed. The three great monasteries were wrecked. The Monlam Chenmo, introduced by Tsongkhapa in 1409, was banned. The contents of the Jokhang, Lhasa's holiest shrine, dating to the seventh century, were smashed. Posters were put up with commands such as:

BOWING AND STICKING TONGUE OUT AS A SIGN
   OF RESPECT SHOULD BE ABOLISHED, AS THESE
   ARE SIGNS OF FEUDAL OPPRESSION OF THE
   PROLETARIAT.
ALL OBSERVANCE OF RELIGIOUS FESTIVALS SHOULD
   BE ABOLISHED.
PEOPLE SHOULD DESTROY ALL PHOTOGRAPHS OF
   THE DALAI AND THE PANCHEN.
THE TIBET DAILY AND LHASA RADIO MUST USE
   THE LANGUAGE OF THE PROLETARIAT . . . AND
   EXPUNGE THE LANGUAGE OF ARISTOCRACY.
ALL STRAY DOGS AND CATS IN LHASA MUST BE
   DESTROYED AND PEOPLE SHOULD NOT KEEP
   DOGS AND CATS IN THE HOUSE.

Pema Wanglha had helped to put up these posters. She was dressed, when I went to see her, in a consciously Tibetan way: a dark-brown *chuba*, coral jewellery, hair braided in long plaits which dropped to her waist. Large, flat gold earrings covered her earlobes. The living room of her house in south Lhasa had a small altar, with images of deities surrounded by candles and water offerings. There was, though, something distant about her, as if a part of her personality had been excised. I had noticed this condition in other people. In a dictatorship, detachment became a way of forgetting. Pema did not want to discuss the Cultural Revolution. I knew that she had been a Red Guard. From the way other people spoke about her, she sounded more like a participant than a ringleader.

At first, she talked about the political currents in Chinese politics in the 1950s and sixties. I tried to pin her down, and she moved on to the later phase of disruption. By late 1966, the revolutionary movement in Tibet had split into two factions, the Gyenlog, made up primarily of Red Guards and their backers, and the Nyamdrel, which was led by Party officials. There were violent, armed street battles between the two factions. Power fluctuated, until in late 1968 Mao ordered the PLA to restore control, and a new wave of 'proletarian' Tibetans and Chinese were put in positions of nominal authority, while members of the old, co-opted ruling class were sent to labour camps. It was not until 1980, when the Communist Party leader Hu Yaobang visited Lhasa and famously announced that officials should radically reform their approach, that liberalisation reached the Tibet Autonomous Region. Hu's visit would mark a major shift in economic and social policy. He told a Party meeting that life for the average Tibetan had not improved under Communism, and that a new emphasis on Tibetan culture and education was needed.

When the factional fighting began, Pema and several other students had appointed themselves Red Guards by making armbands and wearing Chairman Mao medals. By that time, 1967, Lhasa was descending into chaos, and anything was possible, even inventing yourself as a Red Guard. Pema said she would go to struggle sessions and 'act like a leader'. I asked her what she meant by this, and she said that she would persecute other people. If the Red Guards chose a victim, anyone – children, adults, teachers – could beat them during criticism sessions. They would stamp on them. After a while, she had stopped feeling guilty. A Chinese boy was hit with iron rods, again and again, his head wrapped in a sack. Pema did not know if he had survived. The Tibetans were more aggressive than the Chinese during these sessions, she said, but they showed more compassion. Victims who submitted, or started to bleed, would be left. The Chinese always wanted a confession, and continued beating until the victim had terrible injuries.

I wanted to know about the beginning of the Cultural Revolution: what Pema had felt about it, as an idea, when it broke out.

She was only seventeen, a student at Lhasa Middle School. Her family were traders, traditional in outlook, members of the nearest thing that Tibet had to a middle class. One of her uncles was a *tulku*, but not an eminent one. After the Lhasa uprising of 1959, her mother had been sent to prison for harbouring Chushi Gang-drug fighters. So Pema came from a 'bad' class background, but she had not been targeted herself, since she was brought up by a cousin. The authorities did not realise that she belonged to a 'rebel' family; she was, on paper, an orphan who had been taken in as an act of kindness. For her own safety, she was not told the full details of her background until she was an adult.

In August 1966, Red Guards from Beijing and Qinghua universities arrived at the Middle School. They were wearing Mao badges, red armbands and military uniforms. The teachers at the school were frightened, but the students were excited. Using two Tibetan graduates as their frontmen and interpreters, the Red Guards explained that it was necessary to destroy old culture and old ways of thinking. This chimed with what the students had already heard. The speakers were passionate, angry and inspiring. The children of Party officials were particularly enthusiastic about what they said, although they would themselves soon be targeted as capitalist roaders, as the movement spread and split. There were around five hundred children in the school, and about a hundred were chosen as Red Guards. The others, including Pema, were made Students of the Revolution, or supporters of the Red Guards.

Later that month, officials from Xinhua news agency and the Lhasa *Daily News* came to the Middle School and told the students that their revolutionary fervour was an inspiration to others, since they had been the first school to set up a troop of Red Guards. They were advised to intensify the drive to destroy the symbols of Buddhism, since there were still people in Tibet who had 'blind faith' and 'green brains', and were prostrating in front of 'gods and devils'.

The next day, a Chinese teacher at the school told them to go to the Jokhang. Led by two young women Red Guards, they surged out of the school gates, carrying banners showing the name of the school beside slogans such as 'TO REBEL IS JUSTI-FIED' and 'OPPOSE COUNTER-REVOLUTIONARIES'. Pema banged a pair of cymbals, and felt thrilled by the energy of the crowd, but apprehensive about what might happen to her family. Marching down the street, banging drums and waving red flags, they met hundreds of other students and young Red Guards.

By about midday they had reached the Kyamra Chenmo, the courtyard in the front of the Jokhang. A musical group from the school did a rehearsed song-and-dance routine, attacking 'old' ways of behaving. Red Guards dragged chosen elderly people up onto a platform and condemned them for prostrating and worshipping deities. One man was dressed up in an old-style Tibetan army jacket and breeches, like a British military uniform. Some of the women had their *pangdens*, the coloured Tibetan aprons, ripped off, and both men and women had their long plaits cut off. They were told to recant and reform their thinking. One pupil from the school even had to denounce his own mother in front of the crowd, and declare that she was 'steeped in old practices'.

As the size of the crowd grew, several statues were taken from the outer precincts of the Jokhang and smashed by Red Guards. Many of the older Tibetans became hysterical, and the atmosphere grew more intense. The weather was very hot. Red Guards climbed up onto the buildings around the Barkhor and ripped down prayer flags and threw statues from a window. As news of the destruction spread, Tibetan households in the area began to hide and bury their smaller statues, and to smash the larger ones for self-protection, or throw them into the Kyichu river. Pema wanted to warn her cousin-mother what was happening, but did not dare to break away from the ranks of the Students of the Revolution.

By now it was mid-afternoon, and thousands of people had assembled around the Barkhor. It seemed to grow hotter and hotter. Announcements and slogans issued constantly from loud-speakers. Pema was not sure how far the events of the day were organised. At the time, she thought they were spontaneous, but looking back it seemed that they must have been planned in advance. Chinese officials had been to the Jokhang over previous days, and removed the most valuable statues for 'safekeeping'. Many precious objects from Tibet's temples were sent to Beijing around this time, some of which were returned in the early 1980s, while most found their way onto the international art market via Hong Kong, to be bought later by wealthy Tibetophiles in Europe and America.

A line of Red Guards were protecting the four entrances to the Jokhang, keeping the crowd at bay. Late in the afternoon, a mob burst through one of the doors. A second door was breached.

The PLA soldiers did nothing. Pema watched people pour in. Most of them were Chinese and Tibetan 'anti-social elements' (looters and petty criminals) who were not part of the Red Guards, and many came from outside central Lhasa. Pema and the other students from her school joined the mob inside the Jokhang, and watched as chapel after chapel and shrine after shrine was destroyed. Huge butter lamps were tipped over, and pools of melted butter caught fire. Soon the floors were covered in melted butter, *torma* (religious cakes), holy scriptures, *thangkas*, wall hangings and broken statues. People were running in every direction, some trying to destroy and some trying to protect. Monks formed human barricades around the most sacred chapels, the shrines to Jowo Shakyamuni and Palden Lhamo, and many were badly injured.

Pema was nervous about being accused of not joining in, so she helped to drag statues of deities off the altars, and to tip over butter lamps. The experience did not feel real, since she had visited the temple all her life, and could not imagine that anyone could damage the place in this way without suffering immediate retribution. Throughout the destruction of the Jokhang, photographers from Xinhua took pictures of the major acts of desecration. Pema even saw photographers encouraging the mob to smash through the roof of the Jokhang and down into the Palden Lhamo Lhakhang, and to attack the beautiful statue there. Although Red Guards had initially tried to stop people from entering the temple, once it was breached, the loudspeakers announced there had been a great victory over 'backwardness' and praised the actions of the crowd.

Many of the rioters and looters were only interested in stripping the gold and extracting the jewels that studded the deities. Later, Pema learned that the authorities had been worried that photographs of the remains would show that the motives of these people had been covetous rather than ideological, so Chinese members of the Socialist Re-education work teams were sent to the Jokhang that night to smash any remaining statues.

As darkness fell, the students were told to return to Lhasa Middle School. Although they were congratulated by the leaders of the Red Guards for what they had done, most of them felt highly disturbed and unhappy, rather than exhilarated. Smashing the Jokhang had taken only a couple of hours, and they could not believe that such a thing could have happened. Pema was frightened of the possible karmic effect of her actions. The next day, senior local officials came to the school and condemned what had happened, saying that the Red Guards had allowed events to get out of hand. These officials were later accused of being capitalist roaders, and were purged. The Jokhang itself was taken over by the Gyenlog faction of the Red Guards, who turned it into their headquarters.

When Pema told me all this, she was calm and measured, speaking in a quiet monotone. It was only when she listed, one by one, the names of the deities destroyed in the Jokhang, that she began to sob. Her face went red and she covered her eyes and nose with her hands. For five or ten minutes she said nothing, and I wondered if I had gone too far, asking her to describe days that she had not wanted to think of, let alone describe in detail.

Finally she took her hands away from her face, and said, 'I wasn't the only one who did this. It was the other students too ... After it was all over, we couldn't believe what we'd done. Years later, one of the boys from the school – his name was Tsultrim – said to me, "It was the Chinese who killed the sheep, but we were the ones who skinned and gutted it." I feel terrible shame about what happened at that time, all the violence. I can't believe what we did.'

There were many victims of the Cultural Revolution; adults and children, and adults who still carried the weight of the crimes they had been made to commit when they were children.

The Cultural Revolution was not only about cruelty and destruction. It was also about the uses to which the human body might be put to expand and impose power. If you go back to the city of Chengdu, close to where my journey began, and travel south-east for around six hundred miles, passing out of the Tibetan areas and through the poor, mountainous province of Guizhou to the land of another minority group, the Zhuang, you will find that people were eaten by other people for political reasons. Cannibalism has a long and dishonourable history, humans being eaten as an act of triumph in war, and in times of famine, such as in the Soviet Union in the early 1920s. The difference in China in the mid-1960s is that people were eaten to prove a revolutionary point, with the superior organs – the liver for instance – being reserved for senior Party officials.

Despite the best efforts of writers like Zheng Yi, who went to great and dangerous lengths to obtain information for his book *Hongse Jinianbei* (Scarlet Memorial), the consumption of human beings during the Cultural Revolution is still largely unknown, both in and outside China. People who can tell you all about Nazi death camps, or Pol Pot's killing fields, or eminent American serial killers, are content to know nothing about the eatings in China. The very thought of real-life cannibalism is best avoided; easier to relegate it to the realms of horror films and fairy tales.

According to the writer Marina Warner, giving a Reith Lecture, cannibalism is little more than 'a modern myth, easily fulfilling myth's multiple functions, defining the forbidden and the alluring, the sacred and the profane'. People have been eaten 'very rarely and in extremis'. For Warner, the eating of people is, inevitably, a 'deep-seated racial myth', with 'imagery of forbidden ingestion' masking 'powerful longings and fears – about mingling and hybridity, about losing definition, about swallowing and being swallowed – fears about a future loss of identity, about the changes that history itself brings . . . Cannibalism is used to define the alien but actually mirrors the speaker.' And so on; cannibalism for the secure.

In Binyang county of Guangxi Zhuang Autonomous Region, things were different. Between 26 July and 6 August 1968, more than three thousand people were murdered by organised mobs. Stabbing, strangling, drowning, live burial and spearing with pitchforks were considered to be the best methods. The murdered were either 'social dregs', like the gynaecologists, surgeons and pharmacists of Luxu, or 'bad elements', traitors, spies, landlords, rich peasants, rightists and capitalist roaders. Few resisted, for there was nowhere to run. Everyone knew that only those who had been identified in advance by the local Revolutionary

Committee would be killed. As Zheng Yi wrote: 'Despite the random appearance of the beatings . . . Nobody was grabbed from the crowd, willy-nilly, to be beaten to death.'

In nearby Shanglin county, a gang of Party members armed with kerosene lamps would go off at night in search of targets. Finding one, they would hold the victim's arms and legs tightly, and one of the men would slit open the stomach with a five-inch knife. The liver generally popped out with the aid of 'a little squeeze or kick', and would then be cut out, leaving the victim to bleed to death. It was boiled, ceremonially, with garlic and rice wine, before being sliced up and eaten with chopsticks. The meal was supposed to bring medicinal benefits, the livers of the young and unmarried apparently being the most efficacious, curing disease and strengthening the body.

Things were worst in Wuxuan, sixty miles north-east of Binyang. From late 1967, the political leadership in the county had split into two factions, the Big and the Small, depending on which regional leader you supported. There were gun battles and bombings between the factions, and by May 1968 the Big Faction was triumphant. The commander of the Small Faction, Zhou Weian, was chopped into pieces, and his widow Wei Shulan, eight months pregnant, was made to kneel beneath his suspended head and leg in the heat of the day and denounce him. Zheng Yi's most gruesome description is of a gang of old men who liked to feast on that soft, cherished, clever part of the body – the brain. Each man had a metal pipe sharpened to a point at one end.

> Once the crowd had finished cutting away the victim's flesh, they would then slowly advance towards the victim (at that point they had no competitors). After they had pierced the victim's skull with their steel pipes, they would kneel on the ground and suck the brain through the pipe, rather resembling a small group of people in the act of sharing a jar of yoghurt with straws.

As the killings and the eatings spread, and the murderers found they gained notoriety rather than punishment, the practice of communal cannibalism grew. Zheng Yi estimates that at least ten thousand people took part in cannibalism in Wuxuan county alone. The local regime promoted a movement called 'Blow a Twelve-Degree Typhoon of Class Struggle', and as the typhoon blew, more and more people were caught in its wake. They were killed in public during criticism sessions, with red flags fluttering and revolutionary slogans being chanted, their flesh cooked in factory canteens and distributed among the crowds, who believed that human meat – even boiled intestines – would fill them with revolutionary vigour. In Tongling, the school principal and vice-principal were killed. According to a classified official report, 'Around the canteen, under the roof of the dorms, scenes of barbecuing human flesh could be seen . . . Even the air was thick with the smell of blood. The odour of burning flesh was everywhere.' Often all the members of a family were killed, in an effort to wipe out the line, a tradition going back to China's earlier dynasties.

The killings in Guangxi Zhuang Autonomous Region have been documented, as well as they can be in a closed society, but there were similar scenes happening across the People's Republic of China on a smaller scale, often at their worst in areas inhabited by minority ethnic groups. There were nominal punishments in the years that followed – the loss of Party membership, or demotion within the hierarchy – but never any sustained attempt to investigate, let alone publicise, this rolling frenzy of killing and its effect on the mind of the Chinese nation.

Mao got his way. The headquarters were bombarded. The *yang* became the *yin* and dirty became clean. China was inverted. 'In Tibet,' the *People's Daily* reported in November 1968, 'in the past, every household had its clay *Bodhisattva*, while now every house has a portrait of Chairman Mao . . . In the past, the masses used to burn incense and recite Lamaist scriptures every day in worship of the Buddha but now they seek advice from Chairman Mao every morning and make a report to him every evening; every day, they sing "The East is Red".'

Since then, much of this history has been suppressed in China. The live burials in Binyang, the cannibalism in Wuxuan, the eating of human livers at Shanglin, the breaking of Tibet – they have been passed over, these events of 1968, the year in which

'Maoists' paraded through prosperous European capitals and Richard Nixon was elected US President, the year in which the Prague Spring flourished, and was crushed.

SEVENTEEN

We were sitting in a restaurant near the Barkhor called The Third Eye, named after Lobsang Rampa's phoney but influential classic; art imitating art. The cafés and restaurants of the old city offered strange alloys of Tibetan, Indian and American cooking, with dishes on the menu such as curry pizza and yak burger. Lhasa had only one distinctive eating place, the Wonderfl, which served Japanese vegetarian food. It was advertised around town:

WONDERFL VEGETARIN RESTAURANT
Are you wary cancer, cardiopathy and vial hipatitist?
Are you d of obnoxious citgarette smoke, the naeating
stench of putrid urgers, and recurrent bouts of diarrhea
then by all means seek refuge Lhasa's only purely vegetarin restaurant.

Tsering Dorje, a Tibetan man with broad shoulders and a talent for talking, had chosen The Third Eye to tell me about the operating methods of Lhasa's police and security forces. He had been abroad to Nepal for education, and now had his own business, and was trying to put together a deal with a foreign company. Unusually for a Tibetan, he had found a way of taking advantage of the economic opportunities that had opened up in Lhasa in the early 1990s: a generous tax regime, preferential interest rates and other incentives for small businesses, which gave him great plans for his fledgling computer company.

The Third Eye was a good place to talk, since there was music playing and nobody could overhear our conversation. We sat at the far end of the restaurant, drinking sweet, milky tea. Dorje described the cut of the natty suits worn by Public Security Bureau men; PSB women were trickier, since their outfits varied. The Barkhor police – the ones who dressed in peaked caps and rubber boots – could be ignored. Most of them were petty thugs and criminals who had been put into uniform to keep them off the streets. Their job was to patrol the Tibetan ghetto and tip off the authorities if anything like a demonstration or a riot was looming. Dorje's message to me was simple: anyone in uniform was a moron; the threat came from those in plainclothes, and their informants. The authorities had no interest in foreigners, but they wanted to know who foreigners were speaking to. Any hotel or travel company in the Tibet Autonomous Region which interacted with tourists would have at least one informant on its staff, who might be working for money or for favours. Often they had been caught transgressing (there were so many things you could do wrong in Tibet) and had been turned.

The use of unwilling spies was an imperfect way to gather information, but it kept people on edge. Later, I met a man who had been let out of detention a month early in return for becoming an informant. He said that the system was farcical: he would meet his PSB handlers every week or so and pass on innocuous local gossip, but he never told them anything of importance. I felt that he was telling me the truth when he said this.

As Dorje and I chatted, two men came into the restaurant.

They were tour guides, young and cool, dressed in the exile style in T-shirts, bomber jackets and gem chokers. At Dorje's invitation they sat down with us and ordered cups of tea. Both men spoke colloquial English, with Indianisms thrown in, having lived in Dharamsala after escaping across the Himalayas as teen-agers, and spending almost a decade in India. There had been problems with the Lhasa authorities when they returned, they told me, but after paying bribes, everything had been settled. They asked me some questions, checking me out, and when they were satisfied – Dorje said I was a 'brother' – one of them began to tell us some news.

I leaned forward across the table, trying to hear. Two nights before, to mark the start of the National Minority Games, the fantasy games, there had been a protest in the main square in front of the Potala, the place where I had seen truckloads of Chinese soldiers on my first night in Lhasa. He spoke in an undertone, his hand in front of his mouth. A protester had gone there and managed to pull down the Chinese flag from one of the tall flagpoles in the square, and had started to raise the Tibetan flag in its place – the illegal flag with the snow lions and stripes, promoted by the exiles but now adopted inside Tibet as the mark of nationhood and protest – when he was spotted by a traffic cop.

Our conversation stopped. A smartly dressed Chinese woman had come into the restaurant, and was standing by the bar, chatting to the manager. We went back to drinking our tea, not talking.

A little later, when the woman – a PSB officer, perhaps – had gone, Dorje's friend continued with his story. Alerted by the traffic cop, a group of police started running towards the Tibetan man. As they approached, he pressed a detonator linked to a web of explosives that were strapped to his body. It was raining; his clothes were soaked; there was no explosion. He was grabbed by the police and dragged to a van. In the process, his arm was broken and his face smashed. Nobody knew who the man was, but he was now said to be in prison, having been beaten so badly that he was unable to stand. His family and neighbours had been brought in for questioning. The police were on the alert for further bombs or protests.

My heart was racing with the fear of it, the thought of the man planning the symbolic action, preparing the forbidden flag, wrapping the explosives around his chest, managing to pull down the alien symbol, knowing that he was going to die, and then, at the moment of truth, failing to explode the bomb. It made me think of Ngodup and the manner of his death – burning, framed by the orange light, holding up his joined hands – the last throw of the desperate, voiceless man.

We finished our tea. There was a feeling of tension. Everything in Lhasa was unstable, every relationship contingent. As Nadezhda Mandelstam wrote of the Soviet Union, 'leading a double life was an absolute fact of our age, and nobody was exempt'. You might think you knew who was trustworthy, but it was possible you were mistaken.

Tsering Dorje left the restaurant before me. It was better not to be seen in the street with a foreigner.

Some months later, more details came out about the protest in front of the Potala. The man who had tried to raise the forbidden flag was a building contractor in his early thirties named Tashi, married with two young children, one of whom was handicapped. He had won an award for making furniture and classrooms for a primary school near Sera monastery. According to Xinhua, China's state news agency, Tashi had 'confessed all his criminal activities, showing willingness to correct himself'. They did not report the news on 10 February 2000 when, in a squalid Lhasa police cell, he took a smuggled razor-blade, slit his jugular and bled himself to death.

EIGHTEEN

Under the terms of the Seventeen Point Agreement for the Peaceful Liberation of Tibet, signed in Beijing in 1951 by Ngabo Ngawang Jigme and other representatives of the then teenage Dalai Lama, it was agreed that the Tibetan people would 'unite and drive out imperialist aggressive forces' and 'return to the family of the motherland – the People's Republic of China'. Contrary to retrospective popular belief, which casts Ngabo as a solo villain on a frolic of his own, the Seventeen Point Agreement was endorsed by both the Tibetan government and the Tsongdu, the national assembly, and was not repudiated until the Dalai Lama went into exile in 1959.

The only outside observer in Lhasa during the first years of Communist rule was a bright young Bengali diplomat from newly independent India, Sumal Sinha. His reports to New Delhi give an acute impression of Lhasa in the early 1950s, showing how the process of collaboration extended across society, with noble families making fortunes from provisioning the swarms of Chinese soldiers and officials. Although there were individuals who kept their integrity and took risks in defence of Tibet, the conduct of most of the old ruling class was unedifying.

Sinha thought that the young Dalai Lama's government resembled 'an army which has lost all its generals after a series of tactical defeats on the field'.

One is confronted with the unusual spectacle of Tibetan love and enthusiasm for things Chinese; there is everywhere a keenness to imitate the Chinese, to dress, to talk, behave and sing as the Chinese do, and this is particularly noticeable among the respectable bunch of official families in Lhasa, who first succumbed to the spell. The inroad of neo-Chinese culture into Tibetan society whether in music, ideology, dress or speech is truly remarkable, for what was static in this land has become alive and dynamic. There is not a home in Lhasa where portraits of Mao and his colleagues have not found a place in the domestic shrine.

In another confidential dispatch, Sinha wrote:

While most officials live smugly in their ivory towers, leading much the same life of idle dissipation, the common people find the heavy burdens imposed on them insupportable. For them Communism in practice has fallen far short of expectations, and they have derived little comfort from the alliance which the Communists have forged with the ruling aristocracy of Tibet. In complete disenchantment, they ask whether this is 'liberation'.

It was not surprising, then, that many Tibetans resented the old aristocracy, and could be persuaded to persecute its members a decade later, during the Cultural Revolution.

Sonam was a member of the aristocracy, now in her late sixties. We had only just begun talking when there was a sudden noise on the stairs outside her room. Sonam looked afraid. Like many people of her age, she had a child servant, a rosy-cheeked village girl with a shaved head, who planned to become a nun. The girl was sent out to intercept the noise, but the door opened and a wild-eyed man came in, carrying a sack. He had long hair, gold-capped teeth and a rustic air. He turned out to be a young cousin of Sonam's, from a farm near Gyantse, who had come to Lhasa to sell the skull of a revered old monk. The skull was taken out of the sack, and passed to each of us in turn for inspection.

I noticed that it contained dark, dried matter, and passed it on. After a long discussion, Sonam decided that her nephew should take the skull to a monastery near the river, where the monks might want to use it as a receptacle for offerings during religious rituals.

Another of Sonam's relatives was away in a nature reserve collecting *pi-mo*, a small grey seed which was believed to be good for the lungs. So far he had collected two kilos in a month, but Sonam said that he should have collected four. *Pi-mo* sold at US$18 a kilo. Another friend was off in search of a peculiar Tibetan phenomenon, the *yar-tsa gun-bu*, or summer-grass winter-insect. This curious creature is a caterpillar which is consumed by a fungus at certain times of year, and turns into a grass-like stem. The *yar-tsa gun-bu* is greatly prized by the Chinese, who use it as an aphrodisiac, and it is only found at high altitudes.

When the man with the skull had left and the child servant had produced tea and biscuits, Sonam Dorje went on telling me about her life. She came from a minor aristocratic family, and as a young woman in the early 1950s had willingly embraced the Communist Party. Her class background later led to persecution and imprisonment. Only in the 1980s was she rehabilitated.

There was a fluidity of character to Sonam, a theatrical quality which initially made me suspicious of the things she said, with her rings flashing and arms waving, dragging deep on a cigarette. But after cross-checking some of the things she had told me, I felt that her account of the past was reliable. It was clear from the freedom with which she offered current political gossip that she now felt unconstrained. She spoke of the risks she was taking in seeing me, but she did not go cold with fright as others had done when there was a sudden, unexpected noise. I realised that either she was completely fearless, or more likely that she had some sort of protection within the current hierarchy in Lhasa.

Sonam was unbreakable, a survivor. There was nothing destroyed about her. There was one old man I came to know while I was in Lhasa, with a beautiful face and eyes full of pain, who concentrated on making tea and keeping his room neat. The making of tea and the maintenance of order were his handholds, to pull him through the day. He had spent over twenty years in a labour camp. He spoke to me about it once, about the friends he had watched die, but because his experience was so distinctive, I knew that I could not risk writing about it and identifying him. His face had a look of serenity that came after suffering, and he did seem happy, in a way, happy that the life he had now was so much better than what had gone before.

Sonam was different. Anger was her response to the past. When she spoke about the way her sons had been neglected while she was in prison in the 1960s, she glowed with rage and distress, sitting there cross-legged on her high bed, wrapped in a striped blanket, furious, a photograph of sleeping kittens on a low table beside her.

She began by talking of her early enthusiasm for the Party.

'I was sent off to college in Beijing because they thought I was a dedicated student. My Chinese was very good, so I was given a job as a radio announcer, making broadcasts against the Soviet Union. There were great opportunities for a woman like me at that time, although looking back, I realise that no women were ever allowed to reach positions of real power.

'When the Communists first arrived in Tibet, I thought that they had lots of wonderful new ideas about how to develop our country. Without them, I felt we would have been stuck in the dark ages, while the rest of the world progressed. I was very idealistic, and I wanted the best for my people. I married a Tibetan, from a similar background to myself, while I was in Beijing. We had three children. Later, I was asked to translate propaganda materials into Tibetan, including the political thought of Mao Zedong. That was regarded as a great honour. My husband died young, and I was left a widow. I feel numb when I think about those days. I feel that the middle years of my life were stolen.

'When the Cultural Revolution began, I already had political problems. A member of the exiled Tibetan nobility in India had published a book which made a complimentary reference to my late husband's family. When this was noticed by people in authority in China, we came under suspicion and my family was targeted. I was shifted from my job in Beijing, and became a teacher of languages at a college in Lhasa. I remember in 1966 that the whole of the city was covered in Chairman Mao's writings.

Everywhere you looked, you would see his words and phrases – on posters and banners, in books, everywhere. It was a cult, as if he was a deity who had to be worshipped.

'My downfall came in such a strange way. I was trying to be helpful. I didn't want to be accused of not endorsing the attack on the old ways. So I wrote the Tibetan and Chinese script for the big posters at the college. I had always been good at calligraphy. On one poster, I had to write "*Mao Zhuxi Wan Sui*", or "Long Live Chairman Mao". I had done the Chinese characters, but when I was doing the Tibetan words, and was writing the letter "*shi*" – as part of the word "*dhu-shi*", which is the nearest pronunciation we have to the Chinese "*zhuxi*" – a student told me to hurry up. He started to pull the poster away. Some of the excess ink from my brush ran down onto the poster.

'When I was having lunch in the canteen later that day, some students came up and yanked my hair. They said that because of my bad class background I had deliberately smudged the letter "*shi*", to insult Chairman Mao. I didn't know what they were talking about. I was told that I had "crossed" his name. In China, when prisoners have been executed, their names are crossed and displayed on a public notice to show they have been killed. So the crime they were accusing me of was a very bad one. At first I didn't even know what they meant, and when I understood, I explained that it was an accident, and that someone had tried to take the poster away before I'd finished and that I'd spilt some ink.

'I was made to kneel in front of the poster for four hours. Then I was taken for interrogation. The leader of the Red Guards in our district questioned me. At the end, he said there were "bad elements" in our society who had "the hat of counter-revolution" at the level of their knee, and others who had it at the shoulder, but that my crime was so serious that the hat should go straight on my head. It was a label that stayed with me until the early 1980s. He said I had a bad attitude, and that I would have to be "placed under the supervision of the masses". I was given a real white paper hat, which had "COUNTER-REVOLUTIONARY SONAM DORJE" written on it.

'I was taken back to the college and dragged through the

corridors wearing the hat. I was told I had lost my job as a teacher. For the next two days I was made responsible for cleaning the toilets, and given raw grain and raw vegetables to eat, and tea with no salt. On the third day, a meeting was convened to denounce me in the college hall. There must have been around two or three hundred people. I was pulled up on the stage, and the students came up and slapped and abused me. I was wearing the hat saying "COUNTER-REVOLUTIONARY SONAM DORJE" all that time.

'Most of the students were young nomads and farmers' children who had been brought to the city for education. Looking back, I know they didn't fully understand what they were doing. I still see some of them from time to time, when I go out walking in Lhasa. I don't bear a grudge against them, but I do feel bitterness against the leaders who told them to do it. I feel such anger I can hardly speak to you about it. Some of them are still there in the Party, in senior positions, making their fortunes.

'The students had to come up to me one at a time, and shout out a particular phrase, such as, "Sonam Dorje is an aristocrat and she is not happy with the teachings of Chairman Mao! She is a secret supporter of the Dalai Lama and the old ways!" Or it might be, "Sonam Dorje exploited the people and now it is her turn to suffer! She has crossed Mao's name, and now she will pay for it!"

'That was only the start. There were similar *thamzing* sessions two or three times every week. The Red Guards were angry with me because I refused to say I'd crossed Mao's name on purpose. I hadn't, so I wasn't going to lie. It was an accident. I had to eat different food from everyone else, and to clean the toilets every day. After another few weeks, when I still refused to admit my crime, the Red Guards cut off my hair. Like most Tibetan women, I had two long plaits. They cut off one plait, but left the other one so that I could be pulled on and off the stage during struggle sessions. I was not the only one who was targeted. Many people were persecuted at that time.'

Sonam began to talk about the senior Party leaders in Beijing, and how they had suffered. I wanted to get back to her own story, and asked how long her persecution had lasted.

'It stopped in the summer of 1968.'

'But you said it began in late 1966.'

'That's right.'

'You were struggled like that by the Red Guards for a year and a half?'

'Yes. Several times a week. Sometimes it seemed like it was every day. That's what things were like at that time. The whole society had gone mad. After a while, things fell into a routine. There were maybe a dozen people at the college who were labelled counter-revolutionaries, so I was one of the crowd, being struggled and told to reform our thoughts. They would dredge up things that I had said months before, or even jokes I had made, to try to find incriminating evidence against me. They always said they were "digging" my past to discover what else I'd done wrong.

'During the first couple of months I lost all hope, and I wished I was an inanimate object, like a tree or a stone, rather than a sentient being. I thought seriously of suicide at that time, but I knew it would have a bad karmic influence for me. But I admit that I was constantly hoping for death, hoping that someone would go too far during a struggle session and I would die.

'Finally, I confessed that I had "crossed" Mao Zedong's name on purpose. I hadn't, I promise you, but I just couldn't go on any longer. Soldiers from a PLA unit arrived at the college. They were Chinese, from the north-east. They had no connection to Tibet, and were totally different from any soldiers we had seen before. I feel so angry when I think about them. They were criminals, brutes. They came to the school and formed a committee which stayed at the school for several weeks. There were perhaps thirty soldiers. They made a lot of preparations for a big *thamzing* session. Everyone was told it was going to be special, with Red Guards coming from all over Lhasa.

'When it began, they ordered me to say I'd smudged the poster on purpose. I still refused, saying I'd done it by accident. They were all standing below the stage, holding their guns, watching me. Then one of the soldiers pointed his gun right at me and began shouting and screaming. He said that if I made a confession, my punishment would end, but that if I refused, I was going to be shot, as other counter-revolutionaries had been shot. I thought I was going to die, so I made a confession. Afterwards I did not know what to feel. I lost my mind. They said I had been reformed. After that I was sent away, out of Lhasa, to a prison camp.

'I remained there until 1981. I did not see my children for six years. They were looked after much of the time by an old family servant, who was a good friend. When the Cultural Revolution was at its worst, she was targeted too, so she had to let them go. My children were left to run free and live on the streets, out in the cold. They had to beg for food. At one point they were taken into a communal nursery, but they were expelled when it was discovered their mother had been awarded "the hat of counter-revolution".

'I've been told that sometimes people would take pity on them and give them food or shelter, because they knew they were my boys. My friends put themselves at great risk by doing that. The worst time was when I was still at the college, going through the struggle sessions, and I would hear snippets of news about my children. There was nothing I could do, nothing I could do to help them, nothing.'

When stories of the topsy-turvy cruelties of the Cultural Revolution began to leak from the sealed society of the People's Republic of China and across the Himalayas, many Tibetan refugees, and nearly all foreigners, assumed they were exaggerated. Tales of the Jokhang being smashed by schoolchildren, or women being dragged around a stage by a single plait because they refused to confess to imaginary crimes, must have sounded like inflated, McCarthyite propaganda. It was only in the early 1980s, when Tibetans started to be allowed to travel to India, that the full horror of what had happened became apparent.

I found some of the stories of this time so bizarre that I would have had trouble believing them, had I not heard them from the mouths of credible victims. There was one man, from a former noble family, who told me of the events that had led to him spending three years in a hard labour camp. He was entirely apolitical, and not very bright, and even now he could not comprehend what had become of his life.

One day in 1965, when he was sixteen, he and two friends had been using a toy balloon gun to shoot lighted candles. One of the pellets missed a candle and hit a nearby picture of Lenin. The three boys felt nervous about having damaged the picture, so they burned it. A year later, when the Cultural Revolution was underway, one of them confessed at a public meeting. The boys were immediately taken out of school and sent to a labour camp for three years, to be taught a 'class lesson'. I asked the man whether he thought the Red Guards had simply found a pretext to victimise him. He was adamant, as Sonam had been when I asked her a similar question, that it was the action itself – burning a picture of Lenin, crossing Mao's name – that had caused the problem. The frenzied ideological atmosphere of the time meant that the slightest error, particularly from a 'serf-owner', would be construed in an irrational way.

In Sonam's case, it was clear that intransigence and refusal to submit had been at the root of her continued persecution. Confession and self-criticism remain an important part of the Chinese legal system, and her insistence on her innocence worked against her. When I thought back over the things that Sonam had told me, I could not escape a feeling that, as a survivor, she represented only a part of what had happened in the 1960s. She was strong, and had possessed the self-discipline, the stubbornness or the nerve to come through the period of inversion. The accounts I missed were those of the weak and irresolute, the broken, who had seen death as the only escape from the torment of living. This was the underside of the resolution of the survivors: the knowledge from personal accounts that there were innumerable people who had chosen suicide or insanity – mental abdication – as a way out of the communal madness that surrounded them.

I spoke to a man who had been at the Tibetan Minority Institute near Xian during the Cultural Revolution. He told me of his teachers' reaction to persecution: how one man was struggled so constantly and savagely by members of a group calling itself 'Proletarian Vanguard' that he jumped from the top of a building. It was a traditional reaction, the Chinese scholar's response to injustice. The building was too low; he survived, crippled, and later hanged himself in his bedroom.

Let him that loves me, strike me dead.

Not I.

The other accounts I missed, an aspect of history that has been left to one side as unsuitable, were those of the pioneers, the dedicated Party workers who went to Tibet in the 1950s to spread Communism, until the rug was pulled from under them by the Chairman during the Cultural Revolution.

I had met one such pioneer, Mr Wang, on the train from Xining to Golmud, amid peanut shells and jars of green tea, heading to Lhasa on an annual visit to his son. He was erect, gaunt, separate from the other passengers in his austere dignity and his age. His clothes were plain, his hair was clipped short, his trouser legs were rolled and he was wearing brown sandals with lacy white socks, which would have looked camp in any other context. He was friendly but cautious, and instinctively suspicious of what I wanted to ask him. We met by arrangement some months later at his home in an enclosed compound for retired cadres in Beijing, where he spoke fairly frankly about the past.

Wang Zhanpeng was an idealist, that was clear. He had made no money from devoting his life to the service of the Communist Party. His home was a simple fourth-floor apartment: a bedroom, a bathroom, a living room and a kitchen, all painted a peeling pale blue. His wife, Fang Luo, a former soldier, lived with him. Between them they had US$360 a month. Around the living room, the room for greeting visitors, with its balcony where the sunlight streamed in, were medals and scrolls and awards, the symbols of his professional achievement.

Our conversation reminded me of interviews I had done with retired officials of the British Empire. Mr Wang had the same old-fashioned dignity, the dedication of purpose and commitment to the ideal he had served, overlaid by an unspoken sense that he had been overtaken by history, that somehow he had let down the ideal, or maybe that the ideal had let him down. This was far from what I had expected, that the conquerors of Tibet should turn out to be likeable old men rather than arrogant sadists; but after meeting Wang Zhanpeng and several others of his generation, it started to make sense. They had been on an unwanted civilising mission, and it had gone badly wrong.

Mr Wang's family were from the north-east of China; his father had died young, and his grandfather, an office worker and sports enthusiast, was the breadwinner. As a young man, Wang Zhanpeng was angered by the corruption and ruthlessness of the Guomindang regime and, together with other students in his school, became involved with the underground Communists. In December 1948 there was a police raid on his home, but his mother managed to hide his subversive books and he was not arrested. A few months later, with the Reds victorious, he gained a place at the Oriental Institute in Beijing. The city was resurgent after the Japanese occupation. Mr Wang was young and idealistic, waving a flag as the People's Liberation Army marched into town and the People's Republic was proclaimed by Mao from the Gate of Heavenly Peace in Tiananmen on 1 October 1949. The Chinese people had stood up.

Having learned Tibetan at the Institute, Wang Zhanpeng was a perfect candidate to join a new work team that was setting off for Tibet, setting off for the liberation. There were social and natural scientists, Party ideologues, teachers and even a handful of Tibetan Communists such as Dorje Tseten, a young man from Kumbum who went on to become a leading figure in Tibetan politics. Mr Wang described the process of going to Tibet, and the excitement he had felt. He had his first flight in an aeroplane, a long journey into Sichuan by car and truck, and spent days walking in inadequate sports shoes until the team reached the fringes of Kham. They crossed the Jinshajiang, the Gold Sand River, in a goatskin coracle, some of their horses being swept away by the current. The team arrived, eventually, late in the autumn of 1951, in Chamdo in eastern Tibet.

Mr Wang's job was to help begin land reform by setting up a group to spread propaganda in the surrounding villages, and to 'explain and teach' the benefits of Marxism-Leninism. He had to win over local leaders, including nomad chiefs. The process was slow. He compared it to a river sweeping over a rock, saying that only after plenty of water had flowed did people start to think in a new way. His aim was to bring Tibet forward, out of the dark ages, and construct a modern, scientific, Communist society where feudal prejudices and superstitions would disappear. Repeatedly, he emphasised that old Tibet had lacked factories and heavy industry. In the past, the ruling dynasties and the Guomindang had merely hurt and exploited the minorities; it was time to repay that debt.

When the spring came, he and his band of Chinese pioneers trekked through to Lhasa, taking five weeks, pushing up into white mountains and down into dust-blown valleys, enduring altitude sickness, sudden snow melts and long marches over uneven ground. Mr Wang was amazed by the agility and resilience of the Tibetan guides who led him into their land, thinking, at the crest of a pass one day, that it was as if they came from a different species. Sunburnt, possessing little more than they could carry on their backs, the group reached Lhasa. He laughed as he recollected the pleasure he had been able to give Tibetans by greeting them in their own language.

He thought this a good omen, for he had plenty to teach them. Wang Zhanpeng remained in Tibet, on and off, for the next forty-five years. He translated patriotic songs for dance troupes, wrote material for newspapers, was sent to China as a Party delegate. He set up five new schools, and ended his career running a Party institution in the Tibet Autonomous Region. Crucially, this being China, where endorsement and connections are all, he had sponsors within the hierarchy who helped to smooth his rise and break his fall at times of political upheaval.

Initially, Party workers were restricted by the need to set a good example, but in the early 1960s he moved into a proper house. The problems began in 1965. All Mr Wang would say was that he did not know how to describe it, and that for ten years he had been out of a job. He returned to the subject by sticking out his arms at me and holding his wrists together as if he was being handcuffed.

He was in prison for two months, and after that was restricted in every way. In prison, at least he knew where he stood. At other times, all he had was the constant drip of fear, waiting for what might be about to happen. There was surveillance and supervision, which lasted for years. The worst thing was the anticipation. Mr Wang could speak of his fears to no one except his wife, Fang Luo. They whispered when they were alone.

When the Party in Lhasa broke into two factions, the Gyenlog and the Nyamdrel, he lost the protection of his boss, and a group of Tibetan Red Guards came to charge him with 'taking the capitalist road'. To this day, he did not know what they meant. He held his head as he said this, his mouth collapsing in at the memory. Angrily, he asked a rhetorical question. 'What does it mean when someone is taking the capitalist road? It means they think their own thoughts. Nothing more.' They took him to a public struggle session. He tried not to show his fear. When the charges were read out, he repeated over and over to his accusers, 'Show me the facts, show me the facts.' But this enraged the Red Guards. They told him they had no need of facts, and that he was condemning himself by his bad attitude. He was obviously a capitalist roader, who wanted Tibet to return to the feudal serf system. They made Wang Zhanpeng stand up and bend over, touching his toes for several hours in front of a crowd, while they decided what to do with him. He was sent to prison, then put under house arrest, and it was not until the 1970s, almost ten years on, after representations were made on his behalf in Beijing, that Mr Wang's name was cleared.

Despite this, all this, his view of the last fifty years of Tibetan history was overwhelmingly positive. He told me what he termed a 'herdsman's joke'. A Tibetan nomad was asked if he liked the Communist Party. 'Yes,' came the answer, 'I like the Communist Party. It has built such good roads that now I can go to Lhasa and visit the lama temples.' Mr Wang was laughing at himself as he told the joke, but for him the Great Leap and the Cultural Revolution were aberrations, blips on an otherwise constructive record. Feudalism had been abolished, Tibet had been brought back to the motherland and numerous roads, workshops and factories had been built. Life expectancy had soared since 1950. Deng Xiaoping's shift to a market economy had helped people emerge from poverty. In the long term, even if it took a hundred years, a pure Communist society would arise. He did not say how this would be likely to happen; and I realised that it was merely a slogan.

At the end of our meeting, Mr Wang gave me a short homily about the solidarity of the nationalities. I felt he had been saving this up. He said that many of his closest friends and colleagues were Tibetan. When one of them had heard that he had been killed during the Cultural Revolution, he came to Mr Wang's office, weeping, and was overjoyed to find him alive. It was one of his happiest memories, he said, the knowledge that a Han and a Tibetan had been so fond of each other, like brothers.

I went back to see Wang Zhanpeng one more time, puzzled by the philosophy, or the view of life, that had persuaded him to maintain his faith in the Party. At its simplest, he was a man who had cleaved to a strict ideological code in order to retain his sanity. To renounce the faith would have been more painful than to continue. Leading the structured life of a cadre, with its emphasis on discipline, duty, obedience and, most importantly, implacable loyalty to the work unit and the Party, he had always seen himself as a cog in a larger machine. It was too much, perhaps, to expect him to question the virtues of the machine itself.

I asked him where it had come from, his sense of duty. He was baffled, initially, which made me wonder if it had been a meaningless question, given China's long reverence for collective conformity. Mr Wang, being old-fashioned, being courteous, his voice rising in pitch at the end of each sentence and his face flattening as he concentrated, tried to offer an answer.

When he was a child, the country had passed through the chaos of the warlord era, the harsh control of Chiang Kai-shek, the brutal persecution by Japan and the disastrous, enduring civil war between the Guomindang and the Communists. There was a sense in the late 1940s that further disorder had become inevitable, that chaos was permanent. He spoke of his grandfather and his mother at this time, his father dead, and the importance of the Confucian ideal to them. Confucianism, an amorphous concept, more a form of social conduct than a religion, was at the root of how his family lived. Tradition, scholarship, ritual, respect for authority, social order, filial obedience – these were the values they believed in, and they were concerned that social tradition was being swept away by disorder. Although neither his grandfather nor his mother explicitly backed the Communists during the civil war, and were nervous of the risks Wang Zhanpeng took in doing so, they gave him their support.

Looking back, he saw Confucianism as the bedrock of his upbringing and education, as it had been for Mao Zedong. (The difference, which he did not articulate, was that Mao was temperamentally a wrecker and a rebel in a land where conformity was prized.) So for Wang Zhanpeng as a young man, Communism did not represent so much a vehicle for revolutionary disruption and the overthrow of society as a means of re-establishing order. He was suggesting that Communism at this time was attractive not simply for its social vigour and its newness, as it was for those who embraced Marxism in other countries, but for its conservative possibilities, the prospect that it could bring China stability and a return to traditional values. Although many Confucian temples were destroyed during the Cultural Revolution, the continuity of the old ways of thought remained.

The corollary, which I found too awkward to suggest to Mr Wang, but which stayed with me long after I had left his apartment, was that the absolute disruption of that time may only have been possible in a nation which prided itself on the subordination of the individual, and viewed the idea of loyal opposition as anathema. Mao had used the obedience of the Chinese people to shatter them.

NINETEEN

Tibetan attitudes towards sexuality have traditionally been relaxed. Virginity was not prized as highly as in neighbouring countries, like India and Nepal. Back in the thirteenth century, a passing Armenian king, Hetum I, reported optimistically that 'They are temperate in their food and in their marriages. They take a wife at twenty, and up to thirty approach her three times a week, and up to forty three times a month, and up to fifty, three times a year; and when they have passed fifty, they no longer go near her.' More recently, polygamy and polyandry have excited the interest of passing foreign travellers.

Tibet's informal approach came in part from Buddhism's comparatively lenient strictures on sex outside marriage, and also from the cultural prominence of Tibetan women, who were not expected to cover their heads and be demure. A journalist who accompanied the British invasion of Tibet of 1904 worked himself into quite a lather on the subject, reporting that:

> The moral standard of the Thibetan is not high; licentiousness and indecency, far from being uncommon, are rather the rule than the exception. The women are especially erring; their extreme laxity of morals and their utter want of shame are not more remarkable than the entire absence of jealousy or self-respect on the part of their husbands and relatives.

Despite this unconstrained past, the present Dalai Lama has explicitly condemned many sexual acts, whether heterosexual or homosexual. In 1999 he stated: 'I am a Buddhist, and, for a Buddhist, a relationship between two men is wrong. Some sexual conduct in marriage is also wrong . . . For example, using one's mouth and the other hole.' His adamant stand on sexual morality is close to that of Pope John Paul II, a fact which his Western followers tend to find embarrassing, and prefer to ignore. The Dalai Lama's US publisher even asked him to remove the injunctions against homosexuality from his book *Ethics for the New Millennium*, for fear that they would offend American readers, and the Dalai Lama acquiesced.

In the past, Tibetan Buddhist monks often took the Clintonian position that non-penetrative sex did not count as sex. At his home near the Barkhor, Tashi Tsering told me a story of his time as a member of a ceremonial dance troupe in the 1940s. A *dob-dob* or warrior monk had kidnapped him in full view of his friends by a house below the Potala, and taken him as a sexual partner. *Dob-dobs* lived outside normal monastic rules, and were renowned for their aggressive behaviour. They exercised discipline in the monasteries, and would paint rings around their eyes with soot, curl their hair and smear it with butter. They maintained order with the help of a curved blade and giant monastery keys, which were swirled like a martial-arts flail. Since this particular *dob-dob* was notoriously fierce and carried a long knife, nobody could do anything. After a few days, Tashi managed to escape.

As a dancer he had known that he was a target for predators, so the kidnap was not a great shock; but he was angry that the authorities allowed such things to happen. Although Tashi was not homosexual, he was at the time already in a pragmatic relationship with a monk-official. He did not love the older man, but was happy to be his partner, since he knew it would help to further his career. They had intercrural sex, like the ancient Greeks, with Tashi usually being the '*drombo*' or 'guest', as was expected in such relationships. The Japanese traveller Hisao Kimura recorded an encounter with an amorous monk in the 1940s, who told him that apart from any religious prohibition, oral or anal sex 'would be distasteful in a land where toilet paper and bathing were equally unknown, and he explained to me that it is the boys' thighs that provide the necessary friction. The

Mongolians liked their boys front-side up, the Tibetans back-side up.' Looking back, Tashi Tsering said that he viewed the sexual practices of old Tibet as a matter of habit and convention, the socially accepted result of people exploiting loopholes in religious regulations.

In 1950, Communism introduced a new, puritanical edge to Lhasa. Half a century on, that austerity had dissipated and prostitution was booming. Aided by Tibet's traditional cultural tolerance, sex had become gruesomely commercialised. In the past, women who worked in drinking houses and *chang* shops were often sexually available, sometimes for money, but they were closer to hostesses than prostitutes. Party officials in Tibet, far from the supervision of Beijing, were allowing free enterprise in its rawest form to flourish. The selling of sex, like the selling of building permits, minerals and timber, gave easy profits. There had been efforts to curtail the trade, but so far they had come to nothing. A statement on Tibet Radio in 1998 acknowledged that 'since most of the premises used for prostitution are rented property belonging to the Party . . . the first step in the campaign against prostitution must start with . . . effective supervision of the use of the properties rented out'.

Sections of the Lingkhor, Lhasa's outer pilgrims' walk with its shrines and temples, were the new red-light district. Literally hundreds of brothels, each with a blue glass front and a curtain across the door, lined the route. Chinese hookers, mainly from Sichuan and Qinghai, sat in the doorways knitting or combing their hair. Posters of Indian movie stars were stuck to the windows to give a sense of foreign glamour, the most popular draw being the luscious Bollywood actress Madhuri Dixit. The sex trade was controlled by Chinese gangs, who had secured local political protection.

Prostitution was ethnically segregated, and there seemed to be few Tibetan hookers. I went to meet Droma, who worked in a bar in the small Tibetan stretch of Lingyu Chang Lam. She was wearing a grubby *101 Dalmatians* T-shirt and stretchy black trousers. Her face was flat and broad, a country face. The building called itself a bar, but was really only a hut which sold beer. There was a painted cement floor, and the walls were covered with patterned paper, streaked with mould. A poster showed a couple hugging over a bowl of sugar-pink roses. The bar had a table and some chairs, and a tiny plywood cubicle at the back, with a bed in it. Four women, all Tibetan, were expected to work there.

As Droma and I started talking, the owner of the bar, a beefy middle-aged Chinese woman from Qinghai in a purple trouser suit, appeared at the door. I expected her to throw me out, since foreigners are forbidden from entering Chinese brothels under the country's strict laws against sex with aliens, but she was full of smiles, seeming to take my presence as a mark of the establishment's distinction. She said that Droma and the other women used to charge up to US$28 for sex, but since a police raid they now usually settled for US$12. I suspected the prices were being exaggerated for my benefit. They gave the owner half of their takings. This was the usual deal in Lhasa, although some of the Chinese hookers were employed directly by 'businessmen', who rotated them through brothels in western China. In Lhasa, the women serviced the large population of soldiers and migrant workers who were based in the city.

Droma was twenty-three, from a village near Zorge. She spoke in a strong Amdo dialect. Her family were farmers. She had come to Lhasa on a pilgrimage, because she wanted to see the city and its temples, and had worked as a kitchen assistant before beginning to sell sex a year ago in Shigatse.

'It's fine here,' she said. 'I don't mind it. What else can you do if you are poor and have no money? People say Lhasa has become like Bangkok, but I've never been to Bangkok so I wouldn't know.'

I asked her whether she had much contact with the Chinese prostitutes.

'I can't talk their language and I wouldn't know what to say to them if I could. I don't like the look of most of them.'

'What about your clients, where are they from?'

'I don't know. Most of them are liars. Many of the regulars are truck drivers. They drive the route from Lanzhou or Chamdo, and out to western Tibet. They come in groups, four at a time, because they know there are four girls here.'

'Are most of them Tibetan or Chinese?'

'I wouldn't have sex with a Chinese man.'

'Why not?'

'In my village you would never marry a Chinese man, or a Muslim. I would never have sex with a Chinese or a Muslim. Some of the girls would, but I wouldn't. No way, however much they paid.'

I took this to be a political decision, a nationalist's boycott of sex with the oppressor, but as we spoke I realised this was not what Droma meant. Her objection was a social and cultural one, based on the old prejudice of Amdo Tibetans against their ethnic Chinese neighbours, and more particularly against Chinese Muslims.

'It's against our custom to have a relationship with people like that,' Droma said. 'Nobody from my village would have sex with them. People like that are different. They eat different food, and they have different personal habits.'

Droma had the expected dream of the future.

'I'm not staying here doing this for much longer, only another four or five months. I'll save what I can, and then go home to my village to get married. I've not found a husband yet. I want to go back while I'm still in good health, not like the older women here who start drinking and get ill. I could never tell my husband what I've been doing here in Lhasa. A man wouldn't understand, would he?'

Alongside the many karaoke bars and brothels of Lhasa, tucked away, are *nangma* bars. *Nangma* was traditionally a dance performed for the Dalai Lama and the nobility, but has become an important part of Lhasa's new, improvised cultural identity. I visited several, and rarely saw a Chinese, and never sensed fear.

At a *nangma* near the Potala I met people of all ages, dancing and singing together, forgetting themselves, laughing. Mothers and daughters swept across the dance-floor in ballroom style. The atmosphere was a cross between that of a nightclub and a live concert. The room was large, decorated with red lightbulbs,

UV lights and little coloured flags, like prayer flags. There were kitsch pictures: melting telephones, shiny glasses of wine, stylised horses galloping through surf. An elegant waitress in a tight *chuba* filled my glass, handing it to me in a deferential way, without eye contact, and filling it again when I had drunk. This was a performance, done in a courtly, old-fashioned way, a reminder of the Tibetan past.

At the front stood a microphone, with a backdrop of thick, richly coloured drapery. Anyone could go up and sing, and be garlanded with *katags* if the song was well-received. A musician would come on with a flute or a *drab-nyen*, the Tibetan stringed instrument, and play a tune as a woman sang and danced, moving her arms and legs vigorously while keeping her torso stock still, in the old way. Almost all of the women wore *chubas* topped with a modern fitted jacket. Occasionally, someone sang a Chinese song. One man sang about mountains and lost love while wearing the uniform of a PLA soldier. Nobody minded.

When the singing was over, a large screen was carried to the centre of the room to show DVDs of pop videos. The crowd enjoyed this even more than the live singing. Mournful, evocative, romantic songs – some with an unexpected techno beat – joined images flashing up on the screen: pine trees, a bird in flight, mountaintops, grazing yaks, women looking glamorous in elaborate Tibetan jewels or doing folk dances in front of a painted backdrop of the Potala, scenes of snow and ice, sunlit monasteries, *mani* stones, a newborn baby in a nomad's tent, running streams, a waterfall. The images were beautiful, but the visual effects that accompanied them were crude, with pictures randomly rolling, folding and inverting. Many of the songs were by Chinese artists, extolling the beauty of Tibet; others were old Tibetan songs, sung with Chinese words by Tibetan singers. There was no cultural purity here, but there was great enjoyment.

Coming back from a *nangma* one evening past lines of scurrying rats and the inevitable street fight, which would end in reconciliation as quickly as it had begun, I felt that I had seen a moment of rare ease. I had watched Tibetans enjoying an alluring version of their own land, with no subversive implications. *Nangma* gave them an opportunity to embrace everything Tibetan, without risk. It was a way for the citizens of Lhasa to feel at home, to remember their past safely, with no political danger.

I got back to the Hotel Raidi to find a plainclothes PSB officer waiting for me in the lobby. The receptionist was nervous, avoiding my eyes. I knew that the hotel had been under surveillance for some time. There had been an ostentatious inspection of the guest register by officials from the tourism department a few days before.

'Do you have a camera?'

'No.' I had thought it safer not to bring one to Tibet.

'You have an electronic brain?'

'A what?'

'Electronic brain. Computer laptop.' His fingers tapped an imaginary keyboard.

'No. No laptop.' I had thought it safer not to bring one to Tibet.

'You have audio equipment in the hotel?'

I wondered why he was asking. I knew that his officers had been in my room a few days before, and would have seen whatever was there.

'No, I don't.'

He wrote down each answer carefully in a small notebook, and went away.

It was time to move. The next morning I departed for western Tibet on the first bus.

TWENTY

I decided to go as far west as I could, towards Mount Kailash, without joining an official tour group, which would involve restrictions and supervision. Leaving Lhasa, I was pickpocketed for the first time ever. There were three Tibetan boys clumsily shoving their way up the aisle of the big white public bus, but by the time I had realised what they were doing they had melted away. As we drove out through the city, down the straight roads, round the roundabouts, beneath the Potala and past the giant golden yaks, it occurred to me that had I been in any other city in Asia, I would have been guarding my wallet closely. I did not expect to be pickpocketed in Tibet.

The bus carried no Chinese, only Tibetans, wearing wide-brimmed hats and dark glasses, with baskets of food and thermoses of tea. They were prepared for the journey to last all day, maybe longer. Sweets and dried cheese were passed up the bus, to be shared. A little boy with toothache was given a cigarette to smoke, and some of the ash was rubbed on his gum while a cold stone was held to his cheek to ease the pain. His mother, random brown teeth escaping from her own mouth, sang to him, cooing gently.

The road ran alongside the river, which had worn its way low into the valley, with a rush of brown water coming fast from the high cliffs above, splashing along the road and over the field on the far side of the river, where the ground was pale green with patches of grass.

We stopped at a small settlement. Tea and noodles were being served from mud and straw shacks. The bus and lorry drivers, all of whom were Chinese, rolled up their trouser legs and crouched behind their vehicles, smoking vigorously. The Tibetans from our bus settled down to picnics or lay in the sun. As we were preparing to go, some soldiers came in a truck and told the drivers to stay where they were. The road was going to be closed for several hours. An army convoy was expected, and the officers did not want it to be seen by the masses. There had been a military exercise in the west of Tibet, to coincide with a rare visit to Tashilhunpo, Shigatse's big monastery, by the Chinese-appointed Panchen Rinpoche.

We waited and waited, and after four hours, during which I appeared to be the only person who was put out at being kept waiting, we heard the rumble of vehicles crossing a bridge in the distance. We all crowded up to the edge of the lorry park to get a view of the winding road below. Broken bottles and rubbish were strewn across the hillside. The soldiers ran up and told us to get back, but they gave their orders so half-heartedly that nobody took any notice.

A small green truck emerged finally from a rolling cloud of dust, followed by a snake of green vehicles which wound its way through the rough landscape, heading towards Lhasa. By the end I had counted twenty-one trucks, six four-wheel drives, eight lorries with long trailers, five missile launchers (their canvas coverings flapping loose), an army fuel tanker, a bus and a crane. As the bus, filled with PLA soldiers, passed by, some big stones happened to roll down the hillside and smash into the side of it, making a large dent and breaking a window. The Tibetans who were with me laughed so much when this happened that I thought they were going to be sick.

We came to lush, irrigated pasture, and stretches of yellow corn and black buckwheat or *dru-nag*, which grows a deep pink colour and turns dark brown as it ripens. When it was nearly dark we drove round the edge of the Yamdrok Tso, one of Tibet's great 'wrathful lakes', shaped like a scorpion and inhabited by powerful spirits. I could see the shimmer of distant turquoise. It was said that the lake gave spiritual power to the Tibetan nation, and that if it ever dried up the people of the Land of Snows would die. Several monasteries were sited near it, including Samding, the seat of the Dorje Phagmo or 'thunderbolt sow', one of the only female *tulkus* in Tibet, who in her present incarnation had thrown in her lot with the Communists and become a member of the 'patriotic upper strata', like Lhalu and Phagpala.

Reaching the town of Gyantse by night, it was not easy to find a place to stay. I tried the Hotel Clean Cheap, which was dirty and overpriced, and the Hostel of Gyantse Town Furniture Factory, which strangely had no beds, before settling on the Hotel Chan Da, which was filled with criminals, hookers and businessmen, who sang karaoke through the night. Gyantse had a strong Chinese presence. There were two wide muddy streets, with tractors and trucks and motorbikes parked down the middle. At one end, below the towering fort or *dzong*, was a stagnant, polluted lake with a bridge leading to an incongruous bright-red Chinese pagoda, recently built.

One morning I walked up to the huge fort, a long way up, past grinning Tibetan children who clapped as I passed, presuming that I would take their insult as a compliment. The fort had been built on the top of an imposing outcrop of steep red rock, and had been the site of a major battle during the British invasion of 1904. This had given the Gyantse authorities an opportunity to create a museum of sorts, 'THE MEMORIAL HALL OF ANTI-BRITISH'. It contained shoddy relief sculptures of battle scenes, with unintelligible captions, and a long English text painted on a wall:

Tibet is a inalienable part of the motherland. In order to safeguard her unification and unite with every national-ity. Tibetan people one stepping into the breach as another fell ... The British took border matters as an excuse. Yanghusband acted as an envoy and [General] Mcdonald commanded a modern armed troops of about 10 thousand invaders to launch the second invading war in December 1903. After the Thirteenth Dalai Lama issued a conscription order the monks and laymen from every parts of Tibet enthusiastically respond to the call ... To safeguard the sacred territory of the motherland those heroic Tibetan people added an immortal chapter to the annals of anti-invading wars . . .

After the leader from both sides arrived at a dam in Chomik Shingko, introduced each other, and the British troops withdrew the cartridges from bore of guns for showing sincerity of negotiation, and Tibetan troops must to die out the fuse's fire of Tibetan style guns. The Tibetan troops' leaders ordered to die out the fire, at once, but British Army moved troops to encircled Tibetan positions secrety . . . Latingse Dekbon's bodyguard Zhundun found the plot and shouted wrathful, 'They are to kill our per-sens' and he pulled out his chopper cut to death more than ten British soldiers including the British Army-following reporter Edwand Chadler . . .

In this bloody battle, Tibetan soldiers and militias had to withdraw their troops for the reason of lack of reinforcements, but the drive of British troops frustrated and had to cry out in alarm: 'What things can urged Tibetan offensive forward? Actually they were not fear. There isn't any people who looked die as gone back as they did in this world.' British troops trop on crops, set five on the house owned by citizens and also plundered valuables.

The hopelessness of the Communist interpretation of Tibet was all there, in the adjusted facts, the broken language, the shoddy sculptures, the reworking of a half-understood local legend of British duplicity in an attempt to link Tibetan history to modern Chinese nationalism.

I went back down the hill, and after waiting on the edge of Gyantse by the cement factory, watched by Chinese migrant workers with flat-bladed shovels, got a lift with a man and a woman along the road towards Shigatse. If all went well, I would reach the city the same day. There were donkey carts making their way slowly into Gyantse with fresh produce to sell at the roadside market, whole families sitting on the back. Further up, barley was being crunched by a stone roller pulled by a horse on a leading rein. The road was lined with potholes, and we passed a gang of road-menders dressed in stained, ragged PSB waistcoats.

I was travelling in the back of a roll-top four-wheel drive with no suspension, sitting beside a giant saucepan of fermenting barley. We stopped at a typical central Tibetan farmhouse: a farmyard hemmed in by slates to make a pen for horses, yaks, cows and sheep. Potatoes and spinach grew, fed by little irrigation channels which ran off a stream. Above us on a rock face were painted Buddhist symbols and mantras. The farmhouse had a space at ground level for the animals, and a steep metal-lined ladder up to the living area, animals and people close in together, with prayer flags on the roof.

The owner of the house was an old woman, a family friend of our driver, who had pink gums and no teeth. She pressed as much of everything on us as we could eat and drink, refilling our cups constantly. We were given *chang*, butter tea, dried cheese on a string, honeycomb and lumps of rock sugar. There was an old monk there too, with a turned-down moustache and a gold brocade waistcoat, who sat very still with a wet flannel on his head. He drank from a special cup embellished with silver, while the rest of us had ceramic bowls, with a smear of *tsampa* on the side. There were bits of straw around the room, as well as carpets and cushions on a raised dais. The walls were painted with traditional symbols, making the room feel like the inside of a nomad's tent, with the padlocked trunks and boxes to one side.

Being in this house felt good, an idyll, with the amiable smell of burning animal dung and a sense of great, earthy, rustic simplicity. Outside, below a red-green mountain, barley was being harvested fast by hand, men and women singing, hooking up the base of the stems as they cut. When we left, our driver presented the old woman with a gift of a fresh, fatty sheep's leg.

We were now only two hours' drive from Shigatse, and as we headed north-west through the flat, bare, rocky landscape, I thought of the optimistic portrait of the city found in the writings of early European travellers.

George Bogle, a young Scottish official in the service of the East India Company, went to Shigatse in 1774. He found the Panchen Rinpoche 'rather inclining to be fat' (like his twentieth-century reincarnation) and very generous, presenting the visitor with a purple *chuba* lined with Siberian fox skins, a yellow satin cap and a pair of red silk Bulgar hide boots.

> He received me in the most engaging manner. I was seated on a high stool covered with a carpet. Plates of boiled mutton, boiled rice, dried fruits, sweetmeats, sugar, bundles of tea, sheeps' carcasses dried, &c., were set before me and my companion, Mr Hamilton. The Lama drank two or three dishes of tea along with us, but without saying any grace.

Bogle, who seems from his writing to have been an affable, outgoing man, felt an immediate liking for his host:

> His disposition is open, candid, and generous. He is extremely merry and entertaining in conversation, and tells a pleasant story with a great deal of humour and action . . . I never knew a man whose manners pleased me so much, or for whom upon so short an acquaintance I had half the heart's liking.

George Bogle was the first British visitor to reach Tibet, sent there from India by the governor-general Warren Hastings on a 'commission for opening a free intercourse between the inhabitants of Bengal and Tibet'. His visit had been arranged after correspondence with the Panchen Rinpoche's court in Persian, the state language of Mughal India. The Eighth Dalai Lama was at that time in his minority, and the Lhasa government was not willing to deal with the envoy for fear of offending China. The British, like the Chinese, were trying to play on the intermittent rivalry between the courts of the Dalai and the Panchen, the two most eminent *tulkus* in the Gelug hierarchy. The nexus between the two leaders has always been tricky, and ripe for exploitation. Both lamas were spiritually powerful, although the Panchen's temporal control was limited to the area around Shigatse. Crucially, whichever one was the elder was expected to be the religious initiator and guide to the younger, and to help in the identification of his reincarnation. In the 1770s, with a powerful Panchen and a juvenile Dalai Lama, the balance of influence was tipping in Shigatse's favour.

Although Bogle had only limited success in promoting trade between India and Tibet, he was able to gain important new political and geographical information, as well as to record unusual social customs in this distant land, such as the practice of women having several husbands. He coined the word 'polyandry' six years before the first recorded usage in the *Oxford English Dictionary* when he wrote, 'I am at a loss for a name to the other custom, unless I call it polyandry.'

Unlike his more strait-laced successors, Bogle married a Tibetan wife, Dechen, who may have been related to the Panchen Rinpoche. They had two daughters, who were sent to Scotland for their education. Bogle died at the age of thirty-four; Dechen's fate is uncertain, although it is possible that she lived on in Calcutta into old age.

His journey provided useful intelligence, which he reported to Hastings:

> Two Chinese viceroys, with a guard of a thousand soldiers, are stationed at Lhasa, and are changed every three years. The Emperor of China is acknowledged as the sovereign of the country; the appointment to the first offices in the state is made by his order, and, in all measures of consequence, reference is first had to the Court of Peking; but the internal government of the country is committed entirely to natives; the Chinese in general are confined to the capital, no tribute is exacted, and the people of Tibet, except at Lhasa, hardly feel the weight of a foreign yoke.

Bogle depicted Shigatse as a gathering point for Buddhist Asia. He came across Nepalese and Kashmiri merchants and clerks, Mongolian and Manchurian monks, Hindu pilgrims and ascetics, Khambas from the eastern fringes of the Tibetan world, and even Turkis, Kalmyks and Siberians.

Tibet was at this time far from being the isolationist kingdom it became in the nineteenth century: by Central Asian standards, both Lhasa and Shigatse were cosmopolitan. The rapid expansion of British power into the Himalayas would later cause Tibet to close its doors and turn exclusive. Between 1835 and 1865 the British Empire would gain control, mainly by indirect means, of Darjeeling, Tawang, Lahaul, Spiti, Ladakh, Sikkim and Bhutan. The historian Dawa Norbu has written that 'the real reason for Tibet's isolationism and Tibetan anti-Western phobia was the perceived threat that British imperialism in South Asia appeared to represent to the territorial integrity of Tibet if not to the whole Lamaist world . . . Westerners were projected and portrayed as a diabolical threat to the survival of Tibetan religion and the political system that sustained that religion.'

The Panchen Rinpoche in 1774 was a substantial figure, and his world a relatively sophisticated one. Life happened on a grand scale in Shigatse. The Panchen's return to his monastery Tashilhunpo after a trip away was met by a crowd of locals and three thousand monks, 'some with large pieces of chequered cloth hung upon their breasts, others with their cymbals and tabors, were ranked next the palace. As the Lama passed they bent half forwards, and followed him with their eyes. But there was a look of veneration mixed with joy in their countenances which pleased me beyond anything,' wrote Bogle.

The warm tone of the relationship between the Panchen Rinpoche and his visitor, and the stress on social interaction in Bogle's account, sets a marker for later encounters between envoys of British India and eminent Tibetans. Bogle's remark that a senior Tibetan official had told him the Chinese were 'a base, treacherous, and scoundrelly people' (quietly emphasising a common bond between Europeans and Tibetans against the Chinese predator) might easily have been found in the writings of the 1920s or thirties. When the Panchen Rinpoche met a British diplomat in Peking in the 1930s, he told him that they had met previously when he came to stay at Shigatse. The diplomat, who had never visited Tibet, was perplexed, but discovered later that he bore a striking physical resemblance to George Bogle.

The writings of Bogle and other travellers had given me a certain expectation of Shigatse, so it was a shock when I arrived there. There was no sense of impetus, as there had been in Lhasa. The city was resolutely depressing. From a bridge by the river I could see a Chinese settlement stretching away to the south, physically distinct from Tashilhunpo and the ruins of the old *dzong* on the hill. It was hard to see where the old Tibetan city had been. When I reached it, jolting on the back of a hand-cranked tractor through the banana smell of exhaust fumes, there were shops selling onions and cheap plastic goods, and a few sides of sheep hanging in doorways. The streets had the rancid, cheesy stench of poverty. The physical difference between the two sides of Shigatse was manifest: at the Tibetan end there were potholes and puddles and half-destroyed buildings, and there had been no electricity for two days; at the Chinese end there were hotels, shops and restaurants, and the electricity was working.

I spent some time trying to get permission to go further west, towards Mount Kailash. I visited the PSB office, then went to the CITS office, and then went back to the PSB office, where the staff, all Chinese and seemingly with little to do, finally gave me a permit for Sakya and Lhatse. I was not on any blacklist. A photograph of the new child Panchen Rinpoche hung on the wall. The caption said, in Tibetan and Chinese, 'Bring benefit to the nation and to all sentient beings', and at the bottom was Jiang Zemin's signature, with the sentence 'Designed by Tibet Autonomous Region Propaganda Department'.

At Tashilhunpo, where there had been violent suppression in 1995 after the monks opposed the selection of this fake Panchen, I found an atmosphere of fear. The monks seemed to be little more than ticket collectors, and none of them wanted to talk. Their job was to deal with the busloads of Chinese tourists, cheerful with their suits and cameras, who came to look at the monastery. It was rumoured that many were not monks at all, but spies.

Shigatse felt wrong. There were too few Westerners for me not to be conspicuous, and I knew that foreigners had in the past caused problems here. It would be safer if I moved on immediately. Inside a temple at Tashilhunpo, filled with the sweet smell of burning butter lamps, an enormous Maitreya with almond eyes and long gold cheeks looked down at me impassively. Buddhist deities tended to have this reassuring, imperturbable look: watching, turning you back on your own resources, but not judging. I returned to the roadside to wait for a lift out west.

TWENTY ONE

Sheep herders came by, black with grime, and then a donkey caravan, but no vehicles. Finally, a big yellow truck stopped. The driver was Tibetan, a thickset man named Lama in a canvas waistcoat and black slip-on shoes. He had driven all the way from Chamdo, taking over a week, carrying drums of kerosene roped together. We slid and slipped our way out towards the west on bald tyres. It seemed an unnatural way to travel through Tibet, by truck, on a route blasted around the edges of mountains, cutting precariously through rock.

Up ahead, five lorries were stuck in deep mud, and the road had disintegrated entirely. All you could see were pools of mud and water, and impromptu rivulets coming through breaks and gullies. Finally one of the trucks moved, tipping at an impossible angle, as if it must topple over, and then with a roar it righted itself and drove forward. A road gang of Chinese labourers appeared with picks and shovels, and began to dig out the next vehicle. Ahead, a low-axle truck pushed, skidded, turned, sank into the mud, rocked, jerked, stopped, stalled, started, had a length of metal rope attached to it, was pulled free, stopped and started until, as if by some act of will, it rose from its crater and edged on. In the river far below lay the remains of two fallen trucks.

Every hour or so we would reach a checkpoint, a line of soldiers manning a rope across the road. Lama knew where they were, and as we approached I would put on his hat, dark glasses and an anti-pollution face mask, as he had instructed, and slump sideways as if I were sleeping. We were waved through each time with no trouble. Vehicles here generally travelled in fours, like London buses, the drivers keeping an eye out for each other.

We hit a mud slide. The road was not there. The truck slithered, the brakes locked, we slid very, very slowly down, and as we neared the edge of the cliff – a small cliff, but enough to set the lorry rolling – we stopped. Lama said a prayer, smiled at me, stuck out his tongue and laughed as if it was all a game. Slowly, he reversed.

As the sun went down the land became a deep red, and the mountains turned to shadows. We had averaged about eight miles per hour over the day. We stopped at a small Tibetan settlement on an open plain, where there were huts and stacks of empty beer bottles. The people were amazed by the sight of me, a foreigner, and came out to stare. Children in ragged clothes, snot dripping down their faces, poked me to check that I was real. Lama and another truck driver produced a plastic container of *chang*. The food was basic: a bamboo basket of congealed lamb bones and a container of bread, and some lumps of bright yellow butter. A woman in a *chuba* boiled up the butter with tea and salt over a dung fire, joking, flirting, gold teeth flashing, a conch shell strapped to her wrist and a pair of battered trainers on her feet. Dogs came and went, skulking, hoping for a bone.

When I had drunk some tea and people had got used to the idea of me, I was asked the same questions over and over, the same questions that I had been asked whenever I met rural Tibetans, who were far from information. Did I know anything about Kundun, the Presence? Had I seen him? Was he safe? Was he in good health? Would he ever come back to Tibet? I answered yes to each question, with a heavy heart. There was nothing else I could say.

In the morning we drove over the Tsho-la, a high pass, the engine straining, the road falling away. We stopped to release block-printed prayers on the summit. The escarpment was massive, fields stretching out below us, mountain sheep visible in the distance on hallucinogenic patches of red and purple rock. Lama dropped me at a crossroads in the middle of the spreading, exposed landscape, where a few tiny sheep were grazing off scrubby bushes. I waited for a long time, nervous that I would be stuck there overnight. Finally I heard an engine coming. A Land Cruiser rumbled slowly towards me. It contained a pair of government workers, one Chinese and one Tibetan, with cropped hair and bull necks. After long discussion, and advance payment, they agreed to take me.

The two men were delivering computer equipment to remote villages. I pointed out that the villages had no electricity, and so would not be able to run computers. They laughed and agreed, but said they were bringing the computers anyway. They had been allocated to the villages. One of them repeated a well-known propaganda slogan to me, although I could not tell if he was trying to be amusing. 'Without the Communist Party,' he said, 'there would be no emancipation or liberation of the Tibetan people.' The computers sat in the boot, stacked up in their fresh cardboard boxes. Every official here had a scam, a way to get by and get on.

The Land Cruiser was new, and it rose in and out of rivers and passed through the mud easily. Even the tyres were new. The driver went fast, to impress, spinning the vehicle in the mud. Dangling from the rear-view mirror was a picture of Chairman Mao, heavy with braids and tassels. They dropped me at the turning for Sakya, the great monastery that was the capital of Tibet in the thirteenth century, when the country submitted to the Mongol empire.

I had to walk the last few miles to Sakya, wilting in the sun. I could see distant *chortens*, or pointed monuments, on the hillside, wandering yaks and horses, a river with dams to prevent flooding of the fields, a turf and rock stockade around a barley crop to protect it from the rising water, and snow mountains far away. The land was marshy. A woman with a folded umbrella tied to her back trampled clothes in a stream, watched by children. A sheepskin *chuba* was in the water, weighed down with a large stone, rinsing itself. I was followed at a distance by the children, until they went off to persecute a yak, seeing if they could hit its horns with a thrown stone and jump on its back.

In the town of Sakya, dung patties were stacked along every wall, covered with brushwood to keep off the rain. There was an empty official building flying China's national flag, topped by a satellite dish. I found a place to stay. Outside, an aluminium-coated scoop focused the sun to a point on a stand, boiling a kettle with solar power. An outdoor pool table stood nearby, being used by monks with chunky watches and more hair than monks are meant to have. Nearby there were sheds containing a disjointed generator, and drums of oil. In the evening, after several false starts and lots of black smoke and cacophonous noise, lights came on, so dim that you could see only the outlines of things and people. But it was electricity, for three hours. The weather became very cold that night.

I was the only foreigner in town. The next day a wizened old man in a baseball cap saying BOY LONDON came to stare at me. Four young men, with braided hair and trilbies, were flaying sheep by the grain depot, smoking cigarettes while they worked. They peeled off the fleeces easily, like peeling the skin off an orange, using a pair of daggers, one short, one long. The sheep flailed as if they were alive. There was a metal tub filled with blood, and the air was filled with the smell of the blood. Children dressed in rags, with tousled hair and speckled cheeks, played in the puddles. One girl wore shoes made out of a biscuit packet. A slaughtered cow was hanging from a hook, for sale. Before long, only the head was left.

Old men with turquoise earrings and high leather boots circled the monastery, holding rotating prayer wheels. The walls of the monastery were grey, marked with red and white stripes in the Sakya tradition. Prayer flags flew from sticks at the corners of the building. The central part of the monastery had high ochre walls, and behind it across the river were hundreds of derelict buildings from the days of destruction, the Cultural Revolution.

Inside the monastery, I went up a steep metal ladder to a tiny, dark chapel, with an uneven floor and low wooden beams, where monks were chanting and young boys were carrying butter and tubs of *tsampa*. Rice and banknotes were stuck to the deities. An old monk sat cross-legged on a cushion reciting page after page of scriptures, a low, constant, soothing chant, a torch and a thermos by his side. An opening in the thick wall, like an archer's slit, let in a bar of light, enabling him to read. In the darkness I could make out *katags*, *thangkas*, ferocious masks and butter sculptures, all crammed together. There was a sense in the little chapel of something timeless, that had kept Sakya going for centuries, regardless of the violent intermissions. I felt that this was a remote, independent place, a place that was used to running its own affairs and did not want outside assistance.

Down in a chapel by the main courtyard, I watched as a sick child was brought in by his mother. An old monk was summoned, and came and blew on the boy's face as a blessing. Then he touched his temples. The mother passed the monk a rosary; he blew on it too and passed it back. She told me that another monk in the monastery licked affected parts of the body, including growths and open sores, to cure them.

There were eighty-eight monks now, rather than the thousands there had once been. Most of the temples exhibited pictures of the head of the Sakya sect, the Sakya Trinzin, the leader and divinity who lives in exile, and is a close religious colleague of the Dalai Lama. Unlike the head of the Gelug, Kagyu and Nyingma sects, the Sakya Trinzin lineage passes from father to son, or from uncle to nephew, with the position alternating between two distinguished families. I had listened to the current Sakya Trinzin at a conference centre in England. He was a lacklustre performer, despite his high religious reputation, and I found it hard not to compare him to the Dalai Lama. At the end of his talk, having blessed a long line of pulsating Western disciples, he had walked off the stage, unaware that his radio mike was still open. 'Was that OK?' he asked the organiser. 'Yes,' she said, 'but you forgot to ask for donations for our new Dharma centre.'

There was one Chinese restaurant in Sakya, run by a friendly family from Sichuan. While I was in there eating noodles one afternoon, watched through an open window by a crowd of Tibetan children, a four-wheel drive drew up outside. Vehicles were a rare sight here. It carried four Chinese tourists from Guangzhou – a husband and wife who worked for Siemens and Otis, dressed in bright yellow anoraks, with two friends. Travelling with them, for reasons that never became clear to me, was a small man from Kazakhstan called Bolat, who said he was a professional boxer. The Chinese couple had been waiting to come to Tibet for years, saving up so they could travel in style. They had a romantic view of Tibet, similar to that of many Westerners. 'We are not accustomed to the food, but we have always loved the idea of going to Tibet,' the woman told me. 'It's a mysterious, magical land, a sexy place to visit.' They had brought a catering pack of pineapple pastry rolls with them all the way from Guangzhou, six hundred rolls in all, which they now distributed in handfuls to the waiting children.

I pressed on towards the west, getting a lift first on a local tractor and then on a truck which carried crates of beer. In the town of Lhatse, which I reached late at night, my hotel room had a wrinkled red carpet and the heavy quilt on the bed was so damp it felt slimy. In the morning a cleaner threw rubbish, dirty water from the bowl on the washstand, plastic bottles – everything – out of the window. Lhatse was another invented town, a giant truck-stop, neither Tibetan nor Chinese, consisting of a long street, an open drain running down either side, with trucks and prostitutes at one end and shops and hotels at the other. Guarding the town were official buildings, constructed in the familiar way from blue glass and white tiles.

A few months after I had left Tibet, I read a report about Lhatse in the *People's Daily*, an example of the crudity of Chinese state propaganda:

> Tibetan wizards have felt that their time-honoured job is becoming less attractive because the government is introducing modern technologies into the area. For thousands of years the wizards managed major things in a village, especially, when they were said to be able to prevent hailstorms by reciting Buddhist scripture. On most occasions the method failed to work, but villagers, many of them illiterate, continued to employ them as guardians because they had no other choice. The situation changed in 1998 when three meteorological rocket launchers were purchased by the Lhazi county government of Tibet

Autonomous Region. For the first time, Pusha village and Nam village, which were very famous for witchcraft in the county, have survived hailstones and saw bumper harvests. The excited villagers were more practical than dogmatic. The next year they bought twenty-four meteorological rocket launchers at their own cost and operated them with the help of county technicians. The wizards now face unemployment for the first time, and many of them are considering changing their profession.

On my second evening in Lhatse I met a party of Japanese students, with Sherpa guides, who had come all the way from Kathmandu with Land Cruisers and a big lorry. We began drinking together. The hotel restaurant was decorated with a faded poster of a young Tom Cruise. The PSB officials in Lhatse were drunk, so drunk they could scarcely talk, and I quietly joined the party of Japanese students as a fellow traveller. Their minder, drunk too, did not notice, but I knew my time in western Tibet was running out. After a day of hard driving we reached Saga, and I remained unseen. The next morning we set off for Zhongba, which was only a day from Mount Kailash.

One of the Japanese students told me that she had fallen in love with a Tibetan monk, a young exile, while she was in Kathmandu. I thought once again of the Sixth Dalai Lama, Tsangyang Gyatso, the poet with rings on his fingers and braids in his hair, dressed in blue silk, who had sung songs and wooed lovers in Shol, beneath the Potala.

> White crane!
> Lend me your wings,
> I will not go far, only to Lithang,
> And then I shall return.

The Sixth Dalai Lama gave teachings in parks instead of monasteries, and refused to take his final initiation vows as a monk. Although he was living in the early eighteenth century, at a time of religious revival, he declared that he would spend his life as a layman, singing the lines,

> Longing for the landlord's daughter,
> Blossoming in youthful beauty,
> Is like pining for peaches,
> Ripening on the tall peach trees,

Yet his status as a means to realisation, as the living representation of Avalokitesvara, or Chenrezig, the Buddhist deity symbolising compassion, remained unquestioned, so that when he wrote the lines,

> I have never slept without a lover;
> Nor have I spent a single drop of sperm,

with its Tantric implications, it was a claim that his people could believe, and still believe.

The Thirteenth Dalai Lama had talked frankly about Tsangyang Gyatso to the British diplomat Charles Bell, saying:

> He did not observe even the rules of a fully ordained priest. He drank wine habitually. And he used to have his body in several places at the same time, e.g. in Lhasa, in Kongbo (a province seven days' journey east of Lhasa), and elsewhere. Even the place whence he retired to the Honourable Field (i.e. died) is uncertain; one tomb of his is in Alashar in Mongolia, while there is another in the Rice Heap monastery [Drepung]. Showing many bodies at the same time is disallowed in all the sects of our religion, because it causes confusion in the work. One of his bodies used to appear in the crowd in the Reception Hall of the Seventh Dalai Lama. One is said to appear also at my receptions, but I am unable to say whether this is true or not.

The Tuscan Jesuit priest Ippolito Desideri, who visited Lhasa while the Sixth Dalai Lama was alive, depicted him as 'a dissolute youth, addicted to every vice, thoroughly depraved, and quite incorrigible, because of the blind veneration and stupid faith of the Thibettans. Ignoring the sacred customs of Lamas and monks in Thibet he began by bestowing care on his hair, then he took to drinking intoxicating liquors, to gambling, and at length no girl or married woman or good-looking person of either sex was safe from his unbridled licentiousness.'

This was a prurient, Christian reaction to the Buddhist tradition of a wild, intoxicated saint being able to break conventional boundaries in order to attain spiritual liberation, reaching back to the 'crazy wisdom' of figures such as the uninhibited yogi Drukpa Kunley, who when asked by a follower, Apa Gaypo, for a prayer to strengthen his religious resolve, answered:

> Drukpa Kunley's penis head may stick,
> Stick in a small vagina,
> But tightness depends upon the size of the penis.
> Apa Gaypo's urge to gain Buddhahood is strong,
> So strong,
> But the scale of his achievement depends upon the
> strength of his devotion.

The strange thing was that I now wondered whether the rebellious, liberated saint, the odd one out among the Dalai Lamas, may after all have written the prophetic song about Lithang. Michael Aris had thought the Sixth Dalai Lama was unlikely to have been the author of 'White Crane', but other experts on the subject were unsure whether this was right.

Per Sørensen had told me that he thought the song may have been composed during the Sixth Dalai Lama's lifetime, possibly by the Dalai Lama himself, or by members of his entourage, or maybe by one of the drama troupes which were using his life as a theme for performance. The fact that such songs were not recorded in written form did not make them spurious. Sørensen thought there might still be private diaries of the Sixth Dalai Lama in the Potala, hidden away, which would one day clarify the point. Heather Stoddard was more circumspect, answering my queries about 'White Crane' with a query: 'Do you think that any songs can be safely attributed to him without a signed document?' Hubert Decleer, another expert, thought that the songs could have been compiled by a contemporary of the Sixth Dalai Lama, and that he may have lived on after his supposed murder by Mongol soldiers near Kokonor Lake in 1706. His 'secret' biography detailing a later life may not then have been,

as Aris believed, a fake. So the Sixth Dalai Lama, in this interpretation, had a second life, a hidden life, as a wandering pilgrim in
India, Nepal and Amdo.

I wondered now whether this theory, like so many aspects of
Tibet's history, could have been something more than a version
that was hard to dislodge. Memories of the past seemed to be so
fluid, and it was exhilarating to think of the Sixth Dalai Lama
travelling across Asia, living as he liked, while the world believed
him to be dead.

According to the secret biography, he died in Alashan in
southern Mongolia in 1746, in a place which is now part of
China's 'Inner Mongolia Autonomous Region'. His spirit passed
to a boy named Lobsang Thubten Gyatso, and an alternative
reincarnation line known as the Dwagtrul Lamas or Kundrol
Tulkus descended through the abbots of an obscure monastery,
Barun Hyt in Alashan. In 1906, the Russian explorer Pyotr Kozlov
met the incumbent of Barun Hyt, who was 'forty years old and
distinguished by his moral purity, spirituality and clear mind'.
The last known incarnation was called Gegeen of Barun Hyt, who
probably died in 1958. Since then, the trail has gone cold, but
it is possible that the real – or fake – reincarnation of the Sixth
Dalai Lama may today be living in Mongolia, biding his time.

TWENTY TWO

In the twentieth century, it took less than forty years for Tibet to win and lose its independence.

The century began with the Thirteenth Dalai Lama ordering his people to say prayers for the protection of the nation ('100,000-verse Prajnaparamita; various Transcendent Wisdom Scriptures . . .') but his country was soon threatened by the arrival of unfathomable modernity on its borders. The British Empire had invaded. The decision by the viceroy of India to send an expeditionary force to Lhasa in late 1903 was one of the more baffling moves of the late colonial period, with no clear motive but indelible repercussions. The official reason for it was that Tibetans were refusing diplomatic correspondence, rustling yaks, destroying boundary pillars on the Sikkimese border and ignoring the terms of a Sino–British treaty. The real reason was that the hawkish viceroy, Lord Curzon, and his man on the spot, Colonel Francis Younghusband, both believed (wrongly) that Czarist Russia had taken control of the Dalai Lama's government.

Following a bloody military campaign in which the British and their Indian mercenaries killed nearly three thousand poorly armed Tibetans, the army reached Lhasa, only to find that the Dalai Lama, the embodiment of the Tibetan state, had fled. Younghusband cobbled together a treaty with the remnants of his government, stipulating that the British would have the right to station trade agents in Tibet and occupy the Chumbi valley in the south-west of the country for up to seventy-five years, while a large indemnity was paid off. With the failing Qing dynasty unable to offer protection, the negotiators had no choice but to accept these terms: one Tibetan chronicler wrote that they were 'as helpless as if the sky had hit the earth'. The Chinese response to this indignity was to press for renegotiation of the treaty. Conscious of the larger implications of strategic over-extension, the British government backed down and disowned Young-husband. The indemnity was reduced, the Chumbi valley abandoned and Chinese suzerainty (a nebulous term implying, but not accepting, sovereignty) over Tibet reaffirmed.

The invasion served to stimulate China's fears about predatory foreign expansion. After wandering in Mongolia and Amdo and giving religious teachings at Kumbum monastery, the Dalai Lama was summoned to Peking for an audience with the emperor. His travels had given him the chance to develop an understanding of international politics, and when he arrived in Peking in the autumn of 1908 he knew that he was in a weak position. He had been formally deposed by the *amban* during his absence, and although this had been ignored by most Tibetans, he needed to reassert his status. To the anger of the emperor's court, he began to lobby for support among foreign diplomats and journalists, in particular the scholarly American representative William Wood-ville Rockhill.

Conscious of the fracture of the *cho-yon* relationship, the Chinese wished to reassess the status of Tibet. Although the Qing dynasty was collapsing, it paid close attention to the eminent visitor, aiming to diminish his prestige by a thousand cuts. The Dalai Lama was told to perform the *kowtow* before the imperial throne, but since no previous Tibetan ruler had made obeisance in this way, he refused and knelt instead, a compromise which left both sides unhappy. China's dowager empress awarded him a new title, which was designed to reduce his position and assert full Chinese control over Tibet. Rockhill advised him to accept the title in his country's long-term interest, but he appealed against it and departed with the issue unresolved.

The Dalai Lama returned to Lhasa, and less than a year later Chinese troops invaded, using the crimes of the British as their justification. 'There are in Tibet some wicked, aggressive foreigners,' one newspaper asserted, 'with whom intercourse has to be maintained.' The thirty-four-year-old Dalai Lama fled towards India, riding hard over the mountains as his successor would do half a century later. On the way, he sent desperate telegrams to 'Great Britain and all the Ministers of Europe' stating that 'large insects are eating small insects', a Tibetan way of saying that the strong were oppressing the weak.

In February 1910, he reached the embrace of the British Empire. Sergeant Luff, a Londoner who manned a telegraph office on the Sikkim border, was woken by knocking in the middle of the night.

> I said, 'Who the hell are you?' They, 'The Dalai Lama . . . One of the Tibs says, 'Here's the Dalai Lama.' I, 'Which blighter is the correct Dalai Lama? Yer all seem to think yer the Dalai Lama' . . .
>
> There was no mistake he had been very scared, and showed signs of great relief on meeting us and getting under our roof. He sat down in front of the fire. Except one, whom His Holiness told to sit down, the others all remained standing till dismissed; they wouldn't sit down in the presence of the Boss, even after their long day in the snow. After feeling better he looked round our office, finally settling in my bedroom, and after asking all about it and ourselves, asked if he might lie on my bed, a privilege I was only too pleased to grant. He saw I had a service rifle, and asked if we would give him protection if he was attacked during the night.

In India, the Dalai Lama was taken under the wing of Charles Bell, a Tibetan-speaking political officer who was to become a close friend and adviser. A visit to the viceroy soon revealed that although the British would give the Dalai Lama sanctuary, they would offer no political or military aid. After kicking his heels in Darjeeling, coining a Tibetan word for telephone ('ka par', or 'between mouths') and visiting Calcutta zoo, the Thirteenth Dalai Lama was saved from permanent exile by the reverberating fall of the Qing dynasty. He returned to Lhasa, expelled all Chinese troops and in 1912 proclaimed his country's freedom. It was the last time the Dalai Lama would be a guest of the British state until 2000, when, in a different body, he stayed the night at Hillsborough Castle in Northern Ireland with the minister Peter Mandelson, and toured Belfast in the company of 131 police officers, twelve of whom were wearing plain clothes.

Obtaining international recognition of Tibet's new freedom was a harder task than declaring it. A conference was held at Simla in 1914 between Britain, Tibet and China to clarify the Indo–Tibetan border, during which a distinction was created between 'inner' and 'outer' Tibet, the latter being the area under the control of the Lhasa government. China's nominal suzerainty was maintained, but significantly a new border was agreed which absorbed the birthplace of the Sixth Dalai Lama, the Tibetan region of Tawang (now Arunachal Pradesh), into India. This sharp coup was achieved by Bell and India's hawkish foreign minister, Henry McMahon, apparently without the knowledge of London, and was accepted by the Dalai Lama's representative, Shatra Paljor Dorje, either through naivety or the promise of future protection and assistance. A month later, the British secretly sold Tibet five thousand rifles and half a million rounds of ammunition. With virtually no outlay, the British Empire had placed the Dalai Lama in a position of fatal dependence on India, turning Tibet into a useful buffer against Chinese fragmentation or Russian expansion through Xinjiang.

There was one difficulty. China refused to sign the treaty – the Simla Convention – and in the words of the historian Neville Maxwell, 'stated formally, emphatically and repeatedly at the time that she would not recognise any bilateral agreement between Tibet and Britain'.

Despite its abortive status, the Simla treaty was used by the British as the basis for the development of a close, if deliberately ambiguous, working relationship with the Dalai Lama's government. The 'McMahon Line' became, at least on paper, the border between India and China. In the 1930s a senior British official in the Indian government, Olaf Caroe, took matters a stage further. The Simla Convention, having no validity in international law, was not included in British India's diplomatic bible, Aitchison's *Collection of Engagements, Treaties and Sanads*. In an act of astonishing duplicity, Caroe rectified this by arranging for a new edition of the relevant volume to be printed, with the missing text included, and for the new book to be surreptitiously substituted for the original in London's House of Commons library and elsewhere. India and China were to fight a Himalayan war in 1962, and their long border remains under dispute, with India refusing to accept China's reasonable assertion that the unsigned Simla Convention could not have redrawn an international boundary.

In the short term, the Chinese were too weak to challenge the might of the British Empire, and London had no interest in becoming too closely involved in Tibet. It was easier to try to run it by remote control.

After initial resistance from conservative monks at Drepung monastery, Charles Bell visited Lhasa at the invitation of the Dalai Lama in 1920. The invitation was accompanied by a gift of three dead sheep, two bags of rice, barley flour, several dozen eggs, a roll of blankets and a *katag*. Like many frontier officers, Bell had considerable personal sympathy for the Tibetans, and gave the Dalai Lama and his officials detailed advice about how best to defend their shaky independence. The aristocracy of Lhasa held banquets in Bell's honour, with one little girl recording that he had 'a red face, golden hair and a nose like a kettle spout'. He became known as 'Lonchen', the title given to senior Tibetan ministers. After spending almost a year in Lhasa, it was even suggested that he might be an emanation of the Ganden Tripa, a monk who had negotiated with Younghusband, and who had promised that he would be reborn as a foreigner in order to help Tibet.

Initiatives were taken to develop Indo–Tibetan ties. With British assistance, a police force was set up in Lhasa and a secular school opened at Gyantse. The school faced practical difficulties: hostility from local officials, a ban on the erection of new buildings (it would be inauspicious for the Dalai Lama's health) and outbreaks of both smallpox and syphilis among the students. When classes finally got started, the students learned geography, played football and read *Robin Hood*, *The Scarlet Pimpernel* and *The Prisoner of Zenda*. Monastic traditionalists were unnerved by this encounter with modernity, and after only three years the school was forced to close. The departing British headmaster saw such hostility as a bad omen, recording in his diary that the Tibetans would 'regret this decision one day when they are Chinese slaves once more, as they assuredly will be'.

Writing in old age from a position of long experience, Bell had no doubt that Tibet had been 'clearly independent' of China until 1720, and had now reasserted that independence. He had high praise for the Thirteenth Dalai Lama, seeing him as a reformer and strong leader at a time of political flux. Bell's perception of Tibetan society was far from the hell on earth depicted in later Communist propaganda: he reported that 'the Tibetan standard of living is higher than the standard in China or India, and the status of women in Tibet is higher than their status in either of those two large countries'. Like Thomas Manning a century earlier, he was shocked by the 'haughtiness and discourtesy' of the few remaining Chinese officials, and noted that even those who had learned Tibetan (usually from their mistresses, their wives being in China) 'would never speak it in public, for they looked on the Tibetans as savages, and their language therefore as degrading'.

The irony was that, despite his personal feelings, Bell represented a government which was precipitating a reassertion of Chinese power. British policy on Tibet was profoundly cynical, backing its aspirations for statehood – supplying weapons, training soldiers, sending envoys, promoting football and making treaties with this stateless state – while refusing to recognise it as an independent country. Such a strategy had unavoidable repercussions in a wounded, wartorn China. In July 1922, the month in which Wallace Stevens published the lines

> Let be be finale of seem.
> The only emperor is the emperor of ice-cream

the Chinese Communist Party, a fledgling organisation with fewer than two hundred members, which was shortly to produce its own emperor, mentioned Tibet for the first time. The Second Party Congress stated one of the Party's aims as being to 'establish autonomous rule in Mongolia, Tibet and Muslim Xinjiang to turn them into democratic autonomous republics'.

Seven years on, the CCP was still honouring the notion of democracy. Its manifesto vowed to 'overthrow imperialist rule in China', 'unite with the proletariat of the whole world' and 'unify China and acknowledge the right to self-determination of the Manchu, Hui, Tibetan, Miao, and Yao nationalities'. This policy was developed in the constitution of the would-be Communist government, which specifically mentioned the Tibetans and recognised 'the right to self-determination of the national minorities of China, their right to complete separation from China and to the formation of an independent state for each national minority'.

In 1933, a few months before the death of the Thirteenth Dalai Lama, the Communists' tone hardened. Angered by British meddling and worn down by the brutality of the Long March, Mao Zedong sent a telegram to an international conference against war and imperialism in Shanghai, stating, 'In western China, the British imperialists are making use of Tibetan forces to attack and occupy our Xikang and Sichuan provinces, and are preparing to turn western China completely into a British colony.' He went on to claim that 'England wants to set up a Tibetan state in western China.'

In the same year, a British official wrote in an internal report, 'Never in the history of Anglo–Tibetan relations has our prestige stood higher or the Tibetan attitude been more friendly.' But Mao's claim that the British were using Tibetan forces to attack western China was based on partial knowledge. A rumbling border conflict in Kham had recently come back to life, sparked by a battle between two Buddhist monasteries. One monastery was backed by the forces of a Chinese warlord, the other by the Tibetan army. When the fighting spread and Tibetan soldiers (possibly using British-supplied weapons) scored small victories, China's largely powerless Guomindang government in Nanjing reacted angrily, issuing a stream of propaganda claiming that British Army officers were organising the fighting. This was untrue, but it was understandable that the Communists might believe it.

As instability grew after the Dalai Lama's death, all parties to China's civil war made plans to stabilise Tibet. Although the

Guomindang had no influence in Lhasa, and only nominal control over most of Amdo and Kham, they still maintained a legal claim to Tibet. A Communist victory was now likely to mean an end to Tibetan independence. Liberation from the humiliations of imperialism was to become the main justification for an invasion. Mao believed that foreigners were subverting a part of the motherland with a view to turning it into a colony or client state. Although the British ridiculed this suggestion, pointing out that there were barely a dozen Europeans in Tibet, Mao's assumption was logical: a superficial knowledge of British policy in Tibet would give exactly this impression.

With the Second World War looming and Indian nationalism rising fast, the British in reality had no wish to become entangled any more closely in Tibet. They briefly considered protecting what they called its 'de facto independence', when the Foreign Secretary Anthony Eden wrote in 1943:

> if the Chinese Government contemplate the withdrawal of Tibetan autonomy, His Majesty's Government and the Government of India must ask themselves whether, in the changed circumstances of today, it would be right for them to continue to recognise even a theoretical status of subservience for a people who desire to be free and have, in fact, maintained their freedom for more than thirty years.

This passing notion of an ethical foreign policy was soon abandoned.

India gained independence from Britain in 1947, and despite Nehru's protestations of 'Hindi–Chini bhai-bhai' (Indo–Chinese brotherhood), his government happily inherited the mantle of the colonial state. Nehru told the Indian parliament that 'the McMahon line is our boundary . . . and we will not let anybody come across that boundary', despite knowing its dubious legal status. Hugh Richardson, Bell's successor as British representative, renowned for speaking perfect Lhasa Tibetan with a slight Oxford accent, was kept on by Nehru, and India sold Tibet new rifles, Bren guns, Sten guns, mortars, explosives and several million rounds of ammunition.

In October 1950, forty thousand Chinese soldiers invaded Kham. India stood aside and did nothing, nervous that China might question its own recent takeover of Hyderabad and Kashmir. The mild-mannered Richardson was denounced by Beijing as a 'vicious aggressor'. Robert Ford removed the crystals from his radio transmitters. Monks performed propitiatory rituals. Tibet was falling.

The government of the youthful Fourteenth Dalai Lama made an immediate urgent appeal to the United Nations in New York, describing the invasion as 'the grossest instance of the violation of the weak by the strong'. Given the lack of clear information about Tibet's legal position, Britain, the only Western country to have entered into treaty relations with Tibet, was expected to clarify the situation. In the new world order of the early 1950s, the Dalai Lama and his government were easily expendable. The British representative on the UN Security Council, Gladwyn Jebb, wrote with unnerving cynicism to London, 'What we want to do is to create a situation which does not oblige us in practice to do anything about the Communist invasion of Tibet.' To the bewilderment of the Tibetan government, Britain told a UN debate that nothing should be done, since they 'did not know exactly what was happening in Tibet nor was the legal position of the country very clear. Moreover, it could still be hoped that the existing difficulties in Tibet could be settled amicably by agreement between the parties concerned.'

Later, when the Dalai Lama had escaped into exile and the plight of Tibet was again debated at the United Nations, the British attitude was even less helpful. A resolution stating that China should respect 'the fundamental human rights of the Tibetan people' – which was backed by countries such as Canada and Australia – was not supported by Britain on the grounds that its own conduct in its colonies might be culpable. 'Once we concede that the Assembly can discuss and adopt resolutions about observance of human rights in particular territories,' an official noted in a confidential minute, 'we should not have a leg to stand on in the event of attacks on UK policy and activities in, for example, the Rhodesias and Oman.'

'The British government,' wrote Richardson, an upright and

restrained man, some years later, 'sold the Tibetans down the river ... I was profoundly ashamed of the government and continued to be ashamed at their unwillingness to recognise that Tibet has a right to self-determination.'

Sections of British society continued to offer support, in their own quaint way. Tsewang Yishey Pemba, a Tibetan doctor and novelist whose patients included many eminent *tulkus*, wrote in his diary after a visit to London in 1974:

I went to a function and met lots of Tibetan refugee friends. Familiar and unfamiliar faces everywhere. The creme de la creme of the Tibetan diaspora. Those who had done well. Now in the hub of the capital of the empire on which the sun never set. I met a *geshe* [doctor of divinity] who was married to an attractive English woman. She was pressing coins into his palm and instructing him in slow emphatic pidgin English as to which bus he was to catch home and how much was the bus fare. He appeared perplexed. He who had memorised for decades vast tracts of the Prajna-paramita and Nagarjuna's thesis on the emptiness of phenomena now overwhelmed by the bus-routes of Oxford Street. Husbands and daughters of the Raj mingled and ate *momos* and *shabalay* with the children of refugees. If only Tibet had been annexed as a British colony after the Younghusband Expedition of 1904, she might today enjoy the same status as India, Burma, Pakistan and Sri Lanka. The British that day tried to make amends in their own church jumble sales fete style, making polite consoling speeches. Sir Olaf Caroe spoke and so did others. The Tibetan national flag dominated the stage, her national anthem was sung and prayers for independence recited. Much sympathy and commiseration for poor Tibet. Such lovely days ... d'you remember the flowers at Dekyilingka? ... and the Tibetans ... such marvellous people ... really ... it's a terrible shame when you come to think of it ... the poor Dalai Lama ... what MUST he be feeling? ... dreadful.

There was even a raffle.

This nebulous support was the forerunner of the more ambitious, proactive Tibetophile campaigning in Britain at the end of the twentieth century.

With Lhasa under Chinese Communist rule and the Cold War developing, the US took over the role of Tibet's outside arbiter. American motives for involvement were no more sincere than those of the British had been. As part of the global struggle against Communism, the US wanted to destabilise the Himalayas by backing Tibetan irregulars, but without giving Tibet any serious opportunity of securing self-rule. It was understood in Washington that the resistance would have a nuisance value, but nothing more. This was not explained to the Tibetan fighters, who understandably thought that the Americans were trying to help them liberate their country.

Working closely with the Dalai Lama's elder brother, Gyalo Thondup, the CIA began to train Tibetan rebels in a highly secret operation on the remote Pacific island of Saipan, and later at Camp Hale in the Rocky Mountains in Colorado. Around three hundred fighters were taught the art of covert operations: sabotage, ambushes, sending coded messages, reading maps and laying mines. Then they were parachuted into Tibet by night from US planes, dressed in *chubas* and equipped with rifles, mortars, hand-cranked Morse radios and cyanide capsules to be taken in the event of capture. It was extremely difficult for these men to link up with the indigenous resistance movement, the Chushi Gangdrug, and only a handful survived. In the words of one of the few who made it, Bapa Legshay, the operation was 'like throwing meat into the mouth of a tiger'. The Chushi Gangdrug did achieve some small but significant victories over Communist forces. One of their most prestigious recruits was the former head of the PLA artillery in Lhasa, Colonel Cheng Ho Ching, who defected, and later went into exile in India, married a Tibetan and changed his name to Lobsang Tashi.

When the Dalai Lama escaped into the Himalayas in 1959, one of the US-trained fighters, Lithang Athar Norbu, was able to use a Morse radio to send a message to Washington asking for protection. The message was received late on a Saturday night by a senior CIA officer, who immediately put through an urgent call to his boss. Four hours later, the CIA's man in New Delhi sent a wire to Washington saying that Nehru would give the Dalai Lama and his entourage political asylum in India, and this message was relayed back to Athar in Tibet.

Athar, now a cantankerous old man living in a refugee camp in India ('Peace, peace, what is this talk of peace? Are the Chinese peaceful? I want to kill them') had described the moment to me:

> We were waiting for the Dalai Lama by a mountain pass. We had prayed, and taken advice from the deities. His Holiness looked very carefully at us, at our weapons and equipment. There had been an aeroplane drop and we had hand grenades, automatic rifles, charges for bombs, all that stuff. He particularly wanted to see the radio equipment, but we said it was hidden in the mountains. In fact, the men from the CIA had ordered us not to show it to anyone, as they wouldn't know how to use it, and when we explained this to His Holiness, he said he understood and that maybe it was better to show it to nobody, otherwise the Chinese might come. We transmitted the message, and His Holiness went to India.

In the 1960s the CIA changed tactics. Instead of training selected Tibetans in the United States, they set up a larger operation in Mustang, a mountainous spur of land that juts out of Nepal into southern Tibet. The plan was to arm groups of Tibetans with mortars, carbines and 55mm recoil-less rifles, with the aim of setting up guerrilla units and conducting raids inside Tibet. Declassified US intelligence documents show that the CIA was spending nearly US$2 million annually on this operation, and giving the Dalai Lama's private office around US$180,000 a year.

As rumours of the new Mustang base spread among the growing community of Tibetan refugees in India and Nepal, they began to make their way there in their hundreds, anxious to fight. This influx coincided with a ban on covert overflights by President Eisenhower – following the shooting down of a U2 spy plane over the Soviet Union in May 1960 – which meant that supplies could not be dropped to the rebels. The film-maker Tenzing Sonam, whose father Lhamo Tsering had provided the link between the Tibetan resistance and the CIA for nearly twenty years, described it to me as a 'terrible situation. There were more than two thousand people up in the mountains with nothing to eat. They were even boiling their shoes and eating the leather. People died. There was nothing my father and the other leaders could do, until later that year the Americans made their first drop of arms and supplies.'

The Mustang guerrillas were organised along the lines of a proper army, and conducted repeated raids into Tibet. They managed to place an intercept on a PLA radio mast, which provided crucial information for years to come. The most successful raid, near Zhongba on the Xinjiang–Lhasa highway in 1961, resulted in the capture of a significant haul of documents. Forty armed Tibetan horsemen ambushed a Chinese military convoy. 'The driver was shot in the eye,' one fighter, Acho, remembers. 'His brains splattered behind him and the truck came to a stop. The engine was still running. Then all of us fired at it. There was one woman, a very high-ranking officer, with a blue sack full of documents. This was carefully collected by our leader and taken back.' The documents showed the extent of the famine and unrest in China and Tibet created by the Great Leap Forward, and the seriousness of the Sino–Soviet split. Ken Knaus, a former CIA officer, has described the contents of the blue sack, a little optimistically, as 'one of the greatest intelligence hauls in the history of the agency'.

The Mustang fighters lacked the military or financial backing to establish a proper resistance force inside Tibet, and by the late 1960s the operation was mired in internal feuding between the CIA-trained generation of fighters and the original Chushi Gangdrug leaders. American support was gradually withdrawn, and the final blow came with President Nixon's *rapprochement* with Beijing in 1972. The Tibetans were no longer of any use to America, and could be discarded, as they had been by the British two decades before. On the orders of the National Security Adviser Henry Kissinger, all covert funding to the Dalai Lama's office and the resistance ceased. The Dalai Lama sent a taped message to the Mustang fighters ordering them to lay down their arms, but rather than surrender, many preferred to die. One man, a senior officer named Gyen Pachen, slit his own throat with a dagger, and Wangdu, the commander of Mustang, was shot dead in an ambush at the Tinker Pass by the Nepalese army while trying to flee to India. Tenzing Sonam had told me, 'These were men who had been fighting the Chinese since the mid-1950s, people who had grown up with guns and knives, being asked to surrender their weapons. It was the end of everything for them.'

Through these years of suffering and exploitation, the Tibetan people had to contend with a parade of foreign Communist sympathisers visiting Tibet from rich countries, and lauding the policies of the Chinese government. The writer Pierre Ryckmans, using the pseudonym Simon Leys, was the first to expose this phenomenon. In his book *Chinese Shadows*, published in 1974, he wrote of the fellow travellers

> who have come to China regularly for twenty years but have never, *never* taken a bus, or eaten a bowl of noodles at a corner stand, or shared a supper or an informal evening with a family or friends. Why take the bus, when a government car is always at their disposal? . . . These docile visitors – who would never have the bad taste to venture alone in the streets to find out how people live, who never go anywhere without their guide and their interpreter . . . fit superbly into the official plans. Their obedience is rewarded with free trips, which they repay by publishing articles or even books that pretend to describe China.

Tibet's physical isolation made it especially vulnerable to bogus reporting of this sort. Until the early 1980s, it was impossible for foreigners to visit at all without special permission from Beijing. This gave rise to such shameful works of misrepresentation as Israel Epstein's *Tibet Transformed*, Ann Louise Strong's *When Serfs Stood up in Tibet* and Han Suyin's laughably titled *Lhasa: The Open City*, published in 1977. The 'foreign friend' would be plied with dubious statistics and escorted on a short Potemkin tour by Party officials, usually taking in a model farm, factory and hospital. Former 'serfs' would be on hand to tell stories of the evils of the *ancien régime*. The essayist Jamyang Norbu has written that the resultant books and articles 'contain some rather standard fare like the sacrifice of virgins, the ritual murder of babies (a straight plagiarism from medieval anti-Semitic literature), and such gems of the propagandist's art as the accusation that a rosary was made for the Dalai Lama with the bones of 108 virgins'. He concluded that 'all those in this shabby procession of intellectual whoredom are, in the final analysis, nothing more than the grotesque and deformed progeny of such defenders of colonialism and oppression as Rudyard Kipling, without having the saving grace of the latter's sincerity and literary ability'.

Since the 1980s, the procession of intellectual whoredom has almost dried up. However, as recently as 2000, N. Ram, a prosperous Indian press baron, published a long article in his otherwise respectable magazine *Frontline*, based on a five-day official tour he had made through Tibet. He prefaced it with the engaging lines, 'The sky is turquoise, the sun is golden, The Dalai Lama is away from the Potala, Making trouble in the West, Yet Tibet's on the move.' The *People's Daily* was delighted by this rare example of enthusiasm for Beijing's propaganda, and ran a story headlined 'Real Tibet Under Sunshine'. It stated that 'Lam [sic] gave an introduction to locality from six aspects including economy, population, religious freedom and human rights. The article points out: Tibet enjoys prosperous economy, vigorous development of various undertakings, many preferential policies.'

I found Hugh Richardson's phrase 'the mind's Tibet' while I was looking for another piece of writing. It was in the September 1904 edition of the *Monthly Review*, in a poor poem by Henry Newbolt titled 'Epistle to Colonel Francis Edward Younghusband'. Newbolt had produced a triumphalist celebration of the British invasion of Tibet, linking its supposed achievements to his own schooldays at Clifton College, where he had been a contemporary of the young Francis Younghusband.

Across the Western World, the Arabian Sea,
The Hundred Kingdoms and the Rivers Three,
Beyond the rampart of Himalayan snows,
And up the road that only Rumour knows,
Unchecked, old friend, from Devon to Thibet,
Friendship and Memory dog your footsteps yet . . .
Though wide apart the lines our fate has traced
Since those far shadows of our boyhood raced,
In the dim region all men must explore –
The mind's Thibet, where none has gone before . . .
The victories of our youth we count for gain
Only because they steeled our hearts to pain.

Newbolt saw a Tibet of the mind, a pristine land where none had gone before, a dim region where ideas could be projected and dreams could be lived. He was writing with the easy confidence of his age, the simplicity of a generation that had yet to see the twentieth century's world wars and genocides, and the destruction of peoples and civilisations in the name of ideology, a century in which Tibet would be almost destroyed by the carelessness and ambition of passing foreigners. His mind's Tibet was a pure, distant land, far from the Tibet we drove through now in a heavy green lorry in the rain.

A few miles before Zhongba, the convoy turned a corner and reached a Military Area Tourist Stop, a cross between an army camp and an impromptu PSB checkpoint. I was spotted immediately by a gaunt young Chinese officer who, possibly under the influence of the smiling Japanese students, accepted the suggestion that I must have confused Saga with Sakya (which is sometimes spelt Sagya), and had wandered accidentally into the wrong region. Without even a fine, I was ordered to make my way back to Shigatse. I returned, with the usual grinding truck and tractor palaver, and after a day or two of rest in Lhasa, took a flight to Chengdu, over the snow mountains, over Lithang, close to where my journey had begun.

TWENTY THREE

When I arrived in the smog of Chengdu, my eyes noticed short skirts, bicycles and large crowds. There was a feeling of ease and anonymity, almost as if I was in a free country, after the constant, watchful oppression of the Tibet Autonomous Region. Party Secretary Chen Kuiyuan, the ruler of Tibet, who lived in Chengdu and only flew to Lhasa when his presence was required, was shortly to be sacked. His replacement would be Guo Jinlong. Guo would adopt the same stern line, saying that the 'backwardness of the Dalai clique' was Tibet's principal problem: 'The dregs of feudal serfdom ideology and various bad customs and habits are linked together being incompatible with socialist new ideology . . . As Lenin noted, "When the old society died, its corpse could not be placed in a coffin and buried in a grave. It is decomposing, stinking and poisoning us."'

Hundreds of workers in yellow jackets were hosing down the main square. A squad of special police in dark glasses were revving big blue motorbikes outside Kentucky Fried Chicken. Soldiers with long batons were patrolling in step. At the head of the square, behind the statue of Mao, where two months before a giant advertisement for cigarettes had hung, a high podium was being created out of scaffolding. The fiftieth anniversary of the Communist seizure of power was only days away, and the foundation of the People's Republic of China was being treated as Year Zero. The current regime, aware that its combination of economic liberalism and ruthless political control was ideologically confusing, was trying to link itself to past glories.

Long red banners hung from the buildings, bearing slogans:

CHINA 1949–1999
LONG LIFE TO THE MOTHERLAND
LONG LIVE THE UNITY OF OUR NATIONALITIES
LET US PUSH THE CAUSE OF SOCIALIST CONSTRUC-
   TION WITH DISTINCTIVE NATIONAL FEATURES
   INTO THE 21ST CENTURY

Workers were on a week's holiday, and the atmosphere was relaxed and festive, despite the strong security presence. Red lanterns, helium-filled balloons and rubberised light strings were attached to shopfronts and lamp-posts. Thousands of pots of yellow flowers lined the pavements. Hawkers – no longer seen as 'capitalist roaders' – were doing well selling little plastic red flags. Bicycle vendors offered flatbreads filled with beef, ginger and chilli. Mothers wore bright, overdone ruched dresses, bobby socks and high-heeled shoes, and little girls were dressed as airport fairies. Some women, MTV watchers I guessed, with an idea of world fashion, wore stacks and jeans. They chatted into mobile phones, and one or two carried video cameras. Groups of rustics, bussed in for the occasion, walked the streets slack-jawed. Some had set up camp on street corners, spreading out news-papers to sleep on.

As it began to get dark I walked down Renmin Nanlu towards the guest house where I had, with difficulty, found a room. Outside a large hotel, the Jinjiang, a forlorn young hawker stood with a pollution mask stretched across her face. Her cart held a plastic bowl filled with grey noodles, like a tub of wet washing. Feeling in need of good food after weeks of *thukpa* and mutton, I entered the opulent Jinjiang Hotel. Thick pillars obscured yards of marble. A small man in a bellhop's hat was struggling with an oversized parcel beneath a pair of chandeliers. Confused by the surroundings, I stopped in front of a huge, dripping grotto and a kitsch waterfall, and then backtracked towards the cake shop, which offered beige sponge rolls, fatty cream erupting, only to be intercepted by Snow White in a scarlet ballgown with puffy sleeves, her feet encased in dancing pumps.

'I am the Hostess. Please allow me to take you to a seat.'

Regretting it already, I was led to a table by the Hostess. There was a strong odour of floor polish, a surfeit of waiters and penetrating lounge music. The menu offered petty lobster with chess, pork shreds fish smell and spiced cattle with rice crust. I chose a pizza. A banner said: WARMEST CONGRATULATIONS FOR THE GRAND CELEBRATIONS OF CHINA.

Leaving the watery pizza, the Hostess and a symphonic version of 'Whiter Shade of Pale', I descended to the lobby, where a display of photographs showed the various international celebrities who had visited the hotel. I recognised none of them.

Someone materialised from reception, brisk and helpful, to offer captions for the photographs. A name badge revealed her to be Mrs Gao.

'This is Mr Pierre Cardin; this one is a famous businessman from Singapore; here is China's communications minister.'

The poses were repeated in each photograph: the visitor grinning on the steps of the Jinjiang, shaking hands with local officials while junior staff lurked in the background.

'And this one,' said Mrs Gao, pointing at an indistinct figure in a grey suit seated on a high-backed, over-stuffed cerise winged armchair, a squad of aides hovering behind him, 'is a high-up old travel minister from the United States of America.'

I tried to decipher the picture: a pair of spectacles hunched over a sheaf of papers. All was revealed in the next photograph, in which the same man, grinning vigorously, was shaking the hand of a pinguid Chinese official.

It was Dr Henry Kissinger.

'He came here for some business,' said Mrs Gao.

So there he was, the architect of American *rapprochement* with China, doing business in Chengdu. 'Polo I', he had code-named his first secret visit to Beijing, dignifying it with an echo of the Venetian's journey seven hundred years before. By February 1972, everything was arranged. For more than two decades the US had recognised Formosa, later Taiwan, and referred to China as 'Mainland China', as if it was an adjunct to Chiang Kai-shek's little island.

Mao's first overture had been to invite the American journalist Edgar Snow onto the balcony at Tiananmen on National Day, presuming he was a CIA agent. The symbolism was missed by the State Department, who in fact despised Snow as a Communist sympathiser. China's next move was to invite US table-tennis players to Beijing; at this point America cottoned on, and after some secret diplomacy by Kissinger, Richard Nixon went to China.

The *rapprochement* was a monumental climbdown by Mao, an acknowledgement that economic failure and confrontation with the Soviet Union had prevented China from becoming the home of world revolution, and that *realpolitik* demanded an overture to the powerhouse of capitalism. Nixon saw things in reverse, playing the role of supplicant, honoured that he had been invited to the Middle Kingdom. Mao relished the role of the reclusive emperor, receiving tribute; he once received Nikita Khrushchev in his swimming pool, and the unamphibian Soviet leader had been obliged to float about in a rubber ring.

With President Nixon, the compliments flowed, one way. After watching *The Red Detachment of Women*, a wooden revolutionary opera selected for him by Mao's malignant wife Jiang Qing, Nixon said it was 'certainly the equal of any ballet I have seen'. The negotiations had a similar imbalance, as did the final joint communiqué, in which the US abandoned its old ally Formosa. As Kissinger stated later, 'I have always found in dealing with the Chinese that complete frankness is the better course, since they're probably smarter than we are anyway,' an assumption that has since become diplomatic orthodoxy among Western powers.

In the Study of Chrysanthemum Fragrance, Mao deployed his well-honed psychological techniques on Nixon, mixing charm and self-deprecating humour with oblique remarks as a way of drawing out his opponent.

NIXON: The Chairman's writings moved a nation and have changed the world.

MAO: I haven't been able to change it. I've only been able to change a few places in the vicinity of Beijing . . . I discuss philosophical questions. That is to say, I voted for you during your election.

NIXON: When the Chairman says he voted for me he voted for the lesser of two evils.

MAO: I like rightists. People say you are rightists, that the Republican Party is to the right, that Prime Minister [Edward] Heath is also to the right . . . I am comparatively happy when these people on the right come into power.

NIXON: I think the important thing to note is that in America, at least this time, those on the right can do what those on the left talk about . . . Having read some of the Chairman's statements, I know he is one who sees when an opportunity comes, that you must seize the hour and seize the day.

MAO: 'Seize the hour and seize the day.' I think that, generally speaking, people like me sound like a lot of big cannons. (Zhou laughs.) That is, things like 'the whole world should unite and defeat imperialism, revisionism, and all reactionaries, and establish socialism'.

'Zhou laughs.' Nixon could have been forgiven for thinking that the laughter of Zhou Enlai, China's intelligent and urbane premier, was the comradely chuckle of one of Mao's oldest allies. How was he to know that Zhou's dread of Mao was so great that when he had heard, a few weeks earlier, that the Chairman had collapsed during a coughing fit, he shat himself in fear? In the words of Mao's doctor, Li Zhisui, the relationship between the Great Helmsman and China's Eldest Son was that of 'master and slave'.

Mao Zedong's personal charisma, together with the promotion he received from credulous Western writers, concealed the moral putrefaction at the heart of his rule. Even today he remains an acceptable sort of tyrant, and is treated with some reverence. Although he is responsible for more deaths than either Hitler or Stalin, Mao confers status. His face can be seen on badges and posters, in bars and clubs, on Andy Warhol screenprints. His sayings crop up in guides to modern business management. On London's King's Road there is a dumpling and noodle restaurant called New Culture Revolution; a name such as New Holocaust would be considered less congenial.

The romance of Mao, the man who gave fashion journalists the Mao collar and management gurus some catchy aphorisms, has yet to be dismantled. He has been promoted as a statesman, poet and philosopher, rather than as a despot. In the words of C.P. FitzGerald, one of a plethora of sympathetic foreign commentators, Mao's 'remarkable achievement' was 'comparable in its scope to the great religious revolutions ... no Chinese thinker in the period since Confucius has attained the degree of acceptance and authority which Mao has acquired'.

To understand what Mao did to Tibet, and to understand the reasons why he did it, you have to go back to the days before the Communist invasion of 1950. I had noticed that an interview or conversation would often return to him as the arbiter of loss and suffering. All roads led to Mao. The destruction he wrought grew out of the catastrophe of China's early-twentieth-century history, and the Tibetans were, essentially, collateral damage in his pursuit of larger ambitions. Mao had no interest in Tibet. His comments on it were rare and dismissive. The first recorded reference, made in 1919 to the 'Problem Study Society' of Changsha, when he was a twenty-five-year-old student, sets the tone. Some way down a list of issues that were concerning him was 'the Tibetan Problem', a phrase evoking 'the Negro Problem' that was troubling his contemporaries across the Pacific.

When Tibetans sought foreign backing in the 1950s, Mao said mockingly to a Party meeting:

> There's a group in Tibet who want to set up an independent kingdom. Currently this organisation is a bit shaky ... There is a place in India called Kalimpong, where they specialise in sabotaging Tibet. Nehru himself told the Premier [Zhou Enlai], that this place is a centre of espionage, primarily American and British. If Tibet wants to be independent our position is this: if you want to agitate for independence, then agitate; you want independence, I don't want you to have independence. We have a Seventeen Point Agreement.

The historian Roderick MacFarquhar has noted that the decision to crush Tibet after the Dalai Lama's escape in 1959 was not even debated by the Central Committee: 'One must presume that the Tibetan revolt, which had so critical an impact on China's relations with India and, as a consequence, with the Soviet Union, provoked virtually no dissension within the Chinese leadership.' Tibet has never been of significant interest to the Chinese Communist Party; it is a place of trouble, a satellite, a buffer, a resource, and a plantation, which has to be subdued from time to time.

Mao was intuitive, patient and meticulous, with a savage temper and a rustic crudity; a guerrilla chieftain with scholarly tendencies. Although he could be charming, and had powerful affections when he was young, any humanity was burnt out of him by the searing, amoral conflicts of the 1920s and thirties. Even those closest to him, his wives and children, were disposable. Every significant thing that he did in his twenty-six years as China's supreme leader was prefigured before his rise to power. The use of fear and killing as political tools, the purging of close colleagues, the invention of imaginary traitors, the withdrawal and regrouping at times of difficulty, even the subtle, lateral methods by which he achieved his aims, are all reflected from his days as a guerrilla leader. That is, essentially, what he remained. Mao was a key historical figure of the twentieth century, a politician who controlled a quarter of the world's population; but he was also a capo.

Take Mao Zedong in 1911, a poor, stubborn, headstrong seventeen-year-old student in his native Hunan, who reached adulthood in a lawless world of flux and betrayal. Warlords, military cliques and revolutionary social movements rose and fell. When the fighting died down, Mao wrote poetry and read Darwin and Rousseau, and experimented with anarchism and Hunanese nationalism before settling on Marxism. He joined the tiny, fledgling Chinese Communist Party, the CCP, controlled by the Comintern, the international wing of the Soviet government. Mao worked hard as a peasant organiser and union agitator. In 1927, after a journey through rural Hunan in the wake of a bloody revolt, he wrote a report which shocked his colleagues. He described in detail the arbitrary arrests, the violence against landlords and the smashing of sedan chairs, before deciding that 'the broad peasant masses' had 'risen to fulfil their historical mission . . . A revolution is not like inviting people to dinner, or writing an essay, or painting a picture, or doing embroidery . . . To put it bluntly, it is necessary to bring about a brief reign of terror in every rural area.'

He had tasted blood, and realised that unleashing the oppressed on a mission of destruction was the surest way of making revolution. In the same year, the CCP was betrayed by the Guomindang leader Chiang Kai-shek, and thousands of Communists in Shanghai were murdered in vicious pogroms. Fighting, not compromise, seemed the only way forward. A Communist revolt began at Nanchang in Jiangxi, the province bordering Hunan. Although it was a small, localised affair, it would have a lasting symbolism. Mao's biographer Philip Short has called the list of participants 'the *Almanac de Gotha* of the Communist revolution'. Many famous figures were there: Mao Zedong, Peng Dehuai, Zhou Enlai, Deng Xiaoping, Zhu De, He Long, and even Lin Biao, aged only twenty.

The Red Army rose and fell, and came close to destruction several times. Mao's own regiment was a ragtag gang of ruffians, chancers and mutinous peasants, welded together into a fighting force. He developed the canny military strategy of feints and tactical retreats that was to bring him victory at the end of the 1940s.

> The enemy advances, we withdraw,
> The enemy rests, we harass,
> The enemy tires, we attack,
> The enemy withdraws, we pursue.

The Communists were baptised in fire. In the context of China in the years after the fall of the Qing, what happened next, at Futian in 1930, was not unexpected.

There was a purge. Ethical absolutes were put to one side. Traitors who threatened the Party – the members of a secret Guomindang cabal called the AB Team – had to be eliminated. Nobody knew who the AB Team members might be, or indeed whether there was a single one of them within the ranks of the

Red Army, so methods had to be devised to find them. As a leading figure within the CCP hierarchy, Mao was the instigator of the purge, using his brother-in-law Liu Shiqi as his henchman. Soldiers from prosperous backgrounds were an obvious target. Once they had been eliminated, torture seemed the most promising method of locating further traitors. Thousands of supposed AB Team infiltrators were executed, mainly by shooting. Several senior Party figures were arrested, having been named in extorted confessions. The torture techniques were the age-old ones, with colourful names like 'monkey pulling reins' and 'toad drinking water'. (The tradition is still with us: 'golden chicken standing on one leg' and 'old ox ploughing the land' were used to break 1989 democracy activists, despite China's ratification of the UN Convention Against Torture.) The tortured named more senior people as traitors – and it was at this point that the fantasy began to unravel. There was a mutiny, and the suspects were released.

It is astonishing that in the aftermath of the initial purge, the CCP leaders closed ranks and the violence began afresh. Although the pogrom at Futian was caused by factional infighting and personal ambition rather than a genuine external threat, the atmosphere was so menacing that nobody dared to question its basis. By the end of 1931, tens of thousands of people had been murdered. Killing had become an instrument for asserting political control. Afterwards, a veil was drawn over the Futian Incident and the fight for control of China resumed.

After a dispute with other CCP leaders which led to a period in the wilderness, Mao's star rose during the great, brutal retreat called the Long March. By 1937 he was living in some style at Yanan in northern China, and was the recognised leader of the Chinese Communists, who were improving their finances by trading opium. The years in Yanan during the early 1940s consolidated his position. Mao was able to reinvent himself as a statesman during the Second World War, giving interviews to credulous foreign journalists, and establishing a position near the centre of Chinese politics.

Acutely aware of the excesses of the colonial powers during preceding decades, European and American reporters liked to depict Mao as China's nascent saviour. He portrayed himself as a figure from history, one in a line of wise emperors who had led a peasant revolt against a corrupt dynasty. The writer Nym Wales, who was married to Edgar Snow, was not unusual:

WALES: The Red Army has carried out ten years of struggle against feudalism. Do you consider, sir, that this struggle has achieved great successes?

MAO: It has achieved considerable successes. In those places which have been influenced by the Red Army, the feudal forces have been battered by the forces of revolution.

In Yanan, behind the scenes and sometimes in the open, terror continued. Mao propagated his own interpretation of Marxism, a particular form – Maoism, or Mao Zedong Thought – which he claimed was suited to China's conditions. The Yanan Rectification Campaign, as it became known, was nominally about the need to develop an agreed, ideologically pure version of the CCP's history. In practice, it was about crushing opponents. Mao used his favoured, proven technique of 'luring the snake from its hole': people were told to speak freely, and when they did, attacking the hypocrisy and privilege of the Party elite, they were condemned as Trotskyites, spies and Guomindang agents. Tens of thousands were expelled from the CCP; the less fortunate were tortured, murdered or driven to suicide.

Take the case of Wang Shiwei, a young intellectual who had written a satirical essay, *Wild Lilies*, about the inequity of life at Yanan. At his 'trial', comrades took the floor and shouted things like,

I ask that Wang Shiwei express his opinion on the following Trotskyite positions:
(1) Trotsky's opinion on the question of the Soviet peasantry before the Twelfth Congress of the CPSU;
(2) the question of Lenin's Last Testament;
(3) the question of who, in the final analysis, should be responsible for the failure of the Great Chinese Revolution of 1925–27.

Reading these exchanges, it becomes clear that the pursuit of orthodoxy and the persecution of dissidence were the trial's central purpose, hidden behind a cloak of ideological debate. Wang Shiwei was found guilty of being a spy and a member of an 'anti-Party gang'. For a time he was confined, then he was beheaded with an axe.

When the Yanan Rectification Campaign ended, the cult of Chairman Mao, the wise emperor, was promoted with vigour. All that remained was the takeover of China, a prodigious achievement which happened at a remarkable speed. In 1947, Mao was in a nominally weak position, although in the wartime years of partial alliance with Chiang Kai-shek against Japan, the Red Army had gained territory. His rapid victory owed much to the techniques he had honed during the vicious skirmishes of the 1930s: luring the enemy into difficult positions, and giving up territory in exchange for strategic gain. He was also aided by the incompetence of the Guomindang army and the high-level intelligence networks his agents had set up within it. By the end of 1949, Mao's troops were in control of most of China, and Chiang Kai-shek had fled to Formosa.

All of these things – the early writings in praise of a brief reign of terror, the Futian killings, the purges at Yanan – had happened by 1949, the year in which a portrait of the benign, prescient, avuncular Chairman was hung from the Gate of Heavenly Peace in Beijing. Mao was fifty-five years old. His character was set; his methods were known. His attitudes and experiences would be crucial in determining how he would rule Tibet during the 1950s and sixties. Decades later, when all this and more was known about Mao, when the evil of the Great Leap Forward and the Cultural Revolution had fused with his earlier crimes, the portrait of the beneficent father of the nation was still in place in Tiananmen. In 1989 a man from Hunan, Yu Dongyue, threw an ink-filled egg at it, and was given twenty years for counter-revolutionary sabotage, confined, alone, in a tiny, unventilated cell. His release date has been set for 21 May 2007.

On the morning of the fiftieth anniversary, I stayed in and watched Beijing's celebrations on television. Hundreds of thousands of Chinese citizens were involved, choreographed with military precision. Huge floats trailed ribbons, each ribbon held by a symmetrical model worker, in an echo of the 1950s. Detachments of women goose-stepped in yellow boots, holding clusters of pink balloons. There were marchers dressed as stems of wheat, and as sunflowers. A square of women in fitted red jackets, ties, heavy lipstick, mini-skirts and knee-length black boots – not a sex workers' brigade, but a unit of 'civilian militiawomen' – marched in solemn step. A medical float carried doctors probing mannequins, and a giant pink lotus flower opened to reveal four female nurses. Pigeons were released in expanding clouds. Jiang Zemin's portrait was borne on a lorry surrounded by a member of each of China's cheerful ethnic minorities. The parade seemed to me like a national display of lack of confidence.

Jiang stood on a balcony surrounded by the other leaders, blinking behind his giant spectacles and waving his hands urgently at the invited crowd. He looked as if he was astonished that he, a man without qualities, a bureaucrat and back-room manoeuvrer, had become China's paramount leader. To the interest of Sinologists, who wondered what political symbolism was intended by this rare fashion throwback, he wore a Mao suit. At his right hand stood China's reforming premier, Zhu Rongji, conventionally dressed, a man who would have been swiftly purged by Mao as an imperialist running dog. 'Let us hold high the great banner of Marxism-Leninism, Mao Zedong Thought and Deng Xiaoping Theory and march bravely towards our sublime objectives,' Jiang told the crowd. His message to Tibetans was that China's policy on minorities was 'very successful compared to that of other countries', and that he would 'isolate and strike the small group of ethnic separatists'. There had been plans, trailed in the state media, to unveil advances in 'Jiang Zemin Theory' that day, but they came to nothing, because nobody knew what the new theories were.

When Jiang had finished waving, he climbed into an old-style black car with a cut-away roof and was driven slowly over the Golden Water Bridge, once reserved for China's emperor, past block after block of erect soldiers, reviewing them in his capacity as Chairman of the Central Military Commission. 'Comrades, you have been working exceptionally hard,' he shouted, and back came the cry, 'Hello Comrade Chairman, we are serving the people.' Later, a giant picture of Mao Zedong was driven around on a truck, followed by giant pictures of Deng Xiaoping and Jiang Zemin. The message was clear: lineal descent from Mao, through Deng, to Jiang. Only the Washington-based Free China Movement spoiled the Party's party by condemning the celebrations, and stating that 'the Communist regime has been directly responsible for the deaths of over 80 million Chinese citizens'.

In Chengdu, I walked up to the main square to see what was happening. I was with Lobsang, a friend of Pemba, the canny Tibetan woman from Rebkong I had met at the start of my journey, who had just given birth to a baby girl. Like Pemba, Lobsang was a bright, disaffected young Tibetan, who had made a pragmatic decision to operate within the Chinese system for his own economic survival. Rows of police stood in the square, but there was little tension, only apathy as the crowd ignored the speeches reverberating from the podium. Red lanterns, balloons and light strings dangled in the distance, but there were no marching soldiers or revealing lotus flowers here. Lobsang kept up a sly commentary under his breath, ridiculing the amount of money being spent on the celebrations, and telling of the banquets that Party officials would be holding for themselves that night across China. The rally was more elaborate than anything he had seen before, and the flapping banners reminded him of scenes from films about the Cultural Revolution.

I asked him what it made him feel, watching this. I suppose that I was expecting a wrap, a neat speech about the theft of his birthright and the pain of being a Tibetan caught in a false, imposed culture, but he gave me only three words.

'I feel nothing.'

A few weeks later, Jiang Zemin went to Britain on a state visit, the first by a Chinese paramount leader. I thought that I should join him.

I flew out of Chengdu early one morning with one of China's new commercial airlines. The crew held a raffle, handing out greasy biscuits and fluffy toys to the winning passengers. The performance was loud, and I was trying to sleep, but finally they came to the big one, and the winning seat was, yes, 27E – me. I was not inclined to take the prize, until I realised it was a voucher for a free flight anywhere in China. So I strolled up, the passengers craning since I was the only foreigner on board. I made a short speech of thanks on the PA system and bowed once or twice, then explained in English that I had no use for the free ticket, and would like to auction it. When this was translated there was considerable excitement, with offers being shouted up the plane and prospective purchasers streaming up the aisle. I had just got the bidding started when the chief trolley-pusher, Mr Leung, said that what I was doing was illegal and should stop at once. We had a short wrestle over possession of the microphone, but by now the auction was in full swing, with much shouting, waving of banknotes and a stampede towards the nose of the plane. I brought the hammer down in favour of a big woman from Guangzhou in a red serge trouser suit who paid me US$100, and with that we landed in Beijing. There may have been a moral to this incident, but I am not sure what it was.

When I got back to Britain, I stepped down as a director of Free Tibet Campaign. After all I had seen and heard in the Tibet Autonomous Region and its borderlands, I could no longer view things with the necessary simplicity to be part of a political campaign. I doubted whether a free Tibet had any meaning without a free China. There might be other ways I could help Tibetans, by supporting education projects inside the country, or backing the development of indigenous businesses, or promoting the free flow of information. Above all, I wanted to try to communicate something of the complex reality of Tibet's past and present, convinced that the existing approach of the Tibetophile lobby was leading nowhere, and that the Chinese government was simply not amenable to external popular pressure.

As Jiang's visit to London unfolded, I watched with fascination and bemusement, feeling something close to fear at the idea of people daring to protest against him. The PSB, the SSB, or a spy from a neighbourhood committee might be watching. Mental supervision was hard to shake off, and I thought again of Nadezhda Mandelstam's words about those in a dictatorship being 'slightly unbalanced mentally – not exactly ill, but not normal either'. It occurred to me that I had met many people in Tibet who were discontented and desperate for political change, but nobody who had the external knowledge to comprehend how and why their society had been destroyed.

Jiang's visit to democracy got off to a bad start. The British government took the view that, with the handover of Hong Kong complete, it should do all it could to improve the bilateral relationship with Beijing, including some gentle kowtowing, if necessary. Although British exports to China are worth less than US$2 billion a year, and many of China's booming new businesses are corrupt fronts for loss-making government enterprises, and the state banking system is insolvent, and per capita GDP in Britain is thirty times higher than in China, the Chinese market is perceived as an area of massive potential growth. A trip by Jiang to Switzerland earlier in the year had been marked by noisy pro-Tibet demonstrations, and he had lost his temper, barking at the justice minister, 'Don't you have the ability to run this country?' and telling the Swiss parliament it had 'lost a good friend'. The British Foreign Office and the home intelligence service, MI5, both acutely aware of the scope for diplomatic disaster, briefed the London police on the perils of letting Jiang become angry. The police, interpreting this rather zealously, decided to confiscate Tibetan flags and Chinese pro-democracy placards from demonstrators, while allowing the waving of red flags.

On his way down The Mall in a horse-drawn carriage, perched beside Queen Elizabeth on their way to Buckingham Palace, Jiang was intercepted by a pro-Tibet protester, who was promptly arrested. Later, his limousine was blocked by a cyclist draped in a Tibetan flag. Jiang was incensed. Noticing a hostile placard, he turned to the British official seated beside him and said in aggrieved tones, 'Do I look like a dictator?' Over the next few days, in collusion with Chinese security officials, London's police parked vans in front of pro-Tibet demonstrators wherever they appeared, shielding Jiang from the sight of dissent.

All sections of the British media responded with indignation to this interference with the right to peaceful protest. The respected political columnist Hugo Young wrote that the treatment of demonstrators was 'one of the most shocking deployments of state power any British government has authorised to spare the sensibilities of a tyrannical brute with contracts in his pocket'. In a subsequent court case brought by Free Tibet Campaign, the police admitted they had acted unlawfully in seizing flags and banners, and apologised.

At Buckingham Palace, relations were frosty, with one royal aide later describing it as the worst state visit he could remember. During the official banquet, Prince Charles got into a debate with Jiang's wife, Wang Yeping, and Zhou Hanqiong, the wife of China's vice premier. Charles said later that he had felt uncomfortable, and had been shocked by the strength of their hostility. The two women brought up the evils of British imperialism, the brutality of past British monarchs, the virtues of the late Nicolae Ceausescu of Romania (where Jiang had spent two years in the 1970s) and the joys of the Soviet Union under Communism. When Charles tried to discuss Tibet, Zhou Hanqiong repeated the words 'Northern Ireland' at him like a mantra until the prince snapped back, 'At least we try to solve Northern Ireland.'

Two nights later a return banquet was held at the Chinese Embassy, which Charles boycotted ostentatiously in a further rupture of protocol, receiving one of his most complimentary postbags ever from the British public as a result. During the dinner, Jiang entertained the guests by grabbing a microphone without warning and singing the 1930s Broadway hit 'Our Hearts Were Young and Gay', followed by a song from the Beijing Opera. When his karaoke performance was over, the British government felt obliged to respond, and the banquet ended with the surreal spectacle of the stocky and ill-favoured deputy prime minister, John Prescott, leading the guests in a rendition of 'For He's a Jolly Good Fellow'.

The closing diplomatic syrup made little difference to China's verdict on the visit. Jiang Zemin, who had only reached his position as Mao's lineal successor because of his robust role in the Tiananmen crackdown in 1989, was outraged that his time in London should have been marked by street protests. The British government's ill-judged attempts to stop the demonstrations elicited no thanks from him, only contempt. Before leaving Britain, Jiang's spokesman announced that 'these interruptive factors should have been avoided,' and denounced demonstrators against Chinese rule in Tibet as 'high noses' who supported 'the inglorious cause of imperialism and colonialism'.

The visit summed up everything I had come to expect from the Chinese government: arrogance, intolerance, a strong sense of self-preservation, and wilful misunderstanding of foreign customs, as the old, hard-left, nationalist ideology sheltered behind a veil of economic engagement.

TWENTY FOUR

When I went back to Dharamsala later in the year, I stayed in a new hotel at the top of the hill. The monastery at Tsechokling held too many memories for me to want to return there. My elder son Tenzin, aged five, was travelling with me, and the hotel, decked out with gaudy wall paintings of yaks and a sunny terrace which overlooked the mountains, seemed like a better place to base ourselves. Two weeks later it would be a temporary refuge for the fourteen-year-old Karmapa Rinpoche, Ugyen Trinley Dorje, the most important *tulku* remaining in Tibet, who had once been described by Jiang Zemin as 'a patriotic Living Buddha'. The Karmapa's dramatic flight across the Himalayas through the winter snows would deal another hard blow to China's policy on Tibet.

Out on the terrace in the morning sun we ate toast and honey and watched monkeys swinging from trees. At a nearby table a scene was being played out between a plump young Tibetan monk, sage in his robes, and a big-haired Canadian woman in a Himachali embroidered jacket. The gist was that she might like to extend her patronage and sponsor another refugee child through school. It had long been a familiar scene in Dharamsala, the search for a *jindag* or patron, someone who could give finance and practical support to help fulfil an ambition. *Jindags* came in many shapes and sizes, and everyone here seemed to be on the lookout for one, in the *cho-yon* or priest–patron tradition, hoping for the patronage and arbitration of an outsider. The sharper supplicants targeted foreign institutions, especially the ones that were obliged to disburse a fixed annual sum, which could go a long way in the Indian economy.

The adroitness of the monk's pitch was impressive. A decade ago, you would be stopped in the street by a toothless man flourishing a piece of paper and demanding a donation. Now it was done over a cappuccino. 'In Tibetan,' the monk said in flawless English, 'we don't have this word "projecting", but I have studied, you know, some Western psychology, and I think that is what Dolma is doing. Dolma needs to meet with someone who really cares, someone she can really trust.' He got the funding, and that afternoon Dolma was brought to the hotel, a cute little girl who played the role of donee to perfection. Her mother and aunt, who worked in the carpet industry, hovered by the gate nervously while Dolma was paraded around the hotel by the Canadian woman and introduced to the guests as her daughter. 'Daughter?' I thought. 'When did you have her? Who's the father?'

Almost a decade had passed since I had been in McLeod Ganj, the village above Dharamsala. The place was as scruffy as ever, a disarray of loose wires and potholes, choked with open drains, ramshackle refugee buildings, expensive tourist trinket shops and restaurants which sold apple pie and mashed potato. Posters advertised *reiki* classes, freedom concerts, meditation retreats and AIDS awareness, using the slogan: DEAR TIBETANS NEVER FORGET RUBBER TUBE. Developers with muscle and money had put up shops and internet cafés on the once empty road to the Dalai Lama's residence, overlooking the Dhauladhar mountains. Buildings had even spread into the village square, so that buses could no longer turn there, and had to perform elaborate reversing rituals involving Indian boys with whistles.

McLeod Ganj had the same old Tibetan women shuffling to the temple to turn prayer wheels, and young men in beaten-up leather jackets hanging out on balconies, watching for opportunities. An insane man, whose shaved head and thick beard made him look like an extreme Muslim, was begging for food at the roadside as he had been a decade before, but I noticed that the wasteland that had once been his home was now occupied by a hotel. I saw a senior monk I had known, wearing a T-shirt and jeans, walking down the street arm in arm with what I at first took to be a Tibetan woman. At closer range she turned out to be French, dressed in a thick *chuba* and impressive jewellery. They seemed happy – they each had a trophy – and I remembered that in his monastic days he had enjoyed play-wrestling with a big-breasted New Zealander called Carrie, who was doing her bit for the cause by sleeping with as many Tibetans as possible.

There were fewer Indians than before, but plenty of foreigners in varying states of fancy dress: a man with a blond goatee, dressed as a Khampa; another with elaborate braided hair, purple robe and wide sash, riding an enormous motorbike; a woman with hardware hanging from her face and a shaved head, looking like a Gothic Tibetan nun; a decrepit man with piercing eyes, dressed as an Indian mendicant; a skinny woman in half a T-shirt and clown's trousers, covered in Free Tibet badges; a Scandi-navian couple in home-made orange, yellow, green and red robes, presumably representing a religious tradition all of their own. The net effect was of a uniform; the older Tibetans were said to believe that everyone in the West dressed in this way.

Down at Gangkyi, the headquarters of the exiled government, there were new buildings and lines of four-wheel drives, but there was still the same tattered, makeshift air. Staff bustled about pursuing the business of the émigrés. I visited the library, where old acquaintances spoke of a plan for a referendum inside Tibet, and of the Dalai Lama's upcoming tour of the US. There was talk of the armed struggle, a perennial subject of conversation among Tibetans which has gone nowhere since the CIA cut funding in the early 1970s.

Knowing how heavily his followers rely on his face and name, the Dalai Lama has tried to bring democracy to the exiled govern-ment, and allow new leaders to emerge. This has not been a success, since most Tibetans fear any dilution of His Holiness's traditional status. Unlike many exile movements, the problem lies not with an autocratic leader, but with conservative popular opinion. Pema Thinley, editor of the independent monthly *Tibetan Review*, has written:

> I hate to say it, but we have always lacked and still do the most basic requisite for democratisation: willingness

on the part of the people to take responsibility for their own affairs and destiny. Our stock response to all national issues still remains, 'His Holiness knows best,' even though the Dalai Lama has repeatedly emphasised that it is not in Tibet's best interest for the people to depend on him for everything and for ever.

In 2001, with a fanfare, the Kalon Tripa, a chief minister of the exiled government, was chosen by direct election among the refugee community for the first time. The winner, the orator Samdhong Rinpoche, promptly announced that he wanted the Dalai Lama to retain all executive power: 'I would now like to request His Holiness to rescind this decision and continue to exercise his traditional administrative responsibilities in conformity with the provisions of the Charter of the Tibetans in Exile.' The prospect of unseating the Chinese government from power in Lhasa looked further away than ever. When the Dalai Lama went to hospital with stomach trouble in 2002, Samdhong Rinpoche would however start to take a more prominent role.

At the Department for Information and International Relations, I was received with more reverence than I wanted. I explained that I was there as a writer, not as an official guest. It made no difference. There was the same respectful warmth, and the sense that I, as a foreigner with perceived influence, might somehow be able to help in the struggle.

There was a particular subject that I wanted to research: the number of Tibetans who had died under Chinese rule. Data and Tibet do not sit happily together. Some countries enjoy tabulation and statistics; others prefer myths and legends, which mix fact and fluctuating memory, imagining how things might have been in the past. Like Tibet's old theocracy, the Communist autocracy restricts access to verifiable data, which provokes students and academics both in and out of Tibet to concentrate on the apolitical and the ethereal. At a recent meeting of the International Association for Tibetan Studies (the world body for Tibet specialists) I had noticed that out of nearly 230 papers submitted, more than a hundred dealt with religion, a hundred with matters such as linguistics, education, art, literature, medicine, law, social sciences and botany, and only twenty-four with diplomatic history, political history or political science; there was no hint of economics.

The result of this academic hiatus is that bogus information on many subjects is cheerfully traded between the Communist authorities and the exiled Tibetans and their supporters. Basic facts, such as the number of people in Tibet, are unclear and disputed. In earlier times, precise, centralised data was not collected with any rigour in Tibet. There were no correlated population records, and although tax records were sometimes detailed and revealing, they were usually confined to individual monasteries or estates.

The Dalai Lama has long spoken of 'six million Tibetans', although the estimated population of Tibet in previous centuries has lurched from below one million to as high as thirty-three million. Using what information is available, it would appear that in 1950 there were around 2.5 million Tibetans in all, divided fairly equally between the area under the control of the Lhasa government and the multi-ethnic border areas. Today there are approximately 2.5 million Tibetans in the Tibet Autonomous Region, 2.9 million in the Chinese provinces bordering Tibet, and 120,000 living in exile, making a total of around 5.5 million.

Corresponding to the much quoted figure of six million is the claim that 1.2 million Tibetans, a fifth of the supposed original population, died as a direct result of Chinese rule. (Some campaigners claim one-sixth of the population died, which suggests there were originally 7.2 million Tibetans.) This figure of 1.2 million has now passed into popular consciousness, and is often cited as a piece of uncontested fact, not only in campaigning materials but in independent publications. Numerous organisations repeat it in their literature, including the International Campaign for Tibet, the Tibet Society of the UK, the US Tibet Committee and Free Tibet Campaign. During a randomly chosen month, June 2000, I spotted nine references to the figure in the US print media alone. Most of these mentions were automatic, using it as an accepted and accurate statistic.

The difficulty with the figure of 1.2 million is that there were only around 2.5 million Tibetans at the time of the Chinese invasion – which would suggest that nearly half of the population had died at the hands of the Communists. Given the stories of persecution I had heard during my journey through Tibet, this did not seem inconceivable; but I was unnerved by the way that the credibility of the statistic seemed to rest not on any verifiable source, but on hearsay.

When I looked at the origins of the 1.2 million figure more closely, it turned out that it had first appeared in public in the mid-1980s. In response to demands from foreign supporters of the Tibetan cause, the exiled government had come up with the sort of systematically researched numbers that were needed to impress Western legislators. The key thing was to have charts, lists, tables and data – or what looked like data. A commission was established in Dharamsala under a respected official, Kungo Dhakden-la, who sent envoys to the main Tibetan settlements in India, Nepal and Bhutan to examine the claims of recent refugees. At the end of this process, it was concluded that precisely 1,207,387 Tibetans had died between 1950 and 1979 from starvation, fighting, torture, execution, suicide and struggle sessions.

This figure began to be used in the exiles' publications and in the Dalai Lama's speeches. The crucial moment in the development of its credibility as a serious statistic came in 1987, when the US House of Representatives attached a resolution to a State Department authorisation bill which included the claim that 'over 1 million Tibetans' had died 'as a direct result of the political instability, executions, imprisonment, and wide-scale famine engendered by the policies of the People's Republic of China in Tibet'. The Chinese government denounced this resolution in its usual heavy-handed way, but it had lost the propaganda war. The assertion that there were 1.2 million Tibetan victims of Chinese genocide has been repeated again and again since then, with the sheer weight of repetition making it believable.

The exiled government, aware that this figure is generally accepted, has kept a close lid on the original survey and stopped outside researchers from having access to the documentation on which it is based. In media terms, this has worked to its benefit. In her 1990 book *Tibet: Behind the Ice Curtain*, the journalist Vanya Kewley reported that Dharamsala 'had only cross-checked the names of 1,207,487 [sic] Tibetans who had died'. She thought that this figure was sure to grow, since the exiles 'have ready for international verification a list of more checked names of the Tibetan dead. Undoubtedly the Tibetan government-in-exile have additional names and figures but they punctiliously refuse to release them till their exhaustive verification process is complete.' Kewley's approach was not unusual.

After a couple of days of debate within the Department for Information and International Relations, I was allowed to look at the paperwork behind the survey. I was unsure why permission was given to me, but it seemed that new officials in the department favoured a policy of openness, and may have been unaware of the significance of what I wanted to look at. I went through the material slowly, helped by a young member of staff, Topden, who had been born and brought up in exile in India, and was soon to leave for study in the USA. He tried to locate missing sections from the archives, and to explain the accompanying documents.

After looking through the files for three days, it became clear to me that the figure of 1.2 million Tibetan deaths resulting from Chinese rule could not be accepted. The documentation came in twenty-two sections, each divided into the regions of ethnic Tibet: U-Tsang, Kham and Amdo. Two sections were missing, with only the summaries being available. The lists were broken down into males, females and incarnate lamas, and included the likely cause of death. Much of the basic structure of the survey was plausible. Escapees from a particular village or place would report that several hundred people had died of starvation between certain dates, or that a particular number of monks had been executed. The survey was built up by accumulating the evidence of these survivors and eye-witnesses.

There were however no lists of names, as had been promised, and in most cases it looked as if no names had ever been recorded. The most significant difficulties came with the insertion of seemingly random figures into each section, and constant, unchecked duplication. The death tolls in some sparsely populated parts of northern and eastern Tibet were unfeasibly high.

To take some examples: an account of the numbers killed in battle in Amdo was inflated by a bald claim that fifty thousand people had died fighting near Trigan; a document showed 13,574 people dying in Labrang Tashikyil in 1959, but another document listed a further fifteen thousand killed in the same place during the same period; a figure of 69,517 executions in Amdo had no clear origin, and seemed to have been taken from a contentious report issued by the International Commission of Jurists; a claim of 43,286 killed fighting in Kham was accompanied by documentation for only around ten thousand; a single interviewee claimed that twenty thousand people died in prisons near Karong; a table of those tortured to death in Kham included ten thousand who had already been listed under the heading of executions; one informant asserted with no evidence that nineteen thousand people had been executed near Kongbo; a captured Chinese publication stated that 87,884 Tibetan rebels had been killed in central Tibet after the uprising of 1959, but this figure was added to the existing figures for U-Tsang, rather than being treated as a total. Even when I added together all the numbers, credible or not, the total came to just under 1.1 million, rather than 1.2 million.

Most disturbing of all was the fact that of the nearly 1.1 million deaths listed, only 23,364 were female. This would have meant that 1.07 million victims were male, which was clearly impossible, given that there were only around 1.25 million Tibetan men in 1950.

I was left with the unwelcome conclusion that this survey was a well-intentioned but statistically useless attempt to satisfy Western demands for data and tabulation. Briefly, I was tempted to suppress this, and to report that the survey was generally believable, even if there were some gaps in it. But I knew, after everything I had seen in Tibet, that truth was more important than continuing to back the cause in its present form. More realism was needed, not less, when it came to Tibet. It was a land that had suffered for too long from the well-intentioned projections of visiting foreigners.

While I was going through the documents, my emotions turning from shock to something close to despair, Topden had reacted with similar incredulity. He was embarrassed and worried, realising the implications of the crumbling of this central statistic of the pro-Tibet lobby. Although we had been raised in very different circumstances on different sides of the world, we were from the same generation, brought up on a belief in the power of facts and images. We knew that precision mattered in the battle for hearts and minds.

More instructive was the reaction of an old monk who had been involved in compiling the original survey. He was summoned to the Department for Information and International Relations to try to explain the gaps. To my amazement, he did not seem worried by what I had found. Why should it matter if the numbers were not exact? Everyone knew that many Tibetans had suffered death and persecution under the Chinese Communists. Was anybody disputing that? I explained that I was not disputing their suffering, but that I was looking for accuracy rather than propaganda. Even as I said this, I wondered whether there was any point, and whether our perspectives overlapped even slightly. I thought of the old monk again when I read a line in V.S. Naipaul's Nobel lecture: 'the powerless lie about themselves, and lie to themselves, since it is their only resource'.

It is unlikely that a reliable alternative to the figure of 1.2 million will ever be known. The historian Warren Smith, working from shortfalls in population growth, has written that Chinese government statistics 'support the Tibetan claim of massive numbers of deaths rather than the Chinese denial'. He has estimated that over 200,000 Tibetans are 'missing' from population figures for the Tibet Autonomous Region. With the verifiably high mortality rates in Gansu, Sichuan and Qinghai in the early 1960s, it seems likely that the number of Tibetan deaths in the borderlands was at least as high as in central Tibet. If this is correct, it is probable that as many as half a million Tibetans may have died as a 'direct result' of the policies of the People's Republic of China; a devastating enough figure, in all conscience, which in no way diminishes the horror of what was done to Tibet.

I went to see the Dalai Lama. Tenzin came with me. The *bodhisattva* of compassion was standing at the end of a long colonnade, backlit, flanked by officials. I was struck by his powerful, fluid physical presence: the bare arm, the maroon robe, the expressive face. As we approached and he spotted Tenzin, he knelt down, and his entourage knelt quickly too; even at the end of the twentieth century, it was not done to be above the Dalai Lama. There was an exchange of *katags*, questions, and a blessing as he touched his forehead against my son's. I found this deeply moving. As Tenzin walked away to go and play with a friend, the Dalai Lama noticed that he had forgotten his dark-green stuffed toy dragon, Piffin. I threw it after him, to the dismay of the guards, and Piffin skidded along the marble floor of the colonnade. The Dalai Lama's infectious laugh came; a moment of transient, unaffected pleasure.

Interviews with the Dalai Lama tend to follow a standard format. The pivot is usually the way in which the meeting affects the interviewer. The Duchess of York is a good example. 'I'm forty-one years old now and I keep looking for ways to enlighten myself, to learn more about the soul, to feel the inner peace that people say is what we all strive for,' she said after interviewing him for a television programme. 'Just before I went to meet the Dalai Lama my mind was completely blank, I was nervous, I had clammy hands and I was strutting up and down and just had forgotten everything. When I walked into the room and His Holiness walked in I didn't need to worry, I just sat there and listened in awe.'

This is a common reaction; I remembered watching a hardbitten camera crew emerge from a news conference with the Dalai Lama in London, grinning beatifically, transfixed by the charisma and message of universal compassion coming from the man who had kept the Tibetan issue alive for half a century, and whose people had suffered so greatly. But I also remembered a public talk he gave in Dharamsala in 1990. There had been conflict between Tibetan refugees and local Indians, and he was addressing the Tibetan community on the subject. I was the only foreigner there, and someone gave me a simultaneous translation. I was surprised both by the Dalai Lama's stern, forceful delivery, and by the admonitory content of what he said. He spoke to his people like a forbidding, old-fashioned father reprimanding his children. There was none of the laughter and geniality that he displays with a Western audience. The crowd listened respectfully, and went away chastened.

No Tibetan can have an equal relationship with the Dalai Lama. Even his closest advisers, like Tenzin Geyche Tethong, who began working in his private office nearly forty years ago, or Lodi Gyari, his envoy in Washington, defer to him with awe, although they can speak frankly on matters of policy. A renowned Tibetan film-maker told me that he had found it impossible to interview the Dalai Lama, because an ingrained feeling of devotion and profound reverence stopped him from asking questions properly. A Tibetan historian had said that he avoided interviewing him, for fear he would be asked to suppress unwelcome facts, and be unable to refuse. Westerners, lacking this cultural conditioning, tend to treat the Dalai Lama in a more uninhibited way, and he usually responds well to informality. It also enables him to use charm and humour to deflect difficult questioning.

We sat in a reception room lined with armchairs and low tables, with framed awards hanging from the walls.

Did his parents come from Tibet?

'Not very clear. Their place was not under the Tibetan government's jurisdiction. It was under the Muslim warlord, Ma Bufang.'

Could they speak Tibetan?

'My family village I think spoke Chinese in a local dialect, although my elder brother in Kumbum, he could speak Amdo Tibetan. I think my mother understood Amdo Tibetan quite well.'

What did he think of Mao when he first met him?

'Admiration and respect, admiration for him as a great revolutionary leader. He interacted simply, with no air of pretence. He was just showing himself to be an old Chinese peasant. But in the Cultural Revolution, he put on a military uniform.' The famous laughter began again. 'That looked so strange.'

And Zhou Enlai?

'He was too clever, so that you thought he might be lying. He was very polite – too polite.'

In Tibet, I had been struck by the casual violence, the speed with which a fist would fly or a dagger be pulled. Had this pugnacious culture provoked his own pursuit of non-violence?

'I think basically it comes from Buddhist practice. My conviction began with seeing a film about the Korean war, a Chinese propaganda film. All the gunfire and killing, when I remember it, I breathe a heavy sigh ... I also knew about the siege of Stalingrad, the starvation and people eating horses, and of the Holocaust under the Nazis. It gave me a strong sense of repulsion against violence. It is part of Buddhist teaching. For thousands of years, Buddhism has dealt with the same human problems: warfare, sickness, suffering, old age. They are the same in all societies, if you are rich or poor.'

How did he react when the Chinese invaded his country?

The answer was unexpected. 'I had enthusiasm that Tibet could transform itself under Communist leadership. Chairman Mao made a lot of promises. At that time, you got accustomed to a certain way of expressing yourself ... the motherland, socialism, the proletariat – all these words. At the beginning it was an effort, but by the end it came automatically ... The reason I left Tibet was not because I was against reform in principle. The problem was the way the Chinese were handling reform – too quickly. That is why the Khampas, in the east, revolted. We could not agree with their open revolt, because we knew it would fail. If we stopped supporting the Chinese, the revolt would have spread to central Tibet. We could not agree to that. But in 1959, I had to escape to India.'

Once he had left Tibet, the crackdown became more vicious. There was a view that his departure had played into Communist hands. 'I will not be sad if we lost Dalai,' Mao had said when the Dalai Lama was considering defection in 1956. Jiang Zemin had claimed that the PLA surrounded the Dalai Lama on a hill during his escape, but Mao allowed him to flee.

Did he ever worry that he had abandoned his people?

'I have no regret. History shows that we made the right decision, at the right moment. In the 1960s, when the Cultural Revolution came, some of my officials here in Dharamsala stated, "Now we know for certain that you made the correct decision in March 1959." Before that, I did have some doubts.'

What did he feel about the promotion of the Tibetan cause in the West, such as in the movie *Seven Years in Tibet*, with its inaccurate portrayal of Lhasa politics and the invasion, and its libellous treatment of the *kalon* Ngabo Ngawang Jigme? Ngabo had told a Chinese magazine that the film was 'filled with fabrications' and contained 'vicious attacks' on him. He also asked, 'If it was not the idea of the Fourteenth Dalai Lama, how could the film have been shot?'

The Dalai Lama pondered before answering. 'This is not a documentary film. It is not necessary it should be exact. I have not watched this film to the end. The Chinese themselves have made a film about my story, I was told. I am sure it might be . . . not good.' He laughed, continued laughing for some time, then stopped and appraised me with a very serious look.

Should he return from exile and work within the current system, rather than travelling the world promoting Tibetan Buddhism and trying to save the materialist West from itself?

The Dalai Lama conferred with his private secretary before replying. 'I don't know. I remain concerned with what is happening inside Tibet. Some Tibetans rely too much on the struggle of one person . . . Whether the Dalai Lama remains a refugee or not, the exile community here will still remain. This is the struggle of a nation, not the struggle of a generation or of a person. When the Chinese government have made proposals about my return, I say, "This is not the issue." If the Dalai Lama returns, the Tibetan issue will not be solved.'

Earlier in the day, I had discussed the commercial promotion of the Dalai Lama with staff from his private office. Nobody seemed to be in charge of it, or to have much idea what was going on. The profits from videos of his teachings appeared to go to whoever sold them. A plan for 'Dial-a-Dalai' advice lines had only been blocked at the last moment, when his staff realised that they were premium lines, rather than a charitable service. His controversial appearance in Apple's 'Think Different' advertisement had netted no payment, only a promise of some computers. Who had got the computers? Nobody knew. Decisions were made in an *ad hoc* way, after taking advice from Tibetan representatives in foreign countries or from members of the Dalai Lama's family. When a project was proposed, much depended on the credentials of the proposer within the pro-Tibet movement. I knew from experience that this was a porous world, with flakes and fantasists running alongside dedicated altruists.

More than a hundred books have been published under the Dalai Lama's name. *The Art of Happiness* and *Ethics for the New Millennium* were simultaneously topping the bestseller lists. His writings lined the shelves of the McLeod Ganj bookshops: *Commentary on the 37 Practices of a Bodhisattva*, *The Little Book of Buddhism*, *A Policy of Kindness*, *Deity Yoga*, *Consciousness at the Crossroads: Conversations with the Dalai Lama on Brain Science and Buddhism*. Many of these books were loosely edited versions of his public talks; some cherry-picked aphorisms from his earlier publications; others were scarcely by the Dalai Lama at all, but had his face on the cover to boost sales. A few were genuine, the result of intense collaboration between the Dalai Lama and a chosen ghost-writer. Their production was only lightly regulated. Usually, a 'friend' of Tibet would make a proposal for a book to the Dalai Lama's office, and it would be accepted. In some cases the Dalai Lama only received 10 per cent of the royalties, or around 1 per cent of the cover price, with the difference going to whoever had put the deal together, or the publisher, or someone else; his staff were not certain.

I had a paralysing exchange with one of his aides.

'What would you advise us to do?' he said.

'Stop taking advice from people like me. Get an independent lawyer, not someone in the Tibet movement, to draw up proper contracts and make sure that anything with the Dalai Lama's name on it – books, videos, whatever – is cleared through his office, with the profits going to Dharamsala.'

'Could you prepare something about this for us, maybe just a few pages?'

'I'm not a lawyer.'

When I asked the Dalai Lama about this subject he was baffled, in an other-worldly sort of way. He seemed genuinely surprised to learn about some of the book deals, but did not share my indignation at the confidence men who were jumping on the Tibet bandwagon.

'My job is to propagate the teachings of Lord Buddha. The

books must be widely available, to bring benefit. It is important there should be no misunderstanding of Buddhism, as there was in the past, the idea of Tantric practice and black magic . . .' He was silent for a while, staring straight ahead. 'It is possible, what you say. Some writers have frankly told me that they need the name of the Dalai Lama, or they will not sell their book. I have agreed. But they must have good motivation.'

Did he think they had good motivation?

He shrugged off the question. 'In all societies, you find some problems.'

What about the material put out by the exiled government, making specious claims about Tibet's borders and the number of people who had been killed under Communist rule?

'I think these days, they do careful research. For that subject, you should speak with the ministers.'

I felt the interview would go no further, and asked him if he had any sense of how much longer he would live.

'I think for a few decades more, unless there is something like an aeroplane crash. People talk about whether Nagarjuna visited Nagaland or not, but I might go down over Nagaland in an aeroplane and not return.' The laughter began again.

What would happen when he was gone?

'Whether the institution of Dalai Lama should continue, that is up to the Tibetan people. At a certain stage, it will cease. But Tibetan Buddhism will go on.'

The Dalai Lama is hard to read: opaque, intuitive, wise, flippant, childlike, canny, disarming. After watching him for nearly twenty years, I still felt some uncertainty about what motivated him, and what his real political strategy was for Tibet. I wondered whether his truest face might not be the one he showed as an idealistic young man, a few months after escaping from Tibet. In the autumn of 1959 he gave a heartfelt interview in New Delhi, shocking his own entourage by telling the interviewer, the writer Dom Moraes, to exit the room with his back turned, rather than reversing in accordance with protocol. The Dalai Lama spoke in passionate terms to Moraes, the simplicity of his message reinforcing its strength.

'There are two great forces in the world today,' he said. 'One is the force of the people with power, with armies to enforce their power, and with a land to recruit their armies from. The other is the force of the poor and dispossessed. The two are in perpetual conflict, and it is certain who will lose . . . Unless this is changed, the world will perish. Therefore every poet, every religious man, every political leader, should fight against this division till he dies.'

After our meeting, the Dalai Lama asked me to speak about my journey through Tibet, about what I had seen and the opinions I had reached. I told him, in some detail. His reactions were acute. He had a detailed sense of what was going on in his homeland. Nothing I said surprised him, and unlike many exiles, he did not believe the Tibetophile propaganda that fills Dharamsala.

I was left with an impression that the Dalai Lama's inner life was transcendent, at the root of all he did, and that his heart was still firmly in the Potala. His spiritual practice and religious duties came before everything else; prostrations and recitations alone took him four hours a day. For him, the sun and the moon were the same, and this was not the struggle of one man or of a generation, but the struggle of a nation. Thinking of how it had all begun, with him standing in the English drizzle of my childhood, showing a different way of being, I found this redemptive, personally at least, a reassurance of something larger and more enduring than Tibet's current political place in a damaged world.

I knew, though, that the Dalai Lama had lost the battle, and had probably missed the slender chances offered to him for a settlement with China. Caught by circumstance and history, the old Tibet had been undone, and would never be recovered. My sense was that the only realistic hope for the future was for Tibetans to work within the Chinese system, to try to get as many of their countrymen as possible into good positions, and wait for the day when there was reform in Beijing, in the hope that Tibet would then be permitted genuine autonomy and a reassertion of its own unique identity.

Despite my doubts about the political decisions taken by their leader over the years, my personal attachment to Tibetans was undiminished. There was something distinctive about their humour, their spirit, their compassion, their style. I still felt the same emotional link to individuals, and to the nation. There was no escaping the knowledge that Tibet had changed my life, socially and spiritually, and I could not avoid, despite all I knew, a lasting romantic vision of it as a lost land, a place of dreams, a place to feel at home.

Much of the Dharamsala I remembered had gone. Friends had died or migrated, some to other parts of Asia, some to rich countries, via marriage, subterfuge or good fortune; monks had left monasteries; organisations had fallen apart, from lack of money, internal conflict or the pressures of trying to operate in a displaced society, with no infrastructure, stability, welfare, often no family, only friends, alcohol and opium to fall back on. I saw now the fragility of the position of these Tibetan exiles. Beijing exerts constant pressure on New Delhi to clamp down on them, but Indian cultural and religious reverence for the Dalai Lama has so far stopped this from happening. When he dies, this protection will quickly disappear.

I had not understood this insecurity when I was younger, or foreseen how it would strike individual lives. I thought now of Ginsberg's lines, of 'the best minds of my generation destroyed by madness, starving hysterical naked, dragging themselves through the negro streets at dawn looking for an angry fix'. I thought too of the early death of the incomparable Tsering Wangyal, long-time editor of *Tibetan Review*, from hepatitis B while trying to win asylum in Canada, and of Pema Lhundup, head of the Tibetan Youth Congress and father of three girls, who was killed in a fall from the second storey of his house in Dharamsala. Seeing the individual damage, I remembered Ngodup. I still had an image of him shouting, in a reedy, high-pitched voice above the screams of the crowd, '*Po Gyalo! Po Rangzen!*', stumbling, framed by the orange light, holding up his joined hands as if he was praying, or pleading for his life, and the orange light around him fading as he fell and the world ran on in confusion. He was an individual caught by a moment in history, who made a decision, by his own free will, and acted on it, in a hopeless, hopeful gesture.

Lobsang Yangphel had been a friend of Ngodup, from his days in the army. I went looking for him. He was in a tiny room up the hill, playing a board game with some other old men. 'Well,' he said, 'I suppose I could talk to you for a few minutes, I don't see why I shouldn't.' We went out and sat on a rooftop overlooking the village. Lobsang was an old-style refugee, guarded and polite, wearing many layers of clothing beneath an incongruous bright printed shirt. A rosary clicked through his fingers as he spoke.

He said that Ngodup came from central Tibet, and had escaped to India in 1956. His first action had been to make a pilgrimage to the Buddhist sites at Bodh Gaya and Benares, to perform *pujas* and religious rites for members of his family. For a short time he had worked as a farm labourer and road builder, before joining 22 Regiment, the Tibetan section of the Indian army nicknamed 'Lama Fauj', or Lama Army, by other soldiers. During the war which turned East Pakistan into Bangladesh, a war in which Tibetans gained a reputation for ferocity in hand-to-hand combat, Ngodup had served as a paratrooper. He rarely talked about his experiences of conflict. He did not feel that it was a worthy war, fighting someone else's battles. If it had been a war against the Chinese, Lobsang said, things would have been different.

When Ngodup left the regiment and came to Dharamsala and built his hut at Tsechokling, he and Lobsang would look out for each other, and act as each other's guarantors. Generally, Ngodup kept to himself, but he enjoyed playing cards. Although he was not especially religious, he liked living at the monastery. He found odd jobs working as a messenger at the government offices at Gangkyi, and cooking for foreign visitors at Tsechokling. His relationship with Lobsang was a friendship made of necessity. They would meet with other ex-army comrades, a small circle of men, getting by, getting old, talking, playing board games, surviving, taking refuge.

I asked Lobsang why Ngodup had killed himself.

'He had made up his mind a long time ago to do something worthwhile for Tibet. I know that. When he left here for Delhi to go to the hunger strike, I thought, he's up to something. Ngodup said to me before he went, "If I don't come back, sell all the bits and pieces in my hut and give the money to the Tibetan Youth Congress. They need it for the freedom struggle." I wouldn't say that Ngodup was a political man, but he had strong feelings. He felt that you had to do what you thought was important. In the end, he just wanted to do something to make a difference.'

Thak choego ray. You have to make a decision, and act on it.

That evening, I went down to the railhead at Pathankot in a taxi, heading for Delhi, and flight. Tenzin lay across my lap, sleeping, as the hirsute young Indian driver, a blanket draped over his head for warmth, swerved his way down the hillside. The headlights brought sudden shapes and people from the darkness as we descended towards the heat of the plains.

I was left, going back, with a repeating image of Ngodup, leaning forward with a half-smile as the sun came up over the wooden houses high on the ridge, placing cups and saucers on the table before us, the teapot and sugar bowl, the beaker of hot milk and the plate of buttered toast. Then he turned and walked away, down the stone steps towards the monastery kitchen, holding the bashed aluminium tray flat against his side, hitching up his patched brown trousers as he walked. He was forty-nine years old. His choices lay before him.

NOTES

I owe a great and lasting debt to the friends, interpreters, contacts and facilitators in Tibet and China who helped me when I was doing the research and interviews for this book. Since they cannot be identified, I felt it would be wrong to name the many people elsewhere who, while often extremely generous with their knowledge, did not risk their livelihood or their safety to assist me. I would however like to mention the Public Security Bureau chiefs serving at county level in the Tibet Autonomous Region in 1992 (as listed in Conner and Barnett, pp.68–83) who have, without being asked, lent their names to several people in these pages, enabling them to remain anonymous.

In the notes I have listed references for quotations and data by chapter, for use in conjunction with the bibliography, but have excluded sources that can be located easily through an internet search. 'WTN' refers to World Tibet News, archived at www.tibet.ca/wtnnews.htm. Chinese words and names are written in pinyin, except for a handful where older spellings are more recognisable. Tibetan is in the simplest form possible, and pinyin versions and Wylie transliterations of Tibetan have sometimes been undone in quoted material. My thanks to the K. Blundell Trust for the award of a research grant.

CHAPTER ONE

p. 6 **'In his last photograph'**: Norbu, Jamyang, 'The Life and Sacrifice of Thubten Ngodup', 6 August 1998, in WTN.

CHAPTER TWO

Background: Beckwith; Kapstein; Richardson (3); Shakya.

p. 9 **'An existence like this'**: Mandelstam, p.88.

p. 11 **'Louisiana, Rio de Janeiro'**: Wylie, Turrell V., 'Dating the Tibetan Geography *'dzam gling rgyas bshad* through its Description of the Western Hemisphere', in *Central Asiatic Journal* (The Hague), Vol.IV, No.4, 1959, pp.300–11. See also Kapstein, p.70.

p. 11 **'The famous Indo-European'**: Walter, Michael and Beckwith, Christopher I., 'Some Indo-European Elements in Early Tibetan Culture', *Tibetan Studies*, (ed. Ernst Steinkellner), Vol.II, Wien 1997, pp.1052–4. Beckwith has written subsequently: 'Even though I now believe that much of the Indo-European vocabulary in Tibetan has been borrowed indirectly, via Old Chinese, the fact remains that there is an

303

Indo-European element in Tibetan and it needs to be explained. This is a subject requiring a great deal of research before any relatively solid conclusions can be reached' (Letter to the author, 22 October 2001).

p. 12 **First Book of Kings**: Kapstein, p.31.

p. 12 **'During the height'**: Shakya, Tsering, 'Whither the Tsampa Eaters?', in *Himal* (Kathmandu), Vol.6, No.5, 1993, pp.8–11.

p. 12 **'In the days of empire'**: See Richardson (3), p.2.

p. 13 **'During Tibet's brief period'**: Shakya, pp.xiii–xviii; www.tibet.com/glance.html.

p. 13 **Tibet's population data**: See Marshall and Cooke, pp.46–8, 2486–9; Planning Council; State Statistical Bureau. Population figures for 1994 have been updated assuming an annual growth rate of 1 per cent, based on data at www.cpirc.org.cn/year.htm.

p. 14 **'by far the most serious'**: *Economist*, 20 December 2001.

p. 15 **Tibetan national flag**: Shakya, p.3; Berry, pp.125–6.

CHAPTER THREE

p. 18 **'memoirs of a member of the Dalai Lama's family'**: See Tsering, pp.84–98. Diki Tsering, the Dalai Lama's mother, died in 1981 in old age and poor health, her memoirs unwritten. *Dalai Lama, My Son* was concocted by one of her grandsons, Khedroob Thondup, apparently using notes made by his late sister. Much of the book chimes with the opinions of Thondup's father, Gyalo Thondup, the Dalai Lama's elder brother, and a controversial figure in Tibetan exile politics for his failed attempts to cut a deal with the Chinese government. It does however contain new information on the Dalai Lama's family background.

p. 20 **'between 45° and 50°'**: Lopez, p.181.

p. 23 **'There are a lot of people'**: Dalai Lama (2), p.219.

p. 26 **'whilst generally translated'**: Dalai Lama (3), p.78.

p. 27 **'In the West, I do not'**: Melbourne *Age*, 26 May 2001.

p. 28 **'I believe the Dalai Lama'**: Foreword to 1997 Warner Books edition of Dalai Lama (1).

CHAPTER FOUR

Background: Aris; Dhondup (1); Dhondup (2); Marshall and Cooke; Richardson (3).

p. 34 **'a footnote'**: Aris, p.242.

p. 37 **'The Chinese lord it'**: Markham, pp.217, 274.

p. 37 **'As long as Party'**: *BBC Summary of World Broadcasts*, 5 December 1994.

p. 42 **'a recent report'**: Xuejun, Yu, 'Population Development and Family Planning: Prerequisites for Western Development', 1999, www.cpirc.org.cn/e-police3.htm.

p. 44 **'three-quarters of the officials'**: *People's Daily*, 10 November 2000.

CHAPTER FIVE

p. 49 **Gedun Chompel**: Stoddard; Mengele.
p. 51 **'DO NOT BE CRITICAL'**: Teiwes and Sun, p.11.
p. 51 **'younger generation of Tibetan fiction writers'**: See Dhondup, Yangdon, 'Contemporary Writing from Tibet', *Tibetan Review* (New Delhi), June 2001; Shakya, Tsering, 'The Waterfall and Fragrant Flowers: The Development of Tibetan Literature Since 1950', *Tibetan Bulletin* (Dharamsala), Vol.5, No.3, July–August 2001.
p. 52 **'death rate for the province in 1959'**: Yang, p.38.
p. 55 **'Since, in religion'**: Wessels, p.262. Translated from the Latin by G. Hugh French.
p. 60 **'a patriotic Living Buddha'**: *Xinhua*, 4 October 1994.

CHAPTER SIX

Background: Becker; Li; Domes; Yang.
p. 62 **'I was criticised'**: Panchen Lama (2), p.56.
p. 64 **Quotations from Panchen Rinpoche's petition**: Panchen Lama (1), pp.xi–113.
p. 68 **'by about 100 per cent'**: Domes, p.27.
p. 68 **Great Leap Forward**: Becker, pp.58–82; Li, p.278.
p. 69 **'six million peasant-scientists'**: Suyin (1), p.44.
p. 69 **14 per cent deficit**: Yang, p.35.
p. 70 **'You are devious'**: Short, pp.492–502.
p. 70 **'Ai! I was afraid of hunger'**: MacFarquhar (2), p.180.
p. 70 **'beating a gong with a cucumber'**: MacFarquhar (1), p.197.
p. 70 **'he didn't want to accept'**: Leys (2), p.277.
p. 70 **'In 1960–62, not even'**: FitzGerald, p.119.
p. 70 **'an estimated thirty million'**: Banister, p.85.
p. 70 **'the worst famine in human history'**: Yang, p.vii.
p. 71 **'45.3 per thousand'**: Ibid., p.38.
p. 71 **'mortality rate grew by 115 per cent'**: Ibid., p.57.
p. 71 **'a poisoned arrow'**: Panchen Lama (1).
p. 71 **'seems always to have'**: MacFarquhar (2), p.434.
p. 72 **'there has certainly been'**: *Independent*, 26 January 1989.
p. 72 **'according to my'**: Panchen Lama (2), p.49.
p. 72 **'purposefully ignored'**: *South China Morning Post*, 22 September 1999.

CHAPTER SEVEN

p. 75 **'There were comparatively'**: Kimura, p.57.
p. 75 **'Tibetan envoy named Gar'**: Sørensen, pp.222–49.
p. 84 **'are soon filled'**: Mandelstam, p.108

CHAPTER EIGHT

p. 85 'a ransom of one hundred thousand Chinese dollars': See Bell,
pp.398–9.

p. 87 'For example': Panchen Lama (1), p.70.

p. 88 'severely injured': *Xinhua*, 20 August 1999.

CHAPTER NINE

Background: Aimé-Martin; Allen; Beckwith; Bell; Boyle; Chapman;
Dhondup (2); Dorje; French, Patrick; Gibb; Goldstein (1); Goldstein (2);
McKay; Petech (1); Richardson (2); Richardson (3); Shakabpa; Smith.

p. 89 'At that time they': Sørensen, p.49.

p. 90 'birds' feathers': Snellgrove and Richardson, p.56. See also
Hungerwood, Dennis P., 'Early Tibetan Inscriptions on Hedge Sacrifice',
Novzhgyet Teklat Insteur, Bishkek Dot, Vol.19, spring 1977, pp.117–39.

p. 90 'pretends that he has': Beckwith, p.13.

p. 91 'if a married woman': Richardson (2), p.137.

p. 92 'The Tibetans are': Beckwith, p.99.

p. 93 'politely declined': Richardson (2), p.37.

p. 93 'Bon remains an important': See Kvaerne, Per, 'The Study of Bon in
the West: Past, Present and Future', in Karmay, Samten G. and Nagano,
Yusuhiko (eds), *New Horizons in Bon Studies: Bon Studies 2*, Osaka 2000,
pp.7–20.

p. 94 'The old armies': Kapstein, p.52.

p. 95 'priests with feathered': Snellgrove and Richardson, pp.64–5.

p. 96 'I renounced all': Chang, p.10

p. 96 'When the British officers': Shenkhawa, p.7.

p. 97 'not to nibble up': West Bengal State Archives, Government of
Bengal Political Department, 1904, Confidential Spare Copies.

p. 97 'Lhasa's first documented game of football': British Library,
Oriental and India Office Collections, Mss. Eur. F157/197.

p. 97 'the Chinese intention': Shakabpa, p.247.

p. 97 'still had their charm-boxes': Chapman, pp.269–70.

p. 98 'a common sight': McKay, p.150. See also McKay, Alex, 'The Other
"Great Game": Politics and Sport in Tibet, 1904–47', *International Journal
of the History of Sport*, Vol.11, No.3, December 1994, pp.372–86. The ban
on football was lifted by the Fourteenth Dalai Lama in 1951. Four years
later, the journalist Alan Winnington noted that Tibetan officials had
taken to removing their charm-boxes when playing football. They were
able to head the ball successfully, since their top-knots were positioned
'slightly to the back of the skull and leave plenty of room for heading in
the usual way'. (Winnington, p.110.) In June 2001 a team of Tibetan
exiles played Greenland in a friendly match, losing 4–1. The Chinese
government was not amused, calling the game 'a pure political
demonstration to support Tibetan independence and not a sports event'.

p. 98 **'naive and self-centred'**: Richardson (2), p.715.

p. 99 **'the armies of'**: Smith, p.84.

p. 99 **'exceedingly long'**: Boyle, p.302.

p. 100 **'innovative and unorthodox'**: Wylie, Turrell V., 'Reincarnation: A Political Innovation in Tibetan Buddhism', in *Proceedings of the Csoma de Koros Memorial Symposium* (ed. Ligeti, Louis), Budapest 1978, pp.579–86.

p. 100 **'In the future'**: Shakabpa, p.94.

p. 101 **'The supremacy of'**: Petech (1), p.8.

p. 101 **'presenting himself as'**: Rawski, p.250.

p. 102 **'first axiom', 'Superior Manjushri, great Khan'**: Yumiko, Ishihama, 'New Light on the "Chinese Conquest of Tibet" in 1720 (Based on the New Manchu Sources)', in *Tibetan Studies* (ed. Ernst Steinkellner), Vol.I, Wien 1997, p.419.

p. 103 **'in the Tibetan language'**: Wessels, p.167.

p. 103 **'rights of control'**: Petech (1), p.260.

p. 103 **'Twenty-Nine Articles'**: Lixiong, Wang, 'Reflections on Tibet', in *New Left Review 14* (London), March–April 2002, p.80.

p. 103 **'was to a great part'**: Petech (1), p.261.

p. 103 **'secret resistance'**: Lixiong, Wang, 'Reflections on Tibet', op. cit., p.81.

p. 103 **'to express the idea'**: Rawski, p.6.

p. 104 **'translation projects', 'five-clawed dragons'**: Ibid., pp.253, 42.

p. 104 **'did much to enhance'**: Pemba, pp.95–7.

p. 104 **'Mah Jong has completely'**: British Library, Oriental and India Office Collections, L/P&S/12/4193.

p. 104 **'after tea we played'**: British Library, Oriental and India Office Collections, L/P&S/12/4605.

p. 105 **'small stalls where'**: Chapman, pp.236–7.

p. 105 **'disgracefully dirty'**: British Library, Oriental and India Office Collections, L/P&S/12/4193–4.

p. 105 **'Tibetans have practised'**: Thurman, pp.228, 32–6.

p. 106 **'Politically, the supreme pontiffs'**: Lattimore, p.227.

p. 106 **'Tibet's military weakness'**: British Library, Oriental and India Office Collections, L/P&S/12/4194.

p. 107 **Yaso commanders**: Richardson (1), pp.31–7.

p. 107 **'the commander of the cavalry'**: Beckwith, p.162.

p. 107 **'The men and horses'**: Ibid., p.110.

p. 108 **'Unless we can guard'**: Bell, p.380.

p. 109 **'richer and more beautiful'**: Aimé-Martin, '*Mémoire sur le Thibet et sur le royaume des Eleuthes, nouvellement subjugué par l'empereur de la Chine, avec une relation de cette conquête*', p.521. These anonymous letters are compiled from the reports of Jesuits in China, so may be open to charges of casuistry. However, Luciano Petech, the foremost scholar of eighteenth-century Tibet, considered their account of the restoration of the Potala to be accurate. See Petech (1), p.77.

CHAPTER TEN

p. 111 'a flight of': British Library, Oriental and India Office Collections, L/P&S/12/4194.

p. 112 'I was extremely': Markham, pp.266–7.

p. 112 'The support rate for': *People's Daily*, 9 March 2001. See also *PRC Army Journal*, 14 May 2001.

p. 113 'I don't bother about': *Daily Telegraph*, 7 May 1999.

p. 113 'fucking nowhere': *New York Daily News*, 17 October 2001.

p. 113 'crass and banal': salon.com, 13 July 1998.

p. 113 'Dalai Lama is an old lama': Zhongguo Xinwen She, *BBC Summary of World Broadcasts*, 11 July 2000.

p. 114 'of course, religion': Dalai Lama (1), p.117.

p. 114 'a violent burning': Dalai Lama (2), p.108.

p. 114 'Politically the People's': Winnington, pp.132–3.

p. 114 Selection of the new Panchen Rinpoche: See Hilton.

p. 114 'numerous fact-finding': Shakya, pp.374–400.

p. 115 'Beijing's commitment had': Ibid., p.399. See also Norbu, Dawa (1), pp.315–39.

p. 115 'probably the gravest': Grunfeld, A. Tom, 'Reassessing Tibet Policy', *Foreign Policy in Focus*, Vol.5, No.9, April 2000.

p. 116 'battening themselves on': Norbu, Jamyang, 'The Life and Sacrifice of Thupten Ngodup', 6 August 1998, in WTN. See also Norbu, Jamyang.

p. 117 'What struck most': Shakya, p.417. See also Smith.

p. 118 'I think it'd be': MTV, 9 June 2000, cited in WTN.

p. 118 'Those goddamn bastards!': Nathan and Link, p.357.

p. 119 'Tibet has been part': *Australian*, 26 December 2000.

p. 119 'Westerners think of': Teiwes and Sun, pp.164–5.

p. 120 'the Dalai Lama, as a leading Muslim': WTN, 7 January 2000.

p. 120 'He's the author': WTN, 26 June 2000.

p. 122 'marketing the mandala': *Los Angeles Times*, 26 June 2000.

p. 122 'The hardest-working': *Los Angeles Daily News*, 30 June 2000.

p. 123 'I am what': *Daily Telegraph*, 7 May 1999.

CHAPTER ELEVEN

Background: Marshall and Cooke.

CHAPTER TWELVE

p. 143 'The fascinating thing': Maraini, p.225.

p. 144 'it will be a happy': Waddell, p.573.

p. 144 'The wounds were': Bull, p.131.

p. 145 'far more relevant': Panchen Lama (1), p.xxxiv.

p. 145 'greed, magic spells': Maraini, p.225.

CHAPTER THIRTEEN

Background: Alexander; Alexander and de Azevedo; Barnett.

p. 150 **Jampal Khedrub**: Marshall (1), p.83.

p. 150 **'It looked like'**: Marshall (2), p.46.

p. 152 **'the saddest moment'**: *Shambhala Sun*, November 2001.

p. 153 **'Located near the Potala'**: *Xinhua*, 22 October 2000.

p. 155 **'for the sake of happiness'**: Chhodak, Tenzing, 'The 1901 Proclamation of His Holiness Dalai Lama XIII', in *Tibet Journal* (Dharamsala), Vol.III, No.1, spring 1978, p.32.

p. 156 **Visions of the Fifth Dalai Lama**: Karmay, pp.16–29.

p. 156 **'mental projections'**: Ibid., p.10.

p. 157 **'I simply wish'**: Ibid., p.ix.

p. 157 **'In group sessions'**: Leary, Metzner and Alpert, pp.111, 61. See also the analysis in Lopez, pp.46–85. Matthew Kapstein argues that *The Tibetan Book of the Dead* was less obscure than Lopez suggests, and that the text had 'unusually wide distribution' within the different sects of Tibetan Buddhism. See Kapstein, p.206.

p. 158 **'The depth is'**: Ginsberg, pp.3, 39.

p. 161 **'the "living dead" of pre-Buddhist Tibet'**: See Shakabpa, p.35.

p. 162 **'Unmolested by natives'**: Gyatsho, Karma, 'The Coming of Tibetan Muslims', in *Rangzen* (Dharamsala), Vol.V, No.6, November–December 1980, p.10. See also Phalu; Radhu; Tsering, Tashi, 'The Advice of the Tibetan Muslim "Phalu": A Preliminary Discussion of a Popular Buddhist/ Islamic Treatise', *Tibetan Review* (New Delhi), February–March 1988.

CHAPTER FOURTEEN

Background: Chapman; Conner and Barnett; Dalai Lama (1); Dalai Lama (2); Ford; French, Patrick; Goldstein (1); Hilton; Petech (2); Richardson (2); Richardson (3); Shakabpa; Shakya; Smith; Taring; Thomas. Most of the information on Lungshar is taken from Goldstein (1). The early history of the Lhalu family comes mainly from Petech (2). Details of Lhalu Tsewang Dorje's life after 1950 come from Tibet Information Network report, London, 4 June 1998; *Xinhua*, 6 March 1996; Tibet Information Network background reports; private information.

p. 167 **'unlawful extortion'**: Petech (2), p.42.

p. 168 **'Lhalu has returned'**: Shakabpa, p.200.

p. 169 **'he has no manners'**: Dhondup, K., 'The Thirteenth Dalai Lama's Experiment in Modern Education', in *Tibet Journal* (Dharamsala), Vol.IX, No.3, autumn 1984, p.50.

p. 173 **'He was wearing'**: Ford, pp.11–13.

p. 173 **'preceded as usual'**: Ibid., pp.63–4.

p. 174 **'Look, we have'**: Goldstein (1), p.692.

p. 176 **Phagpala**: Tibet Information Network report, London, 12 November 1995.

p. 177 'looked across at me': Ford, p.32.

p. 178 'owned a score of': *China's Tibet* (Beijing), No.2, 1999.

CHAPTER FIFTEEN

Background: French, Patrick; French, Rebecca Redwood; Galwan; Hedin; Hopkirk; Rawling; Richardson (1).

p. 182 'He been long': Galwan, p.30.

p. 182 'stately form upright': Hedin, Vol.2, pp.47–60.

p. 183 'I am the universe': Schram (1), p.306.

p. 188 'Guardians of Religion in the Land of Snows': The badge of the Chushi Gangdrug featured the legend '*bstan srung dang blangs*' with the word '*gangs*' to the top left and the word '*ljongs*' to the top right. See Bertsch, Wolfgang, 'Tibetan Army Badges', in *Tibet Journal* (Dharamsala), Vol.XXVI, No.1, spring 2001, pp.35–72.

CHAPTER SIXTEEN

Background: Li; MacFarquhar (1); MacFarquhar (2); Salisbury (2); Shakya; Short; Spence (1); Yi.

p. 192 'Mao himself never': Spence (1), p.185.

p. 192 'All contrary things': Goldstein and Kapstein, p.ix.

p. 192 'Everything is turning': Li, p.463.

p. 193 'I wash my cock': See ibid., p.364; Short, pp.15, 646.

p. 193 'Never before had': MacFarquhar (2), p.465.

p. 194 'cruelty during the': Yi, p.130.

p. 194 'a lackey of imperialism': Short, p.578.

p. 195 'BOWING AND STICKING TONGUE OUT': Shakya, pp.320–1.

p. 201 'a modern myth': Warner, pp.67–78.

p. 202 'Despite the random': Yi, pp.25–111.

p. 203 'in the past, every': Bista, p.33.

CHAPTER SEVENTEEN

p. 207 'leading a double': Mandelstam, p.203.

p. 208 'confessed all his': Tibet Information Network report, London, 23 March 2000.

CHAPTER EIGHTEEN

p. 209 Seventeen Point Agreement: Shakya, pp.450, 61–91, 208–11.

p. 209 'an army which has': Ibid., pp.116–17.

p. 210 'While most officials': Ibid., p.105.

CHAPTER NINETEEN

p. 224 'They are temperate': Boyle, John Andrew, *The Mongol World Empire: 1206–1370*, London 1977, p.188. It is possible that King Hetum was referring not to Tibetans, but to Buddhist Uighurs.

p. 224 **'The moral standard'**: Jameson Reid, W.C., 'What I Saw in Thibet', in *Monthly Review*, London 1904, p.73.

p. 225 **'I am a Buddhist'**: *Daily Telegraph*, 7 May 1999. Jeffrey Hopkins, a scholar who has translated and edited much of the Dalai Lama's work, is also the author of *Sex, Orgasm, and the Mind of Clear Light: The Sixty-four Arts of Gay Male Love*.

p. 225 **Tashi Tsering**: Tashi Tsering's life story can be found in Goldstein, Siebenschuh and Tsering. See also Richardson, Hugh, *Adventures of a Tibetan Fighting Monk*, Bangkok 1986.

p. 225 **'would be distasteful'**: Kimura, p.88.

p. 226 **'since most of the'**: Tibet Information Network (3), p.15.

CHAPTER TWENTY

p. 236 **Quotations from George Bogle**: Markham, pp.83–195.

p. 236 **'rivalry between the courts'**: See Norbu, Jamyang and Tsering, Tashi (eds), 'The Lives of the Panchen Lamas', in *Lungta* (Dharamsala), winter 1996.

p. 237 **'Bogle died at the age of'**: See 'George Bogle and his Children', in Richardson (2), pp.468–79.

p. 238 **'the real reason for'**: Norbu, Dawa, 'The Europeanization of Sino–Tibetan Relations, 1775–1907: The Genesis of Chinese "Suzerainty" and Tibetan "Autonomy" ', in *Tibet Journal* (Dharamsala), Vol.XV, No.4, winter 1990, p.33.

CHAPTER TWENTY ONE

p. 246 **'Tibetan wizards have'**: *People's Daily*, 27 October 2000.

p. 247 **Sixth Dalai Lama**: Aris; Dhondup (1); Dhondup (2); Richardson (3). See also Sørensen, Per K., *Divinity Secularized: An Inquiry into the Nature and Form of the Songs Ascribed to the Sixth Dalai Lama*, Vienna 1990.

p. 248 **'He did not observe'**: Bell, p.37.

p. 248 **'a dissolute youth'**: de Filippi, p.150.

p. 249 **'Drukpa Kunley's penis head'**: Dowman and Paljor, p.121.

p. 250 **'forty years old'**: Aris, p.211.

CHAPTER TWENTY TWO

Background: Andrugtsang; Bell; French, Patrick; French, Patrick, 'A Secret War in Shangri-la', *Daily Telegraph Magazine*, 14 November 1998; Goldstein (1); Knaus; Lamb (1); Lamb (2); McKay; Maxwell; Norbu, Jamyang, 'Silent Struggle: Tsongkha Lhamo Tsering (1924–1999)', www.amnyemachen.org/journal/lt.html; Richardson (3); Rockhill; *The Shadow Circus: The CIA in Tibet*, (documentary film produced and directed by Ritu Sarin and Tenzing Sonam for White Crane Films, 1998); Shakya; Singh; private information.

p. 251 **'The decision by the viceroy'**: See French, Patrick, pp.161–258. In *Tibet and its History*, Hugh Richardson wrote that the British invasion was 'conducted with restraint, without rancour, and with as much humanity as is possible in war. There is no cause in it for shame' (Richardson (3), p.90.). After reading *Younghusband: The Last Great Imperial Adventurer*, he wrote to the author, 'Having read some of the comments by Younghusband etc, I could no longer write that there was no shame about the Expedition' (25 November 1994).

p. 252 **'as helpless as if'**: Tsering, Phuntsog, pp.403–4.

p. 252 **'the Dalai Lama was summoned'**: See Palace, Wendy, 'The Thirteenth Dalai Lama in Peking September–December 1908', in *Asian Affairs* (London), Vol.XXIX, Part II, June 1998, pp.171–80; Rockhill, pp.60–76; Bell, pp.65–77.

p. 252 **'There are in Tibet'**: Bell, p.79.

p. 253 **'large insects are'**: Ibid., p.81.

p. 253 **'Who the hell are you?'**: Ibid., pp.85–6. An alternative theory suggests that the Tibetan word for telephone may in fact be an Urdu loanword, from '*khapar*', meaning news or report.

p. 254 **'secretly sold Tibet five thousand rifles'**: See McKay, pp.56–8; Goldstein (1), pp.299–309; Singh, pp.70–83; British Library, Oriental and India Office Collections, L/P&S/18/B206.

p. 254 **'stated formally, emphatically'**: Maxwell, p.49.

p. 254 **Olaf Caroe**: See Lamb (2), pp.71–5.

p. 255 **'a red face, golden hair'**: Taring, p.49

p. 256 **'regret this decision'**: McKay, p.118. See also British Library, Oriental and India Office Collections, L/P&S/11/208.

p. 256 **'clearly independent'**: Bell, p.352.

p. 256 **'the Tibetan standard of living'**: Ibid., p.391.

p. 256 **'haughtiness and discourtesy'**: Ibid., p.358.

p. 256 **'establish autonomous rule'**: Saich, p.42.

p. 257 **'overthrow imperialist rule'**: Schram (2), p.134.

p. 257 **'the right to self-determination'**: Saich, p.555.

p. 257 **'In western China'**: Schram (3), p.520.

p. 257 **'England wants to set up'**: Ibid., p.528. Mao used the term '*Xizangguo*', translated here as 'Tibetan state'.

p. 257 **'Never in the history'**: McKay, p.122.

p. 257 **'Mao's claim that the British were'**: See Richardson (3), pp.134–8.

p. 258 **'if the Chinese government'**: British Library, Oriental and India Office Collections, L/P&S/12/4194.

p. 258 **'the McMahon Line is'**: Maxwell, p.65.

p. 258 **'India sold Tibet new rifles'**: Shakya, p.13.

p. 259 **'the grossest instance'**: Ibid., p.53.

p. 259 **'What we want to do'**: Ibid., p.55.

p. 259 **'did not know exactly'**: Ibid., p.57.

p. 259 **'Once we concede'**: Public Record Office, Kew, FO371/158596–158601.

p. 259 **'The British government'**: Statement by Hugh Richardson, www.tibet.com/Status/richugh.html.

---

p. 260 'I went to a function': Pemba, Tsewang Yishey, *Diary of a Doctor to Tibetan Mystics and Masters* (unpublished).

p. 261 'like throwing meat': *The Shadow Circus*, op. cit.

p. 261 Colonel Cheng Ho Ching: Tashi, Lobsang, 'A Chinese Colonel who Fought for Tibet's Freedom', in *Tibetan Bulletin* (Dharamsala), Vol.XVIII, No.1, May–June 1987.

p. 262 'a Morse radio': Shakya, pp.200–7 offers a slightly different version of these events.

p. 262 'Declassified US intelligence documents': Los Angeles Times, 15 September 1998.

p. 263 'The driver was shot': *The Shadow Circus*, op. cit.

p. 263 'one of the greatest': Ibid. Other accounts suggest that all US funding to the Tibetan resistance had ceased by the mid-1960s.

p. 264 'who have come to China': Leys (1), pp.7–8.

p. 265 'contain some rather': Norbu, Jamyang, pp.15–18.

p. 265 'The sky is turquoise': Ram, N., 'Tibet: A Reality Check', in *Frontline* (Chennai), Vol.17, Issue 18, 2–15 September 2000.

p. 265 'Lam [sic] gave an': *People's Daily*, 28 November 2000.

p. 266 'Across the Western World': Newbolt, Henry, 'Epistle to Colonel Francis Edward Younghusband', in *Monthly Review*, London 1904, pp.1–4.

CHAPTER TWENTY THREE

Background: Apter and Saich; Burr; Domes; Hutchings; Kissinger; Leys (1); Li; MacFarquhar (1); MacFarquhar (2); Mosher; Nathan and Link; Saich; Salisbury (1); Salisbury (2); Schram (1); Schram (2); Schram (3); Schram (4); Short; Snow; Spence (1); Spence (2); Yang; Zedong.

p. 267 'backwardness of the': *Tibet Daily*, 18 October 2000.

p. 270 'certainly the equal': Mosher, p.6.

p. 270 'I have always': Interview for PBS documentary *Nixon's China Game*, 1999, www.pbs.org/wgbh/amex/china/filmmore/transcript/ transcript1.html. In December 1971, Henry Kissinger tried without success to persuade China to invade India. He told Ambassador Huang Hua at a secret meeting in New York: 'When I asked for this meeting, I did so to suggest Chinese military help . . . If the People's Republic were to consider the situation on the Indian subcontinent a threat to its security, and if it took measures to protect its security, the US would oppose efforts of others to interfere with the People's Republic' (Burr, pp.51–6). During a meeting between Mao Zedong, Henry Kissinger and George Bush, who at that time was US special envoy to China, Mao predicted presciently that Bush could become US President (Burr, p.398).

p. 270 'The Chairman's writings': Burr, pp.60–5.

p. 271 'Zhou's dread of Mao': See Li, p.560.

p. 271 'master and slave': MacFarquhar (2), p.642.

p. 272 'comparable in its scope': FitzGerald, p.7.

p. 272 'the Tibetan Problem': Schram (1), p.410.

p. 272 'There's a group': MacFarquhar, Cheek and Wu, p.184.

p. 273 'One must presume': MacFarquhar (1), pp.172–3.

p. 274 'the broad peasant masses': Short, pp.172–3.

p. 274 'the *Almanac de Gotha*': Ibid., p.197.

p. 274 'The enemy advances': Ibid., p.222.

p. 274 Futian incident: See Short, pp.265–84.

p. 275 'golden chicken': Saunders, pp.41–2.

p. 275 'improving their finances by trading opium': See *Far Eastern Economic Review*, 7 October 1999.

p. 276 'The Red Army has': Schram (4), p.692.

p. 276 'I ask that Wang': Qing, pp.108–9.

p. 278 'Let us hold high': *South China Morning Post*, 2 October 1999.

p. 278 'very successful': *China Daily*, 30 September 1999.

p. 281 Jiang in London: Private information.

p. 281 'Don't you have the ability': *Boston Globe*, 26 March 1999.

p. 282 'the treatment of demonstrators': *Guardian*, 27 January 2000.

CHAPTER TWENTY FOUR

p. 286 'I hate to say it': *Tibetan Review*, New Delhi, May 2000.

p. 287 'I would now like to': WTN, 5 September 2001.

p. 288 Tibetan population statistics: See China Financial and Economic Publishing House, p.76; Marshall and Cooke, pp.2486–9; Planning Council; Richardson (3), pp.6–7; Samuel, pp.44–6; Shakabpa, p.6; Smith, pp.597–601; State Statistical Bureau; Suyin (2), p.33; Yang. The first census in Tibet, in 1953, produced an estimated population of 1.27 million, but it did not cover the border areas. If this census was accurate, and population distribution in the borderlands matched present trends, an additional 1.47 million can be added, giving a total of 2.64 million Tibetans. Han Suyin, a less than reliable source, claimed in 1977 that the 1953 census counted 2.8 million Tibetans throughout China. Trying to establish Tibet's past population by extrapolating back from current figures (assuming that Tibetans reproduced at the same rate as Chinese) gives a total of approximately 2.3 million Tibetans in 1950, although this lower figure may be caused by a higher death rate. These numbers are all speculative, but an estimated total of around 2.5 million Tibetans in 1950 would seem reasonable. To obtain the current total of 5.5 million Tibetans, I have updated figures for 1994 assuming an annual growth rate of 1 per cent, based on data at www.cpirc.org.cn/year.htm. China's national census in 2000 found a total of 205,000 non-Tibetans living in the Tibet Autonomous Region. Although that figure excludes a substantial number of Chinese migrant workers, the claim by the Tibetan government-in-exile that Tibetans are outnumbered in their own land is not sustainable.

p. 288 '1.2 million Tibetans': The International Campaign for Tibet claims that '1.2 million Tibetans, one-fifth of the country's population, died as a result of China's policies'; the Tibet Society of the UK claims that 'over 1.2 million Tibetans have died in the widespread programme of imprisonment, torture and executions'; the US Tibet Committee claims that 'over 1.2 million Tibetans have died as a direct result of the occupation'; Free Tibet Campaign claims that 'an estimated 1.2 million Tibetans have been killed by the Chinese'. In June 2000, Kristin Gustafson wrote in the Minneapolis *Star Tribune* of 'the 1.2 million Tibetans who have died during the Chinese occupation of Tibet'; Teresa Watanabe wrote in the *Los Angeles Times* that 'about 1.2 million Tibetans have perished under Chinese rule'; Michael Hoffman wrote in the *Mainichi Daily News* that: 'In 1979, Tibet's government-in-exile in Dharamsala, India, estimated that 1.2 million Tibetans had died resisting China's systematic destruction of Tibetan Buddhism. In the twenty years since then, the death toll is believed to have reached 1.5 million.' The Tibetan government-in-exile is presently reviewing these figures.

p. 289 **'over 1 million Tibetans'**: See Smith, p.598. The US House of Representatives resolution is archived at www.tibet.com/Resolution/us8889.html.

p. 289 **'had only cross-checked'**: Kewley, pp.19, 392.

p. 292 **'support the Tibetan claim'**: Smith, p.600.

p. 295 **'I will not be sad'**: Shakya, p.153.

p. 295 **'Jiang Zemin had claimed'**: Jiang Zemin told *The Times* on 18 October 1999, 'I have myself looked up the records to find out what happened.'

p. 296 **'filled with fabrications'**: *China's Tibet* (Beijing), No.3, 1998.

p. 297 **'More than a hundred books'**: In June 2000, Zhao Qizheng, minister at the Information Office of the State Council of the People's Republic of China, told a conference on 'National Research in Tibetology and External Propaganda on Tibet' that 'succinct and well-written works are as effective as missiles in the battlefield . . . The Dalai-related books, such as *The Art of Happiness*, *Ethics for the New Millennium* and *Political Philosophy of the Fourteenth Dalai Lama* (sic) became the US bestsellers in 1999. We cannot underestimate the negative impact of these books on our nation.' Zhao's speech is analysed at www.tibetinfo.co.uk/news-updates/nu160701.htm.

p. 298 **'There are two'**: Moraes, p.88.

BIBLIOGRAPHY

Ahmad, Zahiruddin, *Sino–Tibetan Relations in the Seventeenth Century*, Rome 1970

Aimé-Martin, M.L. (ed.), *Lettres édifiantes et curieuses concernant l'Asie, l'Afrique et l'Amérique, avec quelques relations nouvelles des missions, et des notes géographiques et historiques* (vol. 3), Paris 1843

Alexander, André and de Azevedo, Pimpim, *The Old City of Lhasa: Report from a Conservation Project* (vol. 1), Kathmandu 1998

Alexander, André, *The Old City of Lhasa: A Clear Lamp Illuminating the Significance and Origin of Historic Buildings and Monuments in the Centre of Lhasa* (vol. 2), Lhasa 1999

Allen, Charles, *The Search for Shangri-La: A Journey into Tibetan History*, London 1999

Andrugtsang, Gompo Tashi, *Four Rivers, Six Ranges: Reminiscences of the Resistance Movement in Tibet*, Dharamsala 1973

Apter, David E. and Saich, Tony, *Revolutionary Discourse in Mao's Republic*, Harvard 1994

Aris, Michael, *Hidden Treasures and Secret Lives: A Study of Pemalingpa (1450–1521) and the Sixth Dalai Lama (1683–1706)*, London 1989

Arpi, Claude, *The Fate of Tibet: When Big Insects Eat Small Insects*, New Delhi 1999

Banister, Judith, *China's Changing Population*, Stanford 1987

Barnett, Robert, *La città illeggibile: Storie narrate dalle strade di Lhasa*, Milan 1999

Bass, Catriona, *Education in Tibet: Policy and Practice Since 1950*, London 1998

Batchelor, Stephen, *The Jewel in the Lotus: A Guide to the Buddhist Traditions of Tibet*, London 1987

Becker, Jasper, *Hungry Ghosts: Mao's Secret Famine*, New York 1998

Beckwith, Christopher I., *The Tibetan Empire in Central Asia: A History of the Struggle for Great Power Among Tibetans, Turks,*

Arabs, and Chinese during the Early Middle Ages, Princeton 1987

Bell, Charles, *Portrait of the Dalai Lama*, London 1946

Bernstein, Richard and Munro, Ross H., *The Coming Conflict with China*, New York 1998

Berry, Scott, *Monks, Spies and a Soldier of Fortune: The Japanese in Tibet*, London 1995

Bista, Dor Bahadur, *Report from Lhasa*, Kathmandu 1979

Boyle, John Andrew, *The Successors of Genghis Khan, Translated from the Persian of Rashid al-Din* (vol. 1), New York 1971

Bull, Geoffrey T., *When Iron Gates Yield*, London 1955

Burr, William, *The Kissinger Transcripts: The Top Secret Talks with Beijing and Moscow*, New York 1998

Chang, C.C., *Sixty Songs of Milarepa*, Kandy 1966

Chapman, F. Spencer, *Lhasa: The Holy City*, London 1940

China Financial and Economic Publishing House, *New China's Population*, New York 1998

Conner, Victoria and Barnett, Robert, *Leaders in Tibet: A Directory*, London 1997

Dalai Lama (1), *My Land and My People*, New York 1977 (1st edn 1962)

Dalai Lama (2), *Freedom in Exile*, London 1990

Dalai Lama (3), *Ancient Wisdom, Modern World: Ethics for a New Millennium*, London 1999

David-Neel, Alexandra, *Magic and Mystery in Tibet*, London 1997 (first published as *With Magicians and Mystics in Tibet*, London 1931)

Dhondup, K. (ed.) (1), *Songs of the Sixth Dalai Lama* (translated by K. Dhondup), Dharamsala 1981

Dhondup, K. (2), *The Water-Horse and Other Years: A History of Seventeenth and Eighteenth Century Tibet*, Dharamsala, 1984

Domes, Jürgen, *Socialism in the Chinese Countryside: Rural Societal Policies in the People's Republic of China 1949–1979*, London 1980

Dorje, Gyurme, *Tibet Handbook*, Bath 1996

Dowman, Keith and Paljor, Sonam, *The Divine Madman: The Sublime Life and Songs of Drukpa Kunley*, London 1980

Epstein, Israel, *Tibet Transformed*, Beijing 1983

de Filippi, Fillipo (ed.), *An Account of Tibet: The Travels of Ippolito Desideri of Pistola, S.J., 1712–1727*, London 1932

FitzGerald, C.P., *Mao Tse-tung and China*, London 1976

Ford, Robert, *Captured in Tibet*, London 1957

French, Patrick, *Younghusband: The Last Great Imperial Adventurer*, London 1994

French, Rebecca Redwood, *The Golden Yoke: The Legal Cosmology of Buddhist Tibet*, Ithaca 1995

Galwan, Ghulam Rassul, *Servant of Sahibs*, Cambridge 1923

Gelder, Stuart and Gelder, Roma, *The Timely Rain: Travels in New Tibet*, London 1964

Gibb, H.A.R., *The Arab Conquests in Central Asia*, London 1923

Ginsberg, Allen, *The Dream of Tibet*, New York 1976

Goldstein, Melvyn C. (1), *A History of Modern Tibet, 1913–1951: The Demise of the Lamaist State*, Berkeley 1989

Goldstein, Melvyn C. (2), *The Snow Lion and the Dragon: China, Tibet, and the Dalai Lama*, Berkeley 1997

Goldstein, Melvyn C. and Kapstein, Matthew T., *Buddhism in Contemporary Tibet: Religious Revival and Cultural Identity*, Berkeley 1998

Goldstein, Melvyn, Siebenschuh, William and Tsering, Tashi, *The Struggle for Modern Tibet: The Autobiography of Tashi Tsering*, New York 1997

Grunfeld, A. Tom, *The Making of Modern Tibet* (revised edn), New York 1996

Hedin, Sven, *Trans-Himalaya: Discoveries and Adventures in Tibet* (2 vols), London 1909

Hilton, Isabel, *The Search for the Panchen Lama*, London 1999

Hopkirk, Peter, *Trespassers on the Roof of the World*, London 1982

Hutchings, Graham, *Modern China: A Companion to a Rising Power*, London 2000

Jacquemont, Victor, *Letters from India; Describing a Journey in the British Dominions of India, Tibet, Lahore, and Cashmere, During the Years 1828, 1829, 1830, 1831* (2 vols), London 1834

Kagyu Thubten Choling, *Karmapa: The Sacred Prophecy*, New York 1999

Kapstein, Matthew T., *The Tibetan Assimilation of Buddhism: Conversion, Contestation, and Memory*, New York 2000

Karmay, Samten Gyaltsen, *Secret Visions of the Fifth Dalai Lama: The Gold Manuscript in the Fournier Collection, Musée Guimet, Paris*, London 1998 (first published 1988)

Karol, K.S., *China: The Other Communism*, London 1967 (first published as *La Chine de Mao: L'Autre Communisme*, Paris 1966)

Kewley, Vanya, *Tibet: Behind the Ice Curtain*, London 1990

Kimura, Hisao, *Japanese Agent in Tibet: My Ten Years of Travel in Disguise*, London 1990

Kissinger, Henry, *Years of Renewal*, London 1999

Knaus, John Kenneth, *Orphans of the Cold War: America and the Tibetan Struggle for Survival*, New York 1999

Lamb, Alastair (1), *Tibet, China and India 1914–1950*, Hertingfordbury 1989

Lamb, Alastair (2), *Kashmir: A Disputed Legacy*, Hertingfordbury 1991

Lattimore, Owen, *Inner Asian Frontiers of China*, New York 1951

Leary, Timothy, Metzner, Ralph and Alpert, Richard, *The Psychedelic Experience: A Manual Based on the Tibetan Book of the Dead*, New York 1964

Leys, Simon (1), *Chinese Shadows*, London 1978 (first published as *Ombres Chinoises*, Paris 1974)

Leys, Simon (2), *Les Habits Neuf du Président Mao*, Paris 1971

Li, Zhisui, *The Private Life of Chairman Mao: The Memoirs of Mao's Personal Physician* (translated by Tai Hung-chao), London 1994

Lopez, Donald S., *Prisoners of Shangri-la: Tibetan Buddhism and the West*, Chicago 1998

MacFarquhar, Roderick (1), *The Origins of the Cultural Revolution: II – The Great Leap Forward 1958–1960*, Oxford 1983

MacFarquhar, Roderick (2), *The Origins of the Cultural Revolution: III – The Coming of the Cataclysm 1961–1966*, New York 1997

MacFarquhar, Roderick, Cheek, Timothy and Wu, Eugene, *The Secret Speeches of Chairman Mao: From the Hundred Flowers to the Great Leap Forward*, Harvard 1989

McKay, Alex, *Tibet and the British Raj: The Frontier Cadre, 1904–1947*, London 1997

Mandelstam, Nadezhda, *Hope Against Hope: A Memoir* (translated by Max Hayward), London 1971

Maraini, Fosco, *Secret Tibet*, London 1952 (first published as *Segreto Tibet*, Bari 1951)

Markham, Clements R., *Narratives of the Mission of George Bogle to Tibet, and of the Journey of Thomas Manning to Lhasa*, London 1879

Marshall, Steven D. (1), *Hostile Elements: A Study of Political Imprisonment in Tibet 1987–1998*, London 1999

Marshall, Steven D. (2), *Rukhag 3: The Nuns of Drapchi Prison,* London 2000

Marshall, Steven D. and Cooke, Susette Ternent, *Tibet Outside the TAR,* The Alliance for Research in Tibet 1997 (CD-ROM)

Maxwell, Neville, *India's China War,* London 1970

Mengele, Irmgard, *dGe-'dun-chos-'phel: A Biography of the Twentieth Century Tibetan Scholar,* Dharamsala 1999

Michael, Franz, *Rule by Incarnation: Tibetan Buddhism and its Role in Society and State,* Epping 1982

Moraes, Dom, *Gone Away: An Indian Journal,* London 1960

Mosher, Steven W., *China Misperceived: American Illusions and Chinese Reality,* New York 1990

Mullin, Chris, *The Tibetans* (Minority Rights Group, Report No.49), London 1981

Nathan, Andrew J. and Link, Perry (eds), *The Tiananmen Papers* (compiled by Ziang Liang), London 2001

Norbu, Dawa (1), *China's Tibet Policy,* Richmond 2001

Norbu, Dawa (2), *Red Star Over Tibet* (revised edn), New Delhi 1987

Norbu, Jamyang, *Illusion and Reality,* Dharamsala 1989

Panchen Lama (1), *A Poisoned Arrow: The Secret Report of the Tenth Panchen Lama,* London 1997

Panchen Lama (2), *From the Heart of the Panchen Lama: Major Speeches and a Petition, 1962–1989,* Dharamsala 1998

Pemba, Tsewang Y., *Young Days in Tibet,* London 1957

Petech, Luciano (1), *China and Tibet in the Early Eighteenth Century: History of the Establishment of Chinese Protectorate in Tibet* (revised edn), Leiden 1972

Petech, Luciano (2), *Aristocracy and Government in Tibet 1728–1959,* Rome 1973

Phalu, Khache, *Khache Phalu's Advice on the Art of Living* (translated by Dawa Norbu), Dharamsala 1987

Planning Council, *Tibetan Demographic Survey 1998,* Dharamsala 2000

Qing, Dai, *Wang Shiwei and 'Wild Lilies': Rectification and Purges in the Chinese Communist Party 1942–1944,* New York 1994

Radhu, Abdul Wahid, 'Tibetan Caravans', in *Islam in Tibet* (edited by Gray Henry), Louisville 1997

Rawling, C.G., *The Great Plateau,* London 1905

Rawski, Evelyn S., *The Last Emperors: A Social History of Qing Imperial Institutions*, Berkeley 1998

Richardson, Hugh (1), *Ceremonies of the Lhasa Year*, London 1993

Richardson, Hugh (2), *High Peaks, Pure Earth: Collected Writings on Tibetan History and Culture*, London 1998

Richardson, Hugh (3), *Tibet and its History* (revised edn), Boulder 1984

Rockhill, W.W., *The Dalai Lamas of Lhasa and their Relations with the Manchu Emperors of China, 1644–1908*, Dharamsala 1998 (first published 1910)

Saich, Tony (ed.), *The Rise to Power of the Chinese Communist Party: Documents and Analysis*, New York 1996

Salisbury, Harrison E. (1), *The Long March: The Untold Story*, London 1985

Salisbury, Harrison E. (2), *The New Emperors: China in the Era of Mao and Deng*, Boston 1992

Samuel, Geoffrey, *Civilized Shamans: Buddhism in Tibetan Societies*, Washington 1993

Saunders, Kate, *Eighteen Layers of Hell: Stories from the Chinese Gulag*, London 1996

Schell, Orville, *Virtual Tibet: Searching for Shangri-La from the Himalayas to Hollywood*, New York 2000

Schram, Stuart R. (ed.) (1), *Mao's Road to Power, Revolutionary Writings 1912–1949: Volume I – The Pre-Marxist Period, 1912–1920*, New York 1992

Schram, Stuart R. (ed.) (2), *Mao's Road to Power, Revolutionary Writings 1912–1949: Volume III – From the Jinggangshan to the Establishment of the Jiangxi Soviets, July 1927–December 1930*, New York 1995

Schram, Stuart R. (ed.) (3), *Mao's Road to Power, Revolutionary Writings 1912–1949: Volume IV – The Rise and Fall of the Chinese Soviet Republic, 1931–1934*, New York 1997

Schram, Stuart R. (ed.) (4), *Mao's Road to Power, Revolutionary Writings 1912–1949: Volume V – Toward the Second United Front, January 1935–July 1937*, New York 1999

Shakabpa, W.D., *Tibet: A Political History*, Yale 1967

Shakya, Tsering, *The Dragon in the Land of Snows: A History of Modern Tibet Since 1947*, London 1999

Shenkhawa, Gyurme Sonam Tobgyal, *rang gi lo rgyus lhad med rang byung zang* [*The Pure Unadulterated Copper of my History*], Dharamsala 1990

Short, Philip, *Mao: A Life*, London 1999

Singh, Amar Kaur Jasbir, *Himalayan Triangle: A Historical Survey of British India's Relations with Tibet, Sikkim and Bhutan*, London 1988

Smith, Warren W., *Tibetan Nation: A History of Tibetan Nationalism and Sino–Tibetan Relations*, Boulder 1996

Snellgrove, David and Richardson, Hugh, *A Cultural History of Tibet*, London 1968

Snow, Edgar, *China's Long Revolution*, London 1974 (first published 1972)

Sørensen, Per K., *The Mirror Illuminating the Royal Genealogies: An Annotated Translation of the Fourteenth Century Tibetan Chronicle: rGyal-rabs gsal-ba'i me-long*, Wiesbaden 1994

Spence, Jonathan (1), *Mao*, London 1999

Spence, Jonathan (2), *The Chan's Great Continent: China in Western Minds*, New York 1998

State Statistical Bureau, *China Statistical Yearbook*, Beijing 1999

Stoddard, Heather, *Le Mendiant de l'Amdo*, Paris 1985

Suyin, Han (1), *China in the Year 2001*, London 1967

Suyin, Han (2), *Lhasa: The Open City*, New York 1977

Taring, Rinchen Dolma, *Daughter of Tibet*, London 1970

Teiwes, Frederick C. and Sun, Warren, *The Tragedy of Lin Biao: Riding the Tiger During the Cultural Revolution 1966–1971*, London 1996

Thomas, Lowell, Jr, *Out of this World: Across the Himalayas to Forbidden Tibet*, New York 1950

Thurman, Robert, *Inner Revolution: Life, Liberty, and the Pursuit of Real Happiness*, New York 1998

Tibet Information Network (1), *A Sea of Bitterness: Patriotic Education in Qinghai Monasteries*, London 1999

Tibet Information Network (2), *China's Great Leap West*, London 2000

Tibet Information Network (3), *Social Evils: Prostitution and Pornography in Lhasa*, London 1999

Tsering, Diki, *Dalai Lama, My Son: A Mother's Story*, London 2000

Tsering, Phuntsog (ed.), *deb ther kun gsal me long* [*The Annals of the All-Revealing Mirror*], Lhasa 1987

van Walt van Praag, Michael C., *The Status of Tibet: History, Rights, and Prospects in International Law*, Boulder 1987

Waddell, L. Austine, *The Buddhism of Tibet or Lamaism*, London 1895

Warner, Marina, *Managing Monsters: Six Myths of our Time, The 1994 Reith Lectures*, London 1994

Wessels, C., *Early Jesuit Travellers in Central Asia 1603–1721*, The Hague 1924

Williamson, Margaret D., *Memoirs of a Political Officer's Wife in Tibet, Sikkim and Bhutan*, London 1987

Winnington, Alan, *Tibet: Record of a Journey*, London 1957

Woodcock, George, *Into Tibet: The Early British Explorers*, New York 1971

Yang, Dali L., *Calamity and Reform in China: State, Rural Society, and Institutional Change Since the Great Leap Famine*, Stanford 1996

Yi, Zheng, *Scarlet Memorial: Tales of Cannibalism in Modern China* (translated and edited by T.P. Sym), Boulder 1996

Zedong, Mao, *Quotations from Chairman Mao Tse-tung*, London 1967

INDEX

Gungthang Rinpoche 60
Guo Jinlong 267
Guomindang 220, 222, 258, 277
Gushri Khan 101, 102
Gyalo Thondup 261
Gyantse 233–4
Gyen Pachen 264
Gyenlog 195, 200, 221

Habaling Khache 161–3
Han Chinese 43
Han Suyin 69, 264
Hastings, Warren 236
He Long 274
Hedin, Sven 143, 181, 182
Hetum I, King 224
Hilton, James: *Lost Horizon* 20–1
Hisao Kimura 75, 225
Hitchens, Christopher 113
Hoddle, Glenn 26
homosexuality 225
Hong Kong 137, 281
Hsieh Jen-kuei 91–2
Hu Jintao 36
Hu Yaobang 115, 196
hunger-strike at Jantar Mantar
   (1998) 4–6

illiteracy 42
India 254, 255, 258–9
infant mortality 43
informants 206
International Association for
   Tibetan Studies 287–8
International Campaign for Tibet
   30, 110, 288

Jampal Khedrub 150
Jamyang Norbu 6, 116, 265
Jamyang Shepa 60, 61
Jebb, Gladwyn 259
Jebtsun Damba Khutuktu 104,
   166
Jiang Zemin 30, 37–8, 60, 175,
   278–9, 295; visit to Britain 280,
   281–3

jindags (patrons) 284–5
John, Elton 113
John Paul II, Pope 225
Jokhang 91, 149, 153–4, 155, 168,
   194–5, 197–200

Kagyu sect 60, 100, 101
Kanjur 155
karma 26
Karmapa Rinpoche (first) 100
Karmapa Rinpoche (third) 100
Karmapa Rinpoche (seventeenth)
   (Ugyen Trinley Dorje) 60, 284
Kermo 138–9
Kesang Chompel 45
Kewley, Vanya: *Tibet: Behind the
   Ice Curtain* 289–90
Kewtsang Rinpoche 18
Kham 14, 258, 259
Khrushchev, Nikita 270
King, Larry 120–1
Kircher, Athanasius: *China
   Illustrata* 55
Kissinger, Henry 263–4, 269–70
Knaus, Ken 263
Kochaks 190–1
Kontso 125–6
Körös, Csoma de 20
Kozlov, Pyotr 250
Kublai Khan 99, 106
Kula of Sikkim, Princess 145
Kumbum monastery 85–7
Kumphela 170
Kundun (film) 105
Kungo Dhakden-la 289
Kyibuk 169

Labrang 56–8; monastery of
   58–60
Lama 241, 242
land reform 219–20
Lang Darma 95
language 11, 90
Larry King Live 120–1
Lattimore, Owen 106
Leary, Timothy 157